Re-Creating

The Experience of Life-Change
and Religion

Re-Creating

The Experience of Life-Change
and Religion

VIRGINIA H. McDOWELL

Beacon Press   Boston

Beacon Press books are published under the auspices
of the Unitarian Universalist Association

Published simultaneously in Canada by
Fitzhenry & Whiteside Limited, Toronto

Printed in the United States of America

(hardcover) 9 8 7 6 5 4 3 2 1

Library of Congress Cataloging in Publication Data

McDowell, Virginia H
  Re-creating.
  Bibliography: p.
  Includes index.
    1. Adulthood—Case studies. 2. Self-
actualization (Psychology)—Case studies.
3. Psychology, Religious—Case studies. I. Title.
BF724.5.M28   155.2'5   77-75443
ISBN 0-8070-2732-4

Contents

Acknowledgments

First, I wish to thank warmly those anonymous participants whose patience, candor, and courage made this book possible; my thanks also to William E. Cane, S.T.D., former Director of the San Francisco Cursillo Center, who devoted many hours to a joint conceptualization of the questionnaires.

I am indebted to Professors Frank Barron, Gregory Bateson, Gary Gossen, M. Brewster Smith, and Elliot Turiel of University of California–Santa Cruz; and Professors M. Margaret Clark and Marjorie Fiske of the Human Development Program at University of California–San Francisco. All have made thoughtful and challenging comments.

M. Brewster Smith has been a supportive, enabling, and demanding influence from the conception of this book to its completion, devoting time, energy, and a balancing perspective.

Special thanks are due Rollo May who urged me to complete this book.

Particular thanks to Jane Wachsmuth and Ellen Woods who did the typing, and to Pat Grube and Lona Malcolm who proofread and lent special help in the final preparation of the book. Joanne Wyckoff edited the manuscript with uncommon care and lucidity. For other kinds of help I would like to thank Jim Dunivin, Julie Nash, John Boswell, Coeleen Kiebert-Jones, Lois Bateson, Ingrid Kepler-May, De and George Heeg, and Ann Lopez.

I owe most to my husband, Mike; I am deeply grateful for the support of our four children, Tom, Matt, Mary, and Ann who, with Mike, assumed _all_ housekeeping and caretaking tasks during the final months of writing.

Foreword

The heart of Virginia McDowell's brilliant and valuable book is a set of nine superb case studies of adult personality development, based on her intensive recorded interviews with men and women who had in fact been undergoing very substantial change in directions that most observers would interpret as "growth." These are not randomly selected people; they are extraordinary, in their various ways exemplary people. The cases make fascinating reading, and a close reading of them tells us much about the conditions under which people can become more than they are.

For good reason, Dr. McDowell does not use Abraham Maslow's popular concept of "self-actualizing people," but for readers of Maslovian persuasion, the nine persons to be encountered here sample diverse routes to self-actualization via commitment. It seems to me that reading these personal accounts must have a mind-stretching, growth-inducing effect on the reader, whether student, professional, or thoughtful person-at-large. I would like *my* students to read them. I know of nothing comparable in print.

In the spirit of my teachers, Gordon Allport and Henry Murray, I have long advocated a humanistic psychology that begins to do justice to humanness without casting off its anchor in the aspirations of scientific psychology. Much "humanistic psychology" has been captured by the gurus of quickie mysticism, casual "encounter," and the therapy fads. Virginia

McDowell's book stands forth in contrast as a luminous example of what a humanized psychology can be. In an introductory chapter, she reviews lightly but deftly several contemporary developmental theories that ought to provide, and do, a significant context for approaching the lives that she examines in dialogue. None of the theories of fixed "stages" of adult development does justice, however, to the varieties of development displayed in her interviews, though an intrinsic developmental progression indeed runs through them.

The "cases" presented were selected from participants in an ecumenical Catholic-Anglican religious movement, the *Cursillo*, intent on relating Christianity to the problems of the modern world in the aftermath of Vatican II. The author describes her own involvement in this movement and her present relationship to the religious perspective in the Preface, which should be read as significant context for what follows. Chapter 2 develops a sensitive and acute analysis of the Cursillo as a setting for personality change, drawing upon the powerful formulation of "self-reconstitution processes" by Theodore Sarbin and Nathan Adler. These aspects of the book should make it especially interesting to students of the psychology of religion.

Issues concerning the evolving meaning of religious commitment arise repeatedly and are illuminated. But the book will be just as valuable to readers from a nonreligious perspective. When we speak of growth or development of adult personality, we are implying an intrinsically evaluative concept—unless we use the terms inappropriately for a mere schedule or sequence leading to decrepitude and death. We imply a progression to something that is metaphorically higher or more: *better* in terms of some scale of values. For this way of thinking to go beyond sloppy optimism, we need examples of growth toward better ways of relating self and world; we need a natural history of adult development that displays instances in which the persons themselves (and we as vicarious participants) are convinced that real growth has occurred. It is just this that Virginia McDowell's book provides. And more: as good natural history, it gives us a rich basis for considering the conditions that permit and facilitate growth.

M. Brewster Smith
Professor of Psychology
University of California
Santa Cruz

Preface

At the time I began thinking about writing this book, in the spring of 1973, I was a participant-observer in the phenomena I was proposing to inquire about. I was interested in personal growth in adult life and thought I had been observing it in many who were participants—with me—in an ecumenical, religious growth movement that had developed from the Roman Catholic Cursillo movement (described in chapter 2). Thus, I brought to this book presuppositions grounded in a particular tradition.

In 1973, I placed myself as exceedingly marginal yet committed to Roman Catholic Christianity, an odd position but quite my own. This involvement extended back thirty years, but was not a usual affiliation with institutional Roman Catholicism. As a sixteen-year-old, in 1949, I spent a summer in rural Mississippi teaching reading, writing, arithmetic, and catechism in a black school. I was appalled at the tin-roofed shack that was the schoolhouse, at the poverty of sharecroppers, few of whom had shoes, at the Church's compliance with segregation, and much more. As a young adult, in the early 1960s, I taught Communion classes in a parish for several years and refused to teach an inauthentic Christianity that I thought bad for children: sin lists, a fallen human nature, and hell as a place. Eventually I decided the whole endeavor was absurd and left it behind. I redefined the Church to stay in it and opposed it when I thought it to be oppressive. In 1963 I became involved in the Cursillo movement and worked on several Cursillos, serving on the various leadership committees and workshops that strove to update that movement and make it challenging and substantive. In 1971 I designed and convened women's weekends in an attempt to create an environment in which women could experience themselves and one another as important and creative, able to make choices. The weekends were based on the Book of Ruth—a polemic against legalism and exclusivism, and one of the few places in the Old Testament where Yahweh and other gods and places of worship are given equal value and choice is encouraged.

In 1971 I worked on a women's Spanish-speaking Cursillo, the first Anglo to do so in the San Francisco movement. It was an exhausting (my Spanish was minimal) and memorable experience. Although I continued to participate in leadership workshops for the next year and a half, this was the last Cursillo I worked on. It was during this time that I began to observe adult growth in the Cursillo: some people left jobs they had held for many years and began new careers; men and women returned to school and their self-understanding changed; others became politically involved and questioned their middle-class values. I observed people leaving secure positions and familiar surroundings to work in Africa, to found an innovative school in Spain, and to work in a Mexican orphanage. At the same time, I observed persons coping with the breaking open of an institution that had remained virtually unchanged for hundreds of years; one that they were then committed to as I was.

This book was conceived to focus upon the growing person and the changing institution. A preliminary questionnaire was designed to locate and specify change in persons and institutional meaning. This survey represented a stage of thought, feelings, and hope that I now look back upon from a different perspective. As I began to prepare the survey and then tested it in various groups I made a deliberate decision to remove myself from any participation in religious rituals, meetings, or symbolic groupings so that I might obtain some distance, recognize my presuppositions, and question as well as describe what I had observed. From the questionnaires, I selected for interviews those who had undergone the greatest changes. In 1974, when I began the long interviews from which the life histories were constructed, it was from a position outside of Christianity, a position that respected a tradition of "abbots [and abbesses] and men in rags jeering at the abbots";[1] at the same time a tradition that was no longer meaningful or believable for me. "Such rebellion is as the sin of witchcraft," the Old Testament notes (I Samuel 15:23), and in an earlier age I could not have undertaken the questioning that has brought me to this perspective of curious disbelief.

Having earned some ability to suspend judgment as well as to bring into light "otherness," I do not assume I possess the truth; I do think there are those whose lives reflect successive approximations or attempts to reach truth. My concern is to present those lives for reflection.

Virginia McDowell

Re-Creating

The Experience of Life-Change
and Religion

1
The Growth Experience

Camus reminds us that "The aim of art, the aim of a life can only be to increase the sum of freedom and responsibility to be found in every [person] and in the world."[1] Freedom and responsibility are ideas living in persons in a society. Our age is termed "technological" and many see our technology carrying us to destruction of our planet. This is a possibility and we cannot hide from it. At the same time, scientific technology contains within it the possibility of freeing the world from hunger and other ills, of allowing us to be truly responsible to one another as well as to be more aware of the possible freedom to choose what we shall make of our lives. Certainly the aim of science also is "to increase the sum of freedom and responsibility" and to do so in a variety of ways just as the artist does.

The concern of this book is to present a view of a community and an interpretation of human lives that will increase the sum of our freedom. My focus is upon the process and diversity of personal growth in adult life. By diversity I do not mean a succession of events or details or descriptions of traits; my focus is upon the unique, coherent patterning that enables us to recognize and grasp the quality—the essential character—of this person's being in the world. In setting down the meaning these lives have for these persons I hope to begin a dialogue, a speaking between the meaning of the lived experience and the meaning created by interpretation of that experience by the reader. A high level of personal development in a life history is a fresh way of seeing life; it transforms our understanding, opens up a new world that discloses concrete potentiality as well as the boundaries of our own vision.

Neither our innate capacities nor our behaviors define us, make us human. We become persons at particular historical times which differ as do persons. Becoming human is becoming a person—an individual—within a historically created social system of meaning which directs and orders our lives, pointing them in a particular direction at a specific time. To be human "is thus not to be Everyman; it is to be a particular kind of man, and of course men differ."[2] People differ exceedingly in the meaning they give to the form and direction their lives take. This meaning changes, constituting and mediating further development as one chooses in terms of meaning and creates one's self.

Camus wrote that "personal growth as a choice of what one shall be is both a choice and a creation: a work of art. In this sense every person is an artist moved by his own spirit."[3] The intent of this book is to present the choice and creation of personal growth in actual individual lives.

Theories of Human Development

The ideas we have about human development are part of our culture; they affect us and make us what we are. The boundaries between our innate capacities and culture are permeable and ill-defined. We are incomplete, unfinished, and we complete ourselves through a particular form of culture—not culture in general. Our behavior is the outcome of the interaction between our innate capacities and our particular culture. Literally, if inadvertently, we create ourselves.

The outcome of this interaction between person and culture is not always benign. Our culture provides us with interpretations of ourselves that reflect the dominant values of our society. The importance of the first two decades of life is unquestionable, but nearly exclusive focus upon the adolescent and child leaves us with little insight into the processes of growth in adulthood. If we arbitrarily assume that physical and intellectual maturity are reached at the same time and that this peak is followed by a uniform decline throughout the life span, we limit seriously an individual's theory about his or her capability to develop in the middle and later years of adult life.

The task of the mature adult—learning to live more humanely in the present and to meet a future we cannot foretell—may be a qualitatively different task requiring further development not achieved in adolescence or early adulthood. How can we explore such development and from what theoretical perspectives can we delineate this development? The task is difficult and the outcome uncertain as few, if any, generalizations can be made. We can dismiss the task as impossible on the grounds that there is no adequate theory (my complaint about much of humanistic psychology). The theories I outline—those of Erik Erikson, Jane Loevinger, Jean Piaget, and William Perry—are ones I consider to be *partial* reflections of the developmental thinking that we need, windows that may enlarge our vision.

Erikson is concerned with the achievement of identity through resolution of crises. His first five stages are directed to childhood and adolescence. A more careful reading of these five as well as the three following might suggest their repetition at ever-increasing levels of awareness and complexity over the life cycle. Erikson's first stage is favorably resolved with the development of basic trust and hope as babies learn to differentiate themselves from others, discover a world separate from themselves, and experience impulses and learn to control them. Early and middle childhood are the context of the next three stages whose outcome is the development of a sense of autonomy and self-control; of initiative through play; and of a sense of confidence and belief in one's effectiveness or "industry." The fifth stage centers on the crisis of identity in adolescence which is resolved by choice of a life task. The ability to attain intimacy and the capacity for enduring love are presented as the struggle of the sixth stage. Generativity, care, and responsibility for others is the desired outcome of the seventh stage; it is the accomplishment of the mature adult. In old age, Erikson confronts us with the final task of achieving integrity and a wisdom that is able to be detached, yet actively concerned with life as death approaches.

Each of the eight stages has a "failure" or unfavorable outcome that may result—taking the stages in serial order—in mistrust, shame or doubt, guilt, inferiority, role diffusion (instead of identity), isolation, stagnation, and despair. My questions about the order of the stages center on identity through discovery of one's life task and then the attainment of the capacity to love. I see the two as growth outcomes of adolescence occurring over the same period for both males and females. Trust is not settled in infancy and I do not

think Erikson would have us think so. If his developmental crises are taken more loosely and not age-
restricted, they can then add to our understanding of
development in adult life. If they are bound to particular ages and life events (marriage, child rearing, old
age) then they do not contribute to our understanding
of the decades of maturity that precede old age. I do
not think Erikson is usefully interpreted in so narrow a
vein.

Jane Loevinger describes ego development in
terms of stages or milestones. Her Presocial, Impulsive,
and Self-Protective stages center on infancy and childhood. Although Loevinger posits higher stages, she
sees her next stage—Conformist—as most common
among adults in this society. Loevinger's conformist
lives in a conceptually uncomplicated world of stable
and unchanging things that are always right for
everyone, to be adhered to by all. This Conformist
Stage precedes the Self-Aware Level, the transition to
the higher Conscientious Stage. Self-Awareness
moves the person out of this conformity as exceptions
are perceived and permitted. The perception of actual
alternatives occurs with the awareness that one does
not always live up to one's conception of an idealized
person established by social norms. She does not state
whether not meeting social norms is by choice on the
part of the individual or is negatively perceived as a
failure of oneself to "measure up." Characteristic of
the Self-Aware Level is the expression of emotion in
banal terms—"loneliness, embarrassment, self-
consciousness"—which refer to interpersonal or group
relationships. Loevinger considers consciousness of
self to be a prerequisite for the acquisition of self-
evaluated as opposed to group standards.

The Conscientious Stage is characterized by the

internalization of rules which are chosen for oneself and are not absolute. One is responsible for oneself and others and obligations and rights are accepted. Achievement is measured by internal standards, not competitive norms. Right and Wrong are more complex and differentiated as are the emotions; the person at this stage experiences a rich inner life. Transition from this stage to the Autonomous Stage is marked by a greater sense of individuality as well as concern with emotional dependence, now recognized as separate from physical or financial dependency. Tolerance of self and others grows and enables the person to accept and cherish individuality, the mark of the Autonomous Stage.

The Autonomous person is able to acknowledge inner conflict and cope with it rather than projecting it; transcends polarities and sees the complex and multifaceted aspects of reality; recognizes the need for autonomy on the part of others; values relationships; and considers self-fulfillment more important than achievement. The person at this Stage is expressive, sensual, humorous, and concerned with social ideals such as justice and equality.

Loevinger describes her highest stage, Integrated, in a brief paragraph:

We call the highest stage Integrated, implying some transcending of the conflicts of the Autonomous Stage. It is the hardest stage to describe for several reasons. Because it is rare, one is hard put to find instances to study. Moreover, the psychologist trying to study this stage may acknowledge his own limitations as a potential hindrance to comprehension. The higher the stage studied, the more it is likely to exceed his own and thus to stretch his capacity. For the most part, the description of the Autonomous Stage holds also for

the Integrated Stage. A new element is consolidation of a
sense of identity. Probably the best description of this stage
is that of Maslow's Self-Actualizing person.[4]

Loevinger notes that most of Maslow's Self-
Actualizing people were over fifty. In an earlier work
Loevinger stated that she and her colleagues detected
no increase in level of ego development between ages
twenty and fifty and in her stages of ego development she does not directly address her stages to
the decades of adult maturity. Considered in its entirety, her stages are a challenging conceptualization
developed within a broadly psychoanalytic perspective. I have sketched Erikson's and Loevinger's approaches because of their suggestiveness for developmental thinking. I cannot use the psychoanalytic
theory that underlies them. Even these modern re-
visors of Freud carry over from Freud a view of human
nature as an arena of conflict between biological drive
and social imperatives. This view doesn't do justice to
the interactive, spiraling process by which people
emerge into personhood.

A different approach to development, termed
"cognitive-developmental" is discussed by Jean
Piaget, who believes that we create our world (our definition of physical reality) through interaction with it.
Piaget believes that knowledge does not arise from nor
reside in objects or persons, but from interactions—
from birth on—between the persons and objects. His
developmental theory stems from the presupposition
that knowledge is an extension of biological activity,
that knowing shares certain characteristics common to
all forms of life: the ability to organize and adapt to the
environment through assimilation and accommoda-

tion. In order to know the person must act upon or with an object and transform it: The infant and child pull and push things, take them apart and attempt to put them together; later on, the adolescent carries out mental activities such as joining together, putting things in order, or a one-to-one correspondence, and makes comparisons by reversing his or her thought. Knowledge, for Piaget, is always linked with interactions involving actions, operations—resulting in transformations of the intellect. He regards this knowledge resulting from interaction as richer than what the person or object could provide alone. Knowledge is never a copy of an object or the accumulation of information but is always an "inventive construction" characteristic of all living thought.

For Piaget, intelligence is organized—structured—and these structures interrelate to form a whole, a stage. The stages have an invariant sequence. That is, one must pass through Concrete Operations in order to attain Formal Operations. First one learns to have opinions, to argue in their favor (concrete thought); later one learns to follow the form of the argument as well as its context (formal thought). Here, one may agree with the conclusion and, at the same time, infer that the framework within which the conclusions are presented is not logical. Formal thought (abstract thought) is able to generalize. Thus, once one has acquired the concept of "class inclusion" one knows that a bouquet of nine roses and three daisies does not have more roses than flowers (the young child does not make this distinction) and one does not need roses and daisies to think about this concept. Piaget's final stage, Formal Operations, is achieved in adolescence. It does not follow from his work that this stage is automatically the culmination of the person's interaction with the environment; it is a theoretical construct that individuals or peoples may never attain.

In his study of intellectual and ethical development William Perry notes his reliance on Piaget's concepts. He also notes his departure from Piagetian concepts when they fail to consider emotional and aesthetic aspects. Perry's study is a description of students' evolving interpretations of their lives drawn from their reported experiences. It is a study of students, mostly males, in a particular context (Harvard College) that is hardly representative. Nevertheless, I have found useful his conceptualization of the shift from a dualistic view of oneself and the world to acceptance of a multiplicity of viewpoints, and thence to relativism and commitment made in the context of a relative world. In my observations of what I thought to be growth, one of the more obvious issues that I saw people confront was their recognition that they had made a commitment, had *not* questioned it, and now were facing remaking it as they perceived a relative world.

Perry's open-ended interviewing led to a variety of content which at first appeared to preclude any order. Gradually, the investigators perceived a sequence of challenges emerging which the students responded to in their own individual style. Perry's sequential development proceeds through nine positions beginning with a basic dualism in which the world is seen in dichotomous terms of "we-right-good" as opposed to others who are wrong-bad. There are right answers for everything and they exist as absolutes, possessed and understood by those in authority whose role is to teach the truth they possess. Knowledge and goodness, acquired by hard work and obedience, are quantities one accumulates or collects.

Next, diversity of opinion is perceived and ac-

counted for by judging those in authority to be confused or incompetent, or the diversity is seen as an
exercise set up in order to teach one to find the right
answer. Then, diversity and uncertainty become temporarily legitimate, confined to areas where the right
answer remains to be found by experts. Thus, multiple
perspectives are perceived; uncertainty and diversity
do exist; perhaps others have a right to their opinions
in certain specified areas. However, there is the remaining domain where authority's possession of truth
prevails. Here, relativism is subordinated to prescribed
areas. Following this subordinated relativism, knowledge and values are perceived to be relative
perspectives—frames of reference—and dualistic
right-wrong thinking and Authority become subordinated. Thus, relativism and a relative world are accepted and persons perceive the necessity of orienting
themselves in that world by some form of individual
and personal commitment. A commitment is made in
some area and identity is affirmed and realized as a
process which unfolds and is expressed individually,
through Developing Commitments, Perry's final stage.

Implied in Perry's scheme is the qualitatively different construction of reality and knowledge from
within these various positions. Although Perry is ad-
dressing students' epistemological stances, he suggests
that his "progression of forms in which a person con-
strues his [or her] experience" can be generalized to
represent a variety of human experiences. Perry's system cuts across psychological, sociological, an-
thropological, and philosophical disciplines. It appears
to adequately interpret a theme present in a variety of
experiences as it presents three modes of being in the
world: a standpoint or dualism; a movable view or mul-

tiplicity; and a moving viewpoint or frames of reference that unfold a new position—possibly a higher-level "standpoint"—from within which one must begin again.

From a "standpoint" one has a correct and immovable position from which to view and judge the world. It is a position the person is not aware of as it is "natural" or god-given. Roles, patterns of relating to others, duties, and responsibilities are defined by external authorities or experts who know what is true, right, and good, and what is wrong. Further, they know what attitudes are appropriate in new situations and toward new questions. The person does not perceive the self as origin, that is, as independent or creative in thought or action from this position.

A movable view becomes possible when this standpoint is broken into through awareness of pluralism of authorities and values and the apprehension of historical tradition, concepts of culture and world-views, recognition of socialization to roles, and so on. The person becomes aware of diversity; at the same time truth, authority, and value are still thought of as being outside oneself. They exist independently and the person's new task is to defend a particular position or to find another correct place to stand where things are rearranged and reworded to take into account new awareness and new questions. Those in authority—the President—may be dishonorable, but there is the hope that this will be taken care of by the new President. The movable view runs the risk of looking for the absolute in a new place, person, movement, or institution (secular or religious), in a search for relevance or correctness outside the self.

A moving viewpoint comes into being with the

recognition that growth will take place not by finding a new reality outside, but by entering into a new relationship to knowledge, persons, situations, and institutions. The uncertainty and relativism of the moving viewpoint changes the nature of commitment, i.e., commitment to a cause no longer ensures one's values and there is a freedom to choose how and where one will be involved.

Perry sees relativism as a point of no return, i.e., it is revolutionary and represents a paradigm shift wherein one cannot return to one's previous ways of thought. This is consistent with Piaget's concept of abstract thought as independent of particular objects and constituting a form of thought. To return to my earlier example of class inclusion: there is no return to the innocence of childhood where the bouquet (of nine roses and three daisies) obviously has more roses than flowers. While the sequential incorporation of past structures into a new whole may occur, I do not think it is generalizable to all of life. Perry's paradigm shift is repeatable, I think; embeddedness is always a possibility.

The lives we will examine certainly illustrate individual patterns of movement that fit the simpler scheme I have extracted from Perry. Yet while, as we will see, this movement may generally permit us to talk about growth or development rather than mere change, there will be difficulty in applying any rigid conceptions of stages, whether those of Erikson, Loevinger, Piaget, or Perry. The next chapter will focus upon the *source* of these people who are undergoing significant change in their lives, change to be regarded as personal growth.

2

A Setting for Change

The Cursillo[1] is a little community in time—a religious movement characteristic of the period in which it came into being, the 1960s, and the society in which it existed. The beginning of the Cursillo movement in San Francisco[2] coincided with the beginning of the Second Vatican Council which called into question the certain and unchanging world-view that had characterized Roman Catholicism since the Council of Trent in 1545. Traditionally, Roman Catholicism had been a safe haven from doubt and uncertainty: one adhered to formulas, adopted prescribed conduct, picked one's way through a maze of rules and regulations, and thus preserved one's faith and transmitted it intact.

In keeping with this tradition the Cursillo experience at the San Francisco Center in 1962 was one of a structured, total milieu, designed to convert the individual by providing a profound experience of both community and marginality—of being on the threshold of a new life. The person was ritually separated from everyday life, isolated for three and a half days, placed in a culturally strange environment, led to participate in religious rites, and thus initiated into a new Christian community requiring a new commitment and high involvement of the self—a community that possessed a group-consciousness, a homogeneity in terms of accepted common meaning or belief system.

The ritual separation occurred at 8:30 p.m. on Thursday evening when visitors were required to leave. Those "making" the Cursillo were told to put away their watches for the next three days and to maintain strict silence until breakfast the following day. The group of from forty to sixty men or women (coeducational Cursillos were not instituted until the 1970s) then filed outside and upstairs to the chapel to listen to a reading of the "Prodigal Son" followed by a talk on "repentance." After an interminable time those making the Cursillo went downstairs in silence and prepared to go to bed in a culturally strange environment. The Cursillo Center was located in a run-down hall with a hundred or so beds, in rows, filling two thirds of the area. The neighborhood in the inner city was poor and largely black. The sound of sirens was a frequent occurrence. Despite the lack of talking few slept well and many not at all.

After a fitful night's sleep at best, the silence ended at breakfast as each person, in turn, introduced the neighboring person to the group at large and was then assigned to a table with seven or eight others. These little groups remained together for the next three days. Meals took place at different hours than were customary and were prepared and served by a team that included clergy and laypersons. The dining area occupied one end of the dormitory, the beds the other.

The team that conducted the Cursillo was composed of clergy, nuns, and laypersons and had a priest as "spiritual" director, and a layperson in the position of authority as leader or Rector/Rectora. Over the course of three days fifteen talks were given by both clergy and laypersons, breaking down the stereotypic perceptions of both as did the sleeping arrangement that placed priest next to layman and sister next to laywoman. Here the norms governing dressing and undressing in privacy fell aside of necessity—a matter of little consequence to those with military service, but quite difficult for the sisters and laywomen.

Contact with the "outside world" was limited to one walk around the block on Saturday and those making the Cursillo did not have access to media or to their families, except in an emergency. The only telephone was located in the kitchen. It was, in the early 1960s, a total milieu using such procedures as isolation, fasting, and ritual singing. One became a "Cursillista." That is, one made the Cursillo and committed oneself, before the group, to a new life by accepting a small crucifix as one's name was called.

One might say that it was a resocialization process akin to brainwashing. This issue was raised by the Cursillo leadership. In response, professional theologians participated in Cursillos and revised the four talks given by clergy as theology took a different emphasis in the years during Vatican II; laypersons met and reconsidered their topics in light of their changing conception of self and their commitments; thus, "Piety" became "The Choice to be a Christian," and so on. Prayer is hardly spontaneous when carefully planned and carried out by a team; authoritarianism is not reduced unless decisions are arrived at by consensus; testimony is hardly authentic when each is required to testify—so the questioning continued. The nature of the content changed over the years and became an attempt to relate the updated theology of Vatican II to the daily life of a Christian in the world.

Although the Cursillo was conceived as a program to revivify the parish and the parishioner—to reinitiate the person into parish life—which it did in its beginning years, its ultimate effect was to encourage disaffection with parish involvement, to stimulate the creation of experimental communities and the development of forms of ministry concerned with social and community service.

While the emphasis, in San Francisco, was upon self-development, self-liberation, and personal growth, the Cursillo was, first and foremost, an experience of community. It engendered a commitment to participation in continued learning and religious communal development. In this respect it differed from sensitivity and encounter groups which tend to end up with a weekend "high"; it also differed from current secular or quasi-religious movements (such as est) as it emphasized the interdependence of the caring community that was formed in the Cursillo and that community's responsibility to the outside world.

Each Cursillo became a communion of equal individuals. Titles, status, occupation, and social class differentiations were not considered relevant to the formation of the Cursillo community, a common occurrence in situations of "communitas." Relationships which have previously been institutionalized or structured by norms of society change drastically when those cultural norms are dissolved in "communitas." When this dissolution and transgression of norms happens suddenly and spontaneously the new realizations of relatedness are accompanied with high affect. The self and other are face to face without the former definitions of status. "Communitas" means being with all, and each, as persons, all turning to, moving toward a common goal. Metaphorically, this experience of purification may "burn out" or "wash away" the di-

visions, separations, and alienating effects of structured
relationships and institutions. At the same time, one
becomes "liminal," stands upon a threshold, and enters into an unknown place where all that is familiar is
left behind; it is an experience accompanied by feelings
of "unprecedented potency" which are almost
everywhere considered to be *the* experience of the
sacred or holy.[3]

Such also are the characteristics of millenarian or
religious movements (and of some secular ones in our
times). These movements usually appeal to the
alienated, the uprooted, the oppressed, or the marginal persons in a society. While participants in the Cursillo were diverse in social class, race, and ethnicity, the
majority were very middle-class suburbanites. They
were selected or invited to participate because of their
demonstrated commitment to their Church and because of their potential to perceive the responsibility of
the Christian to the modern world.

Before analyzing the Cursillo as a setting for personality change I would qualify the foregoing account
from ten years of participant-observation in the Cursillo. I cannot depict an "average" man or woman who
chose to participate in the Cursillo. While the majority
were certainly middle-class, the minority who were not
(about 15 percent in the early and mid-1960s) had an
impact that is suggested by the post-Cursillo social
concerns of the middle class participants. The early
Cursillo teams were purposely and carefully diversified
to include a laborer as well as an educator; bilingual,
Spanish-speaking men and women; a mother or father
of several children and a single man or woman;
Roman Catholics, Anglicans, and Christians of other
denominations; nuns of different religious orders; the

very poor man or woman on welfare or jobless; Blacks
and Filipinos; people from the city and from the
suburbs. The team was made diverse in order to relate
to the diversity of those attending. Composition of the
Cursillo tables was planned with this same diversity as
the uppermost consideration, and bed assignments in
the dormitory were similarly made. Underlying the diversity was a common commitment to a religious tradition, a commitment that was to be reoriented in the
Cursillo experience of "rebirth" or reconstitution of the
self.

Theodore Sarbin and Nathan Adler[4] direct our attention to the conditions, the "identifiable sequence of
events" they perceive to be components of the "self-
reconstruction process" of conversion, a process
which, in their view, is essentially non-rational. Sarbin
and Adler suggest that most models of behavioral
change have been rationalistic and have focused upon
"verbal transactions" or talk as the "mediator of ra-
tionality." Thus, any departure from the apparent ra-
tionality of polite talk—methods of behavioral change
that applied theological metaphors or utilized such
procedures as isolation, ritual, dancing, fasting,
prayer—were considered by social scientists to be un-
scientific and not worthy of serious study. Sarbin and
Adler trace five communalities or themes that they
have isolated as sequential steps in the process of reconstruction of the self. The particular system or model
used for self-change is incidental. Significant reorganization of conduct will occur when the person (trainee,
client, convert, patient, and so on) becomes actively
involved in this "identifiable sequence of events."

First is symbolic death and rebirth. In some sense
the self is perceived as needing to be reborn because

one is, in some way, deadened. This deadening is denied initially: the person coming to the Cursillo comes to "get the experience" rather than to face futility in one's life or to experience despair. The first evening of the early Cursillo focused upon repentance (later changed to reconciliation) and persons were encouraged to participate in a sacramental ritual of Confession covering the entirety of one's life. This process acknowledged the self as in need and desiring to set aside past ways. The following day, Friday, was characterized as a Day of Faith or waiting, of being in "limbo"; people felt exhausted, uneasy, and most wished they were anywhere else but sitting around a table hour upon hour. By design, the day was somber and any singing or other escape was discouraged. Over the course of the day people began to know one another; on Saturday, the Day of Love, fatigue and familiarity encouraged informality. Those making the Cursillo were taught some of its Spanish songs, encouraged to relax, and the group began to cohere. The sense of rebirth and group consciousness was the theme of the songs and prayers. The last day of the Cursillo was a Day of Hope and willingness to fulfill one's newly perceived responsibility *beyond* the Cursillo. This day concluded with people who had previously made the Cursillo arriving to hear the testimony of "rebirth" of the new Cursillistas.

The second theme in the conversion process considers "The Group and Other," noting that in a religious or millennial culture the group provides the actual setting for change. Not only does the group provide role models that furnish specific objects to emulate, imitate, and identify with, it also conditions the environment so that certain performances or behaviors are *demanded* from the initiate or trainee. An "other" is required as a role model and as a source of information on how to carry out or enact these new roles. This mediating "other" or teacher is perceived as an esteemed member of the group in which the person seeks membership. The role of teacher in Cursillo was filled by a team of esteemed others—laypersons, nuns, and clergy who guided the Cursillistas through the process of death and rebirth. Prior to the Cursillo, this team had met for several months to prepare themselves for this experience and to familiarize themselves with the structure and content of the Cursillo, to become reinforcing agents and partial creators of the group consciousness that constituted the Cursillo. At the beginning of the Cursillo the esteem of the teachers created social distance, but this distance was reduced as the Cursillo continued. The whole group then took on the mediating role of the teachers and expressed concern that "everyone" make the Cursillo. They used the same techniques of positive regard, affection, encouragement, and openness that had been modeled by the team members. As the group became a total community it provided its own reinforcement.

The third theme, "Ritual Behavior," overlaps and mediates between the themes of death-rebirth and the group. In the conversion setting ritual functions both as an activity in itself and to manipulate time. Rituals have a "time-binding" component: the use of ritual activities manipulates time into concentrated, limited, and intense spans of individual attention. Setting aside time prepares the person for the setting aside of previous specific roles and begins a stripping away of achieved status, a prerequisite for "dying."

As I described earlier, time was structured in the

Cursillo in a disorienting manner. It enhanced separation from one's previous life as one gave up responsibility for one's own timekeeping. Ritual activity flowed back and forth between the little groups at their tables and the whole group and was specifically religious in content at intermittent intervals. At other times, ritual involved learning the songs of the movement, its history, and the telling of jokes. During the course of the Cursillo, ritual activity and "time-binding" initiated the person into a more active and participatory role and a sense of being an agent, illustrated by one refrain: "Prayers do not change things; prayers change persons and persons change things."

The fourth theme is "Proprioceptive Stimuli," that is, stimuli arising from within the body. Attention is shifted to within the self by fatigue states, sleeplessness, long periods of kneeling, silence, increasing involvement in ritual, and attention to one's table. One's view of one's environment is strange and baffling. One can then begin to *feel* strange and baffled. These feelings are aroused by the Cursillo experience and at the same time, reduced by positive regard, calm, support, and nurturance on the part of the team and later by the group-at-large. Periods of high involvement are followed by quiet and short periods of rest, or fruit and coffee breaks. A variation in stimuli brings about shifts involving emotions and physical and cognitive states. There is an oscillation between such emotions as awe, serenity, empathy, joy, loneliness, anxiety, dread, and emptiness.

Finally, the theme of "Triggers" was found in all the reports of self change. Triggers are events that are likely to promote or augment the process of self change. A trigger is a "high value stimulus." The Cursillo was structured to contain several events that emphasized and contributed to the sense of community. Other events were designed to enhance the person's sense of self and his or her relatedness to a transcendent God. A key event of Saturday was a three-to-five hour talk on sacramental theology, emphasizing biblical themes of "a chosen people," deliverance, and love. A liturgy followed in the little conference room, on a bare table with the priest facing all those standing around. The impact of this intimate sharing was felt by all, and for many was a first experience of *communitas*. This day ended with singing and candlelight setting the scene for an *Agape,* a ritual brought to the Cursillo by two laywomen, that consisted of breaking a large loaf of bread, passing portions to one another to eat, and the drinking of one small glass of wine.

If the Cursillo could be said to have a "trigger" it would be the various events that conveyed to the person that he or she was both loved and a part of a loving community. This perception made God believable and it was this perception of self and others that the individual experienced as conversion.

Sarbin and Adler began their report on "conduct reorganization" by deploring the resort to rationalism to explain conversion. Agreeing with them I would add that my account has been a rationalistic analysis of an essentially incommunicable experience, the outcome of which always remained in doubt. Many people did experience the Cursillo as a "conversion"; some simply enjoyed the weekend and largely forgot it; a very few found it dreadful and said so.

Between its introduction in 1962 and the time I surveyed this group, in August of 1974, approximately eight thousand people in the San Francisco Bay Area had participated in the Cursillo. About three thousand remained actively involved, in varying degrees, at the time of my surveys and subsequent interviews. These people include those most enduringly affected by the Cursillo, or most attached to the values it exemplified. They do not represent mainstream Roman Catholicism or Episcopalianism. They are people who chose to participate in a religious growth movement and have continued to do so. To those in the movement, the Cursillo became an initiation into a world of personal and social relatedness; at the same time it functioned as a separation rite from the rule-governed Church. Through the Cursillo they left the Church of their childhood, a Church that took care of them from birth to death and beyond. The self-sufficiency of traditional Roman Catholicism resided in an externally given "whole": directives for the good and virtuous life were explicit, shared, and unquestionable. Roman Catholics, along with other denominations, shared a state of mind, an ethos, that was called into question and broken open in the 1960s.

Meaning is called into question in persons. World-views or outlooks on life are modified because the self-understanding of the person-in-the-world has changed. Responses to a short survey[5] indicated that these people tended to perceive themselves as less authoritarian or ethnocentric, more concerned with society's problems and involved in social concerns than they had been in their adult years prior to participation in the Cursillo Movement. They saw their personal religion as less fundamentalist but still largely oriented to an anthropomorphic vision of God: their view of God seemed quite resistant to change. A longer, more searching questionnaire[6] (mailed to a selection of per-

sons whose responses to the first survey indicated substantial changes in their lives) suggests that the institutional Church had largely ceased to be meaningful to
these Cursillistas; increasing social involvement and interpersonal relationships provided new sources of
meaning for many. Attitudes toward sexuality were reported to have shifted toward liberalism—a frequently
qualified liberalism: while three fourths of those surveyed indicated their approval (sometimes or always)
of premarital cohabitation, parenthetical notations
such as, "But not for *my children,*" were not infrequent. Many were searching for other ways of living,
questioning the meaningfulness of their work, wondering about the future existence of Christianity, and im-
agining other possibilities for themselves.

I have focused here upon the Cursillo as a *source*
of people who are in the course of significant change,
change to be regarded as personal growth. I have
analyzed the setting of the Cursillo as a model for producing such change and examined some of the pro-
cedural features common to settings or environments
that seek to induce change of self. In the following
studies of individual lives we will be concerned with varieties of change and understanding the process of
change whether related to Cursillo or not. The kinds of
change for which interviews have been selected are in
the direction the Cursillo sought to promote; the
people interviewed were ones who had made the
Cursillo.[7]

Each one should decide his own conduct for himself. If it is good, then he can be proud of what he himself has done, without having to compare it with what someone else has done.—*Galatians, 6:4*

3
Deciding for Oneself at Fifty

THOMAS VAN DYKE

People make decisions daily. Wittingly or unwittingly these are ethical judgments insofar as they involve a decision as to the worthwhileness of one's values, time, self, things, relationships, and thinking processes.

These decisions are made from cultural referents that are also interpreted as religious laws. Historically the Judeo-Christian tradition has viewed its code of laws as delivered from a transcendent God, valid for all time and to be obeyed without question. The Ten Commandments have served as the truth which separated good from evil. In this tradition, ethical judgment was a matter of obedience to the law and any "deciding for oneself" was a deciding whether or not one's behavior was right or wrong in light of a particular law. The law itself or the nature of laws in general went unquestioned as did the origin of truth and authority: law, truth, authority, and God were one. What is of interest in this book is the process whereby a number of very obedient persons come to question—persistingly—and then to begin to decide that this questioning is a legitimate activity. This in turn leads to further questioning until gradually, for some—not all—rules become differentiated from truth, truth is pried loose from authority, and authority de-divinized.

Reliance upon an externally defined morality has been characteristic of Christianity. Knowledge of good and evil was delegated by God to civil and ecclesiastical authorities. This attitude is epitomized in the Thirteenth Rule of Orthodoxy in *The Spiritual Exercises of St. Ignatius*, founder of the Jesuits:

To be just in all things, I must be prepared, when I see something that is white, to believe that it is black if the hierarchy of the Church decides that it is so.[1]

The notion that one might not "know" whether something was good or evil was not an issue. The issue was that the Church had the authority to "know." Now, if laws, truth, authority, and God get pried apart, then just how does one know if something is right or wrong? To pursue this question it seemed useful to ask it, and to search people's replies for the locus of moral judgment. If the nature of authority and truth came to be called into question, the milieu in which the questioning occurred was probed, to note the issues, the context, the pattern and process of "deciding for oneself" in adult life.

Tom Van Dyke mused over the way "things used to be" in the "authoritarian Dutch tradition" in which he was raised. The fourth in a family of six children, he had just begun college in Oregon when he developed tuberculosis. He spent the next three and a half years in and out of the hospital taking correspondence

courses "to utilize time and not waste it." After miscel-
laneous jobs he went to work as a salesman in an Eastern timber company. At thirty-three he met his wife,
Ann, and shortly thereafter left the timber industry,
"kind of a doggy business, and not much prospect of
expansion for me." Tom went to work for the large
and nationally prosperous Mixor Corporation as a
salesman and was transferred to the Bay Area in 1968.
Tom, Ann, and their six children moved into St.
Jacob's Parish and "that began my first involvement
with *any* community affairs and that encompassed my
entire life." Tom continued:

I was at Mass one Sunday and John Carls [priest] announced that he wanted to form this social justice group.
About that time Ann was a little restless for something to do
which she thought could be valuable and she went herself,
then talked to me about it and I agreed to accompany her to
this meeting where there were two other couples. We got
acquainted with Tom Winters who had this awareness program where he was trying to get the Anglos aware of the
Mexican-American community problems. There was a
weekend put together—a group of us were supposed to visit
various Mexican families and spend the weekend in their
homes, which we did.

Well, it came across to me, it was an education for me,
as it came across to me it was apparent that all of—or a great
deal of—the problems of the Mexican-American and the
poverty they experienced was associated with employment
opportunities or lack of them. It all seemed to come back to
that one thing, employment opportunities. So I got an education about it. It came across to me!

Thomas Van Dyke described the effect of his immersion in the ghetto in language that conveys the impact of undergoing what Goulet calls the "shock of

underdevelopment." Statistical reports of low income, poor housing, disease, high mortality, and underemployment provide knowledge, but not necessarily understanding. Understanding comes as a result of the "shock," a sudden awakening to the hopeless predicament of the poor. One sees from inside the situation rather than from outside. One experiences the hopelessness and powerlessness of poverty as if they were one's own.

Tom's experience in the ghetto shocked him and moved him to act, and in so doing to experience the vulnerability and sense of powerlessness which prevail in the ghetto.

There was some discussion of employment opportunities in this group I was in—we'd meet every three to four weeks. So I got an education about it.

See, I'm working for this organization that has a reputation of being a progressive in all social matters: employment of minorities, women, discussing the issues on TV, and backing all these good causes and so forth, and a very highly publicized position on minority employment. So at the facility I worked at which was semi-autonomous we had 150 in sales and service and a few clerks and there was not a single minority there!

So I just naturally, because of a beginning of this awareness that was growing upon me, I asked a couple of people—first-line managers—why they weren't employing minorities and no one was able to give me an answer as to why when they were making such a big appearance in this area. "We've been hiring at this level and until someone instructs us or encourages us, why should we do that when there is no one bugging us to do it?" That was the answer.

I wanted to take that one step higher and ask somebody they reported to as to why something wasn't being done. But before I did that I wanted to research what the company's actual policy was—the real policy about employing Blacks or Mexicans or minorities in field offices. So I used a question box channel that we had for such things and mailed my inquiry back East. So I just sent my inquiry to them. I wasn't doing anything surreptitiously—it was just research and I wanted to let my own manager know that I was investigating something I had an interest in and I was going to pursue the thing a little bit to see if I couldn't help the company to implement—in this area—what its policy was in general. So I sent my manager a copy of the inquiry and in the margin I said I just wanted him to know I had an interest in this area and I'd be pleased to be of help wherever I could.

Tom paused here, emphasizing that he wanted to be certain that I understood what he was about to tell me.

I don't know if you can understand what I'm telling you at this point—there wasn't anything in my mind that was controversial. At that time I thought this was the type of thing that the company encouraged. It seemed reasonable to research the situation before I made any direct offer of what I could do and lo and behold I get this reply—this written reply. He rakes me over the coals for having made the inquiry.

So that is the beginning. He made it clear that I was in direct opposition to branch management by having made this inquiry and he sent copies of this letter to me to other management people who directly influence my career, putting them on notice—"Look, I am citing this man for a serious failure in my estimation," and he is putting all these people on notice that this is his evaluation of me and you can imagine what this does to my career.

It became right or wrong when I received the reply from my manager to my initial inquiry and he castigated me for having made the inquiry. He was penalizing me for having made the inquiry. That is something I was aware enough about to realize I would fight to the end. That would have to be rectified. That was a decision made at that time. As a matter of fact when I got that letter I was staggered by it. I couldn't believe it. I showed it to Ann and I told her what this means to me is that I am forced to respond to this and get it cleared up and that we face the possibility of getting in over our necks about this thing and before I do that I want her to realize what I am doing and she was with it all the way.

During this time Tom had a "fantastic year" and achieved 1,050 percent of his budget which put him close to thirty thousand for that year and placed him as the top salesperson in the area. Before he mailed his "inquiry" East, Tom had been slated for a task-force assignment prior to a management assignment. His manager attempted to have Tom removed from the task force without success. After completing the assignment, Tom returned and found his manager still opposed to discussing what could be done at the branch to make way for minorities to be hired there.

He had already taken a position from which he would not back down. Damage had been done to my career and it was permanent damage. He was intractable about it so I began to develop defenses as well as aggressiveness about the matter. One of my combined aggressive-defensive moves after I had gotten my answer back from the East, was to put together a written proposal on what the branch should do about employing Mexican-Americans, a formal, written proposal which I submitted to the branch manager who was over my manager. They accepted the proposal. They had to. It was written and he couldn't go on record as being opposed to that. He refused to implement it and the months rolled by and the months rolled by and nothing was being done . . . so I got a little pushy. Four months after I made the proposal he agreed to allow a recruiting seminar to be held but in two parts. The first part was to be a hearing of community representatives and the second was to be to develop an affirmative action plan. Well, the first seminar was held but the second part of it was not.

Six months more and nothing was happening. What sparked it was on January 1, we became a full-fledged branch and had to increase employment by about 10 percent which meant sixteen people—up to the time this guy had been saying, "We can't do it because we aren't hiring anybody." So they hire one Mexican-American and here was this opportunity. . . .

So we [the group Tom had been meeting with all along] talked it over and decided to get the Confederación into it, and the EOC [Equal Opportunity Commission] wrote letters addressed to this man. It came as a shock to him because here was a public organization citing him and his organization for neglecting a public duty—in being a representative of a major corporation which had this image . . . and copies went off to Senators and Representatives and the State Board and the President of the Company.

When he got that he called me into his office—the way he did this—was he called me into his office with a couple of other minor management people and proceeded to tell me that I was going to stop it right now or else. Then the manager got up and walked out—just long enough for his righthand man to tell me if I didn't stop what I was doing he was going to fire me—and then the manager walked back in.

So it was a very serious situation and it proceeded from there. He wrote a formal request for my termination. Before the end of the year they got rid of this man but they could not admit he had taken a wrong position. So I hired an attorney and filed my own individual case under Title VII of the Civil Rights Law and the EOC decided to come along. I'm going to continue the court battle which is coming up this winter—we have a trial date now.

You have to understand the conflict was not a right-or-wrong situation; that wasn't the issue *here* [emphatically]. It wasn't a question of right or wrong about minority employment. You have to understand that it was company policy to encourage minority hiring and I was just simply working within—I thought—that policy. It was just the expeditious thing to do. If I was working with a group of people who said: Let's all make a little bit of effort to help to get a few people employed—so my little effort is just to go and say: "Look, Mr. So-and-so, our company says we should be hiring people so let's put on some." I am not talking about any sacrifice or any moral issue. I was talking about something that was expeditious for everyone else. That I think is the confusing thing about all of this. A lot of people want to look at that as a moral issue. It really wasn't the case. It was a political case, it was an economic issue, but it wasn't a moral issue. It became a moral issue—the only moral issue was when he began to penalize me for something I had a right to do. Then it became a moral issue, as far as I was concerned. How do you decide whether or not something is right or wrong or a moral issue? [laughs]

You tell me—you get a different answer to that for almost every stage of life, I think. The older I get—yeah, I don't think truth changes but your appraisal of what is right or wrong does change. The older I get the more inclined I am to say—you don't know what is right or wrong. The younger I was the more positive I would be in making a decision.

Well, how do you decide if something is right or wrong now? Well, I'd say that I probably won't be able to give any complete answer to that until I finish my life because that's always a question in my mind. How do you determine what is right or wrong? I give you an example: when I was younger . . . we raised our first kids—we disciplined them very strictly. We disciplined them very strictly! At that time that appeared the right thing to do. You take a look at this spoiled three-year-old. You realize that there has been a great change, at least in my thinking. You're not absolutely certain. I'm more so that way today than I have been in the past and getting more so. I don't mean by that doubt or uncertainty. I don't mean—I'm saying that in regard to the other party involved in the dispute—I can be pretty certain of my position but that doesn't mean that the other person is wrong. That is what I am trying to tell you—it means that the other person may be looking at it from an angle that I haven't seen or there may be some basis for that person holding that position which mitigates the circumstances or explains that position or gives a little bit of validity to it. The more I understand about that position the more inclined I'll be to find a common ground. I can take that position with the Arabs and the Jews, for example. I can see that each side of that has got a valid position and I can see that each side has got a wrong position, too, apparently from this viewpoint.

Another example is what the Church says is right or wrong. Well, that is probably the area of *greatest* change in my thinking in my lifetime. The *greatest* area of change there has come within the last ten years, maybe even more restricted to the last five or six. Once again, it's not—I'm a Catholic as you know—it's not a position of having much of a change in my thinking of what's right or wrong. In other words, the Catholic ideology still makes sense to me. But the opposing ideology makes more sense to me all the time. That is what I'm saying. The Protestant theology—I have much more respect for the Protestant theology all the time.

An example comes from my association with people in groups like this interfaith group that meets for breakfast on Tuesday mornings. I was just never that close to people like this before. Their thinking is good thinking. It is Christian thinking. It isn't doctrinal thinking; it is Christian thinking. That is the thing I dislike about the Catholic procedure—this tendency to doctrinize everything. In other words, instead of proclaiming the basic teachings of Christ on love—to translate that in terms of "love means not eating meat on Friday" or "love means . . ." I don't know. It becomes form. It means, "love means going to Mass every Sunday, just being there, or not entertaining couples who married invalidly" . . . this type of thing. I know that is not doctrine but that is the interpretation of it. This is the old family approach to things that I became acquainted with. It's distorted. Just plain human laziness to take this great flexible law of Christ to love your neighbor, and to translate that into a few lines of if you do this, if you do this, if you do this you're guaranteed a slot in heaven or something like that. That type of thing brings ridicule upon Christianity.

The next thing that enters into this is when you say "what the Church teaches." Now—when you use that phrase it has a different meaning today than it had to me ten years ago. At *that* time there *was* something very positive in my mind. What the Church teaches is a certain—concrete, immobile—something . . . you could always go to page 22, line 7 and you'd get the answer to every situation. Now that is no longer true. The Church is the people and what the Church teaches—now—is not a question of turn to page such-and-such and listen to what this theologian has to say. You're listening to the whole Church, you have to listen to what all of the Church is saying and you do still, ultimately, have a decision to make yourself. In other words, it used to be in my mind that the Church made the decision—all you had to do was look and say: "Church, what do you say? Right or Wrong?" That's the simple way, the easy way, the way a lot of people would like to have it. The mature way and the way I'm sure Christ intended it to be is that it is not easy. Before you can make a decision on any of these things we've been talking about you have to listen to all input and make your own decision. And this is further complicated by the fact that you don't know when even that rock-bottom teaching of the Church that the Pope is always right—that isn't even a certainty. When he is speaking from authority with his red hat or whatever—even that is something you have to make a decision on. When is he the voice of the Church? Or just a fallible human being? In the same respect, you have to listen to him and then you have to decide from your other input whether that is the voice of the Church.

After his employment at the Mixor Corporation was terminated, Tom sold his home, got a real estate license, and worked at real estate for a year and a half. The income wasn't enough, however. So he built on his previous experience with remodeling to become a journeyman carpenter—"not a very good one," he said—and he alluded to the physical strain. "It's not a very desirable thing to break into late in life—you have to go on unemployment and all of that."

I anticipated that it would not be easy to go out and make that kind of money but I have developed a philosophy that you have to take risks and my particular philosophy is such that it accommodates poverty if that is your lot or wealth— it's nicer to be wealthy. It's also boring and degrading and everything else. There is more to life than security. . . . there isn't much to be afraid of. Unless you are talking about being afraid that you won't eat steak instead of hamburger or you are afraid of driving a ten-year-old car instead of a brand-new one. That's a different kind of fear. That's a social fear. And social fears have never bothered me very much. I don't know why, but they haven't. Besides, anyone with his health does not have to be that concerned—he can make ends meet. That doesn't apply to the Mexican-American or the Black in a ghetto. Well, I want to modify that—if you have your health and the opportunities that are afforded to the privileged white American male—is what I should have said . . . it is an entirely different thing. You take an uneducated Mexican-American, living in the ghetto, who has no contacts and can't even speak the English language and has burdensome responsibilities—it is a different situation.

Just thinking of my own situation—the family responsibilities—it's a burden even for me. When you get seven children it is quite a burden. Six is a burden. The seventh was quite a surprise. Ann had been infertile after the last child and from that time until this last one, we didn't use any kind of contraceptive. She was on some medication for thyroid and all of a sudden she was pregnant. It was during that pregnancy that the decision was made that she couldn't go through that again. For one thing, it is quite a burden on the woman to bear the child after you have had that many and after that to raise that child. The time has come in her life—she should be able to relax, she is still a young woman.

At the time of her pregnancy we didn't consider abortion. I don't think that I personally have actually faced that issue squarely yet in my life. Let's say squarely—I'd say I faced it indirectly in the way I was telling you. That I can see an opposing view now has more potential for merit than I would be inclined to say otherwise. On balance, it seems to be something that has great potential for damage—terrible damage. Abuse and potential for abuse is probably the greatest thing to be said against it.

All right, if you set aside the possibility of abuse and face it just on the issue of its own merits or not—the issue of whether that fetus is life, is human life or not. I'm not sure in my own mind what the answer to that is. This is one case where I give considerable amount of weight to the doctrinal position . . . it does seem to me that the life once begun is life and it is wrong to terminate it at any point beyond that. And yet, the sperm and the egg separate[ly], are they not life themselves before and if they join? That's another question exactly when—why is it more life after they join than before?

In other words, before they join you call it contraception and after they join you call it abortion. Are they not one and the same thing?

That points out the limits of my personal thinking—how far it's gone. I haven't carried that thought out that far except we did have a discussion with our oldest daughter on that exact situation—if she were pregnant—what would you say to the daughter? How would you react to that child? I think that we explained that a year ago. The action would be: what can I do to help you?—it would be that question, what can I do to help you? I think the fact that this happened represents a certain degree of tragedy . . . you've got, you're faced with a problem concerning life and you don't know if you have the means to sustain it, or the proper means in the normal fashion. With a thirteen-year-old raising the child, you know, a contradictory situation. So I can't feature myself, at this *particular* time, ever counseling anybody to have an abortion. I cannot feature myself at this time with that advice as a solution . . . but . . . well, in the first place, my not being a woman, I never have to make that decision. I never am going to be in a position in my life where I ever have to make that decision on abortion. The only thing I could do would be influence somebody's decision. Unless I have complete authority over somebody which I don't feel I have over anybody, including my own children, except for this youngest one, who has no ability to accept responsibility on her own. So, I don't think that I have that complete authority—I sometimes exercise it, though!

So where I am—if you are married you couldn't advise it, but then if a woman is raped it is right to have a D. and C. . . . All of this, of course, relates to contraception. The old doctrinaire approach on that was—marriage is for the raising of families and nothing should interfere with the procreation of children—I think there is a citation from the Old Testament that dispersing your seed upon the ground, something like that. I think that is the one used. And then the argument

is raised if every couple in the world had six children and so
forth and soon there isn't going to be room on earth or food.
And the answer to that is of course, grow more food, fish for
more fish, and we'll worry about that when that day comes.
A doctrinaire answer, a real doctrinaire. I have to say it
makes more sense to say that God gave a couple the ability
to have ten children because if two survived because of wars
and famine . . . but today that attrition isn't happening so
obviously man is going to bring planning to this, too. The
last stumbling block is whether it is chemicals and condoms
or the rhythm system. That is the final stumbling block when
someone is making that rationalization or conversion. That's
a proper decision. As a matter of fact, today, in explaining it
to the children I would lean towards the explanation that
was always used by the proponents of contraception—that
under certain circumstances it was an admirable thing. Making that decision . . . well, it was the pressure of circumstances and nature. We had talked about it before, so it was
nothing new . . . it was at the time . . . about a year before I
was terminated—we came to that decision. You ultimately
have to make that decision yourself.

In going back over this period, Tom could not
pinpoint any time when he questioned what he called
"the doctrinaire" position and separated it from what
he called the Catholic ideology. However, he was quite
clear about making decisions to *act*. Acting is a matter
of "expansion."

It was a matter of taking a risk if there was to be any expansion, otherwise I would have been stalemated the rest of my
life which I didn't want to do.

And that meant making decisions. Tom felt the basic
Catholic ideology had always been there but they
taught the "chaff" instead of the "wheat." He emphasized the important change had been in the area of

"what the Church says" and he now questions the
Church as *teacher* of *a particular* position. This arose
when he said that his children had been in a parochial
school in the East, but when they moved out here
there was a year or so waiting list:

So with the waiting list we just never found it desirable. Now,
that is something that I've done a complete about-face . . .
I'm more likely now to say it is a *bad* thing. I am less and less
inclined toward anything that sets up barriers between
people. Now, if you got a better education it might be
OK but I'm not certain of that, and besides the Church
isn't in the business of giving better education. It is in the
business of getting people to think, at least from my point
of view.

While the institutional Church has lost meaning
for Tom, God has become "more incomprehensible,
but more certainly real." The Liturgy has never been
particularly meaningful to Tom; nevertheless, he generally attends Sunday Mass, with some feelings of ambiguity, but:

As a rationalization for it, we ask ourselves as parents guid-
ing kids . . . no matter what you say it comes out best by way
of example. The question is, is it something to demand or
encourage? I'm inclined . . . ceremony doesn't mean anything to me. Never has. But I still have the belief that there is
a need for some sort of discipline. Whether Mass satisfies
that or not is a question. We still have a need for some kind
of formal recognition or display of our acknowledgment of
our all being one and having to pay allegiance to God, our
Creator. As some sort of a minimum requirement the person
has need to satisfy that. Now, it would be better to do that in
a way God created him to understand. One way, not necessarily the best—it's good until something better comes
along—is Mass.

Tom notes a tendency that is new "to measure all things against the standards that Jesus set." Again, it is the *deciding* that is important. Tom said he is easily moved to tears "not [by] something sad, that wouldn't make me cry, but someone who has made a difficult decision—then finally does it, that's a happy situation, brings tears to my eyes. I am less affected by tragedy, isn't that strange?"

"Something else now," Tom adds: "I would stand up for the rights of any individual . . . I would stand up for the right of any person much more so than I [once] would have." His encounters with the Mexican-American community have had a definite impact of "experience versus knowing about something." Tom and Ann had been aware of racial discrimination in the East but were never in any direct contact with minorities. "We knew it before on an intellectual level, but there was never any opportunity for contact." Tom had always felt the dignity of the person to be important. "You can't give . . . I don't think you give minorities—anybody—dignity. People have to *take* dignity. A person who is denied the visible aspects of dignity, who reacts to that, gains dignity. You cannot be denied dignity. The person has it and demands it."

Tom discussed the difficulties of standing up for his own rights and opposing the Mixor Corporation, and the lack of empathy among his co-workers.

You have to remember in an organization like that people are selected for that type of work for their aggressiveness and the most highly successful salespeople are highly aggressive and will step over anybody to get where they are going—a sad situation but true. I would say I am competitive and I don't hesitate in a competitive situation to win, which is to say the other person loses. The thing I hesitate about is doing it by stabbing somebody in the back. I would prefer to have a good clean competition. Work my tail off to beat him—to a certain extent that would be unfair competition, you know, if you work twenty-four hours a day to nail down a contract and win it away from someone else who is only given a normal day's work to do it in—to a certain extent that is unfair competition. But that is, for the most part, the dirty trick that would be involved. The art of selling is a strange thing. The all-important thing is to get someone's name on the bottom of a contract and sometimes very questionable practices might be used. In the process of selling someone something, if I honestly believed that that person would benefit by the product I might withhold information from him that might influence him not to sign an agreement. Technically, that's not right, but I wouldn't hesitate about doing that if I figured I was doing the right thing by him. That is probably a rationalization but it is true.

Thus, given the competitive and aggressive nature of sales work Tom was not surprised that "there was no rush to support me. The few I did discuss it with did not share their honest opinions with me, I think. After I was terminated, some did cooperate by giving depositions." In 1972 Tom had been fired, he and Ann had an unexpected baby, and earlier in the year Tom had attended a Cursillo and subsequently worked on one. That was also the year in which he and Ann made the decision to use contraceptives. Tom does not think any of these events are related to each other: "they are separate situations." As far as the Cursillo was concerned, Tom had been involved in the Cursillo movement long before he attended one: he was surrounded by people deeply involved in the Cursillo movement, social justice, support for the Farm Workers' Boycott, and as he recalls it, "by happenstance." His choice of St. Jacob's Parish was accidental in that he found a home which happened to be within the parish. At this time, Ann "just decided she wanted to do something else . . . she had been in the Rosary Society and National Conference of Catholic Women and she stopped by the Rectory to see about doing something else. She saw John Carls who suggested we come to the Sunday Folk Mass in the Hall, not the Church. From there one thing led to another—the time was ripe."

In 1970 St. Jacob's was moderately polarized with an exceedingly conservative pastor and two very liberal assistant pastors who were involved in the Cursillo movement, were bilingual, and were committed to the cause of the Farm Workers. By the end of 1972 both assistants had left, one to marry and the other to go to another parish where he remains involved in community concerns. The atmosphere was "challenging" as Tom remembers it. It was during this period that Tom began going to ecumenical Tuesday morning breakfasts. He could not remember who had invited him to come along: "It was a very informal thing with a few ministers, dedicated people, some women interested in women's liberation." It was a good experience "being with people who were concerned about social issues . . . though I had to leave that when I took up carpentry."

While the challenge of those years was important to Tom, he now believes the most important challenge facing him is the need for a change "between these two partners in the marriage."

One thing that takes on greater importance in my life involves Ann. If we could roll back the clock—attempt to develop different roles for her other than mother and housewife all the time. At this stage when things are all firmed up—all firmed up, and no preparations made, yet there is a need for change in this life and these two partners. How to accomplish this is the biggest challenge that faces us over the next two years.

We've got one miserable woman here, with her realization that there is nothing she can do other than housewife—here with the kids. I don't know if she is going to make it. She uses the argument that if she goes out to do something she will just have to pay someone to take care of this and won't be ahead. I think her mental health is worth it: the purpose here is not to make money but to change the scene. I wish there was something I could do to help. She needs to do it herself. These coming two years before this little one is in school—this coming year . . . I am really not sure she will make it!''

Tom's concern was very evident as was his feeling of helplessness about the problem. A quiet, calm, and dignified man, Tom evidenced strong feelings when talking about his wife's present role. His worry was apparent as had been his anger as he talked about receiving the initial letter from his manager. These were the only two areas where Tom's feelings disturbed his usual articulate, thoughtful manner of speaking.

Looking back over this period with Tom it is difficult to point out any one event or factor as "cause" for his taking on the corporation, and modifying and altering his belief system about almost everything—except his conception of truth as existing concretely. Tom does not perceive himself as a liberal. Prior to the Cursillo, Tom thought those in authority should be obeyed. After the Cursillo, but not necessarily as a result of it, Tom's concern was with "effectively opposing the unwarranted use of power by whosoever resorts to it." He does perceive his enculturation as lacking critical thought: it is no longer possible for him to "pick a theologian" to believe. Diversity and pluralism are positively valued in his life now. For Tom, the "shock" of underdevelopment provided a learning experience and suggested to him an area in which he might do something. His experience of an extraordinarily successful year reinforced his knowledge of his own competence and may have influenced his decision to take the issue of his termination to court.

Deliberate, articulate, and thoughtful, Tom weighs his words, examines his rationalizations with humor, and moves on. Tom's life is not governed by fear, either of loss of status, money, or security. Indeed, he regards his present uncertain situation as an opportunity to "try out some contracting and take a few law courses at night—see what opens up."

4

A Radical Nun

RUTH McCARTHY

Perry notes that aligning oneself with authority leads to a dualistic structuring of the world:[1] a we/they viewpoint. As we/they-ness is sensed and ambiguity regarding authority's possession of the whole "truth" is experienced, possibilities of outright opposition to all authority or some sort of expedition to find the "right" authority arise. This latter move may appear timid when compared to a global denouncement of authority. But by virtue of its totalism, outright opposition can cause one to resubmit to another authority. Such a simplistic rejection of authority avoids the "working through" process. The searching expedition, though a far less radical move, can begin a journey where there is room to grow. This assumes, of course, that while those in authority "know," they have announced that there are areas where one must "work it through" for oneself. Thus, the journey is begun out of obedience and with the belief that some rules, laws, or whatever have a human tradition while others are of divine origin. Obviously, those made by persons may be rethought; those of divine origin are not subject to such a process and can only be interpreted by the "right" authority.

If the person embarking on this journey is also *in* a position of authority and she/he perceives the meaning and nature of authority as changeable while in this position, creativity and originality may flourish. There is also the possibility that the disintegration may be more than the person can bear. Happily, that is not the outcome here.

Ruth McCarthy was the fourth and last child born to an Irish immigrant couple who raised their family during the Depression. There was little money and a constant struggle to find work. The family lived "very simply and by their convictions," Ruth remembers:

There were always people in our home. There was never just the six of us. There were uncles and cousins or somebody from Ireland or anybody who was down and out. Their home was open . . . and people would say to my mother, "Why do you let people come in, you know you don't have enough food for your own children?" But they just lived that way.

One of the things I always sensed from my parents was . . . even as a small child . . . they really trusted me. They would tell me if I did wrong, or if I didn't meet their standards. But at the same time, when the chips were down, I knew they trusted and believed in my goodness. My dad came through very, very strongly, in any decisions that I made . . . like the decision to go into the convent . . . and my mother tried to cover all the bases by saying "Feel free to come home, we'll still love you."

Subsequently Ruth was appointed to two positions of responsibility and ultimately was elected to head the religious order she had entered. Ruth describes those years of responsibility as "the hardest and most freeing of my life" and thinks that being in those positions, particularly when she led the order, enabled her to come "to a slowly-formed realization that I was a self-determining person, that I could make decisions, with regard to my own life and that would affect the lives of others. And a sense of my own goodness in doing that . . . a sense of believing in that."

Self-determination, autonomy, and responsibility are valued in our society. However, the idea of becoming a self-determined nun is a rather new one as far as Roman Catholic religious life is concerned. Taking a vow of obedience and living with a group of people and a superior who have taken the same lifelong vow is hardly the environment one would expect to generate self-determination. Although the communal living of the convent has been viewed as a respected alternative to private family life, even as better than married life, in practice this alternative became institutionalized powerlessness—submission to one's superior who in turn obeyed the bishop's commands. There have always been some exceptions to this docility but their fate has been rather uniform.

Daly notes that in medieval times abbesses had the power to suspend clergy under their jurisdiction, wore miter (headpiece) and cross, and carried a staff as bishops did. Until the last one died in 1809, the abbesses of Conversano, Italy, received homage from the clergy under their jurisdiction. Large abbeys in Germany, Italy, England, and Spain, some including double orders of monks and nuns, were ruled by abbesses.

These instances of abbess rule were rare and exceptional, of course. From 1289 on, papal decrees and church legislation imposed *strict* enclosure (cloister) upon all religious women. This meant that once a woman became a nun she was enclosed in the convent for life—a condition which lasted until the early 1960s. There were occasional revolutionaries who attempted to break open this prison. One was Angela Merici (1474–1540) who founded the Ursuline order which survived her but not as she had planned. Angela had wanted a company of women who were not bound by the cloister or the habit. She wanted women to live a virginal life while at the same time laboring in the world.[2] The hierarchy, including the Cardinal Archbishop of Milan, Charles Borromeo, disapproved, and after Angela's death dispatched her company back into cloister, habit, and vows of obedience. A similar fate befell the plans of Jeanne de Chantal and Francis de Sales for the Sisters of the Visitation and many, many more, including religious orders attempting to break out of the old forms in the 1960s. Suppression, censure, and decrees from Rome awaited the reformers of the sixties, among them Sister Ruth, known then as Mother St. James.

When Ruth entered religious life in 1940, being a nun almost meant not-being. Life was regimented and regulated from the moment one awoke to a bell until after night prayer when the "great silence" began— not to be broken until the next morning's bell called one to prayer. Once a woman entered the convent, she could not visit her home or any other home except when carrying out some act of mercy. Visiting hours were strictly regulated and the nun could see her family for a few hours one Sunday a month—except during Lent. Of primary importance was obedience to the "Rule" laid down by the founder of the order. The intent of the Rule was to foster charity and other virtues in a dedicated community, as indicated by this excerpt from the prologue of *The Rule of St. Benedict* (480–550):[3]

We are therefore about to establish a school of the Lord's service in which we hope to introduce nothing harsh or burdensome.

However, in practice, religious life was burdensome. The emphasis was upon obedience to a massive amount of ritualized trivia including such things as "custody of the eyes" (keeping one's eyes focused down so as not to be distracted by others and thus be drawn away from the presence of God), how to bathe oneself modestly, how, when, where, and what to pray or read, how and what to eat, how to put one's habit on and how to take it off.

Authority was held in awe and reverence because authority came directly from God. One would become *free* to carry out God's *will* by *obedience* to the rule. Nuns lived under vows of poverty and chastity as well as obedience. Poverty did not mean lack of anything, it meant one did not own things and a "poverty of spirit." Chastity meant no friendship and instant repression of any sexual feeling or thought. Nuns did not have friends because "particular friendships" were expressly forbidden.

Failure to comply with any aspects of the rule were made public in a ceremony called the "Chapter of Faults" in which the individual nun accused herself, in the presence of her community, of the rules she had failed to obey: dishes dropped, sleepiness during prayers, habit askew. The emphasis was upon obedience, charity, meekness, humility, self-abnegation, sacrifice, and service, all defined and decided by au-

thority. Emotion, creativity, thinking, and any asser-
tiveness were repressed. Socialization to the rule was
conducted by a novice mistress who lived with the
young women in a separate building for the two-year
period of initiation into the order.

The mistress of novices held an important position, one in which she could profoundly influence
others. The young sisters were dependent upon her for
their image of themselves as sisters. Ruth remembers
not only her own relationship to her novice mistress,
but also the effect upon her when she was appointed
to that same position:

I had gone from the dependence of the home to the dependence of the community. I entered at seventeen and a year
later at age eighteen I was teaching and I felt the responsibility of growing and developing in that area and at the same
time being told, "This is the way you are as a sister and this
is how you grow as a person." I had a great dependence
upon my novice mistress because I had just transferred from
mother to novice mistress and even after the novitiate [two-
year period of initiation] still treasured her friendship. I
taught first grade for *ten* years because . . . the novice mistress thought for me . . . I trusted what she thought about me
more than what I . . . and I hated teaching first grade. I liked
to play with the little kids but I did not like to teach them and
I finally realized that I was going through agony every September when we'd start another crowd of first graders and
my superior said, "If you don't say something to get out of it
I am going to say it for you. This is really terrible. It is not
good for you and it is not good for the kids."

Ruth's novice mistress remained her model for
about eight years until Ruth went to Los Angeles for a
community event and "saw her for the first time from
an adult viewpoint and was shattered, really disap-

pointed in what I saw. She wasn't the ideal that I had believed in and I think that there I began to trust my own judgment. That was a shattering experience but it was a growing up."

The role of a model or "mentor" in the life of a young adult is very important. The mentor is a guide who regards the young person as a younger adult, not as a girl/boy or a daughter/son, and who supports the young adult's "dream" and helps her or him to put it into effect. The mentor is a non-parental career role model who helps the young adult overcome the parent-child polarity. Lack of a mentor may hinder development. However, imitating a model may necessitate shrinking the self in order to fit the model. Ruth's novice mistress was more role model than mentor and as such was a developmental handicap.

I think there is a big lacuna in my own growth and development, which was the early period of my religious life—I would say from the age of seventeen to maybe the age of twenty-seven or twenty-eight. Those years where I really accepted the whole guru idea. I really accepted the wisdom of other people. I think I was doing a lot of my own thinking on the way, but not trusting it. And probably during that time I made a lot of right decisions by accepting someone else's decision.

Then, when I was about twenty-nine or thirty I was appointed superior and principal. It was a sort of graphic sense of what I began to come to—the realization of my own personhood. There was the growing sense of responsibility I got from my community of being superior and principal and really feeling the closeness of sisters in community for probably the first time. I think that during that time of being superior, to a great extent, I let go of other people's values and began to assert my own.

For example, in community life, friendship and all that smacked of love relationships between sisters was really looked down upon. I sensed that that wasn't good.

The rule wasn't good. Probably I had never really lived it in my own life except that I have a certain amount of detachment that I think is part of the discipline of those years but may also be part of the Irish temperament. I don't know what it is but I was able to live through it. But when I sensed that this was a time that I had something good to give . . . maybe I had a sense of right and wrongness and I felt I had a right to be myself. One sister in particular, who was going through a lot of really hard troubles . . . and was really fighting. She had gone through surgery for teeth and for three days and three nights she had no sleep . . . after the surgery she had such pain and she had such a low threshold of pain, that she got absolutely no rest. Finally I called the dentist and I said—it was Easter Sunday—"You've got to come and do something for her." So he came, he gave her a shot, and she was on her way out. I was sitting by her bed and she kept saying: "You're so good, you're so good. God must be good because you're so good." It was the first person outside of my family that had felt I was good. And I think . . . that was the *first* insight I had about what the gospel . . . the message really was. Telling someone else that they were really good and helping them to appreciate the depths of their own goodness. I would say that was the starting point of my own growth.

That incident occurred after I had been given the responsibility or authority . . . I've often thought that I might not have grown if I hadn't been given the authority by the community. Well, you know, I guess I was the good religious kind. I think I was trusted. At age thirty I had been living in the community for twelve years. So, you know, I think I had a sense of trust from the superiors, both those that dealt with me directly and the higher superiors. Those tasks at that time were appointive. In a sense it was from . . . I believe that authority comes from the community—within the group. And in a sense I think it was true that it came from the sisters I lived with and dealt with.

So I think that had a big influence on me. Another thing that had a big influence . . . and this is strange because this was a whole negative kind of thinking. But I had an experience during that time [of being principal and superior of a convent] of a major superior telling me that I was doing all the wrong things. I think that was the very first time I really took a different stand from the person who had been my superior. I just recognized that if I was doing things wrong she would have to take me out of office. I had to be who I was. I think she was trying, probably, to get me to conform more to standards.

Another thing that I think had a profound influence on me was when I was appointed novice mistress and went to the novitiate, and was dealing with young people who were trying to seek a rationale for the life I had accepted twenty years before. This was 1962 to 1964. I went to the novitiate with fifty young seventeen to eighteen year olds who asked why, why, why to everything I had been doing for twenty years. They really helped me because they questioned everything about religious life. At first it was just driving me mad . . . I was driven up a tree because I had taken everything for granted by this time. Then I remember saying to them: "Please keep questioning me. I might not have the answer and I might only be able to say to you—'That's the way we do it.' But don't stop questioning me."

It became *very clear* to me just how much I had assimilated that had *no* meaning to me. Reasons that I had been given twenty years before just didn't hold water. For example . . . one of the most difficult things, I think, that I ever had to try to explain was the community Chapter of Faults. This kind of thing, you know, was something you had to do if you were a novice mistress. I spent more time talking about that, and explaining it away . . . since then they've done away with that . . . than in helping them to come to an honest deal with themselves—and each other. I think this was probably the basis of what the Chapter of Faults was all about. But it was put in such a phony external kind of humiliating, debasing framework. . . . People never internalized the core of what the thing was about. I think what I was asking for was: give me the freedom in which to operate, and the same thing will come about. But why do I have to waste time explaining the full formulary of I am sorry for doing something and then . . . and then they talk about *things*. Novices would talk about things of no importance: breaking dishes, being late, and what-have-you. And never get to the things where maybe they were crunching another person or stifling themselves—say by keeping the atmosphere from the growth-producing atmosphere of acceptance that you wanted to grow—well, the opposite was happening. It's so much easier to just hide behind the framework of "dos" and "don'ts."

I think those two years prepared me for what probably was the most freeing experience of my life even though it was the hardest experience of my life which was to be *mother general* of the order.

In 1964, Ruth was elected to lead her order during a time of upheaval and polarization within Roman Catholicism. The church had called for renewal and reform, a plea that was taken seriously by several heads of religious orders who had begun to communicate with one another about the formation or socialization of sisters to religious life. In many, many instances the hierarchy reacted to *any* change in religious life with instant condemnation, threats, and calls for "obedience."

The Glenmary order's confrontation with Archbishop Alter of Cincinnati exemplifies the attitude most of the hierarchy had about attempts by religious orders to change their living situation in order to be of service in the world. The Glenmary sisters wanted to live with and serve the urban and rural poor in southern Ohio. Archbishop Alter reacted by restricting the sisters' hours and limiting their contacts with laypersons. In the months following his orders in the spring of 1967, about twenty-five sisters left the order. In August a mass exodus occurred. Fifty sisters left indicating that the attitude toward sisters in the Church made it impossible for them to continue to work as sisters; they would continue their work as laypersons.

It was in this climate that Ruth took office and set out to obey the call for renewal. At the suggestion of some of her sisters who were involved in the Cursillo, Ruth made the Cursillo. The Cursillo "opened up a whole new world of relationship . . . outside the clerical world. Through Cursillo I met many people who were striving for the same things that I'd been dreaming about." The Cursillo was one "turning point" for Ruth. "The most *extraordinary* experience of my life" followed:

It was coming into contact with Ivan Illich . . . going to Cuernavaca, coming into contact with Illich and Daniel Berrigan . . . there were two workshops lasting a week. Georgia [a sister who was one of Ruth's advisors] and I grew close together during the workshops. . . . Mind blowing . . . just mind blowing . . . they were really tremendous people that we met during those institutes. [They] opened up my whole thought processes to something beyond the so-called American dream . . . *and* the so-called Catholic Church having all the edge on truth. They challenged the thinking that I had been brought up on. Definitely challenged the whole authority

thing. The reason I was down there. . . . the reason I went to
Mexico was just responding to get American religious down
to South America to "save the Church in South America"
type thing. I went out of *complete* obedience to the Holy
Father and just by Illich's own life and hearing him speak of
his own experience and recognizing . . . he gave us the
whole background of how that came about. . . .

In 1961 the Pope issued a call for North American
clergy and religious to send 10 percent of their personnel to Latin America to offset a critical shortage of
clergy; at the same time the Alliance for Progress was
launched. Illich was cynical about what he labeled "an
alliance for the progress of the middle classes" and at
CIDOC (Center of Intercultural Documentation) in
Cuernavaca he ran numerous institutes and workshops designed to keep all but the most open and progressive out of Latin America and to "de-yankee"
those who did go on as missionaries. Illich de-mythed
both "The American Dream" and "The One True
Church" as he showed the socio-political consequences of the missionaries' well-meant venture into
Latin America.

   This is the "whole background" Ruth experienced:

He gave us the whole idea of how the commands to American religious to send 10 percent of all our sisters to Latin
America came about, and I *still* went ahead and sent them. It
was strange because I was ambivalent at the time. I really
saw it as a good, but also it was still very much that whole
mystical kind of thing—you know *Christ speaks* to you
through Peter and through your superiors and through the
bishops . . . and so forth. I was still acting on that and at the
same time realizing that maybe *I* was a part of this whole

process too; all the rest of us were. Maybe we didn't have to wait for answers from on high. Now Christ speaks.

A lot through going away by myself and reflecting . . . but in the reflection it's never a solitary thing. It's like a part of the people I have been in contact with . . . much more through everyday happenings . . . between other people and myself. It's really strange, because as you ask me that question I hadn't realized . . . how . . . how *diametrically* different is my response right *now* to what it was—say nine years ago I was really waiting for the answers from on high and only trusting that . . . but also thinking my way through most things probably. Most of the time I've had superiors who were deeply listening and intelligent people who would listen to me. I think I had idealized Church authority as being the kind of authority I had experienced . . . again my mother and father were the authority in the house . . . they were so good. They bred in me a respect for authority. I don't mean I don't have respect for it anymore, but I don't see it as coming from the top. I see it as coming from within the group. To do that . . . the thing that gives me peace in that is to know that I had to let a lot be destroyed within *me*. In order to grow, a lot had to be destroyed.

I guess the whole sort of mystical response to God and to Christ and to church. A kind of having it in sort of safe categories, which, as I look back now I recognize as a kind of cumulative fantasy! It was handed on and it was sort of comforting. It *is* kind of comforting to know, to believe, to really deeply believe, that there is a God out there with a *master plan* and all *you* have to do is respond to it. When you don't believe that any more you've lost a deep sense of comfort. That stopped . . . I didn't believe that. It probably happened during those years of decision when I was superior general. Up to that point there had always been a . . . someone that I could talk this over with and say, "This person has authority from God, and therefore I can believe." But, as superior general, I was going through that whole process of recognizing that *I* had to make decisions and finding, at a point, that there were decisions which I could *not* make in conscience that the so-called hierarchal Church was making such as the whole incident with the Immaculate Heart sisters. I think that was the first time with a big issue that I had to take a stand. I felt the people who were making decisions in Rome were not aware of the human dimension of what was happening.

The Immaculate Heart sisters, one of the more progressive religious orders during this period, were located in one of the most conservative archdioceses, Los Angeles. Their steps to move were blocked and fought by Cardinal McIntyre who headed the archdiocese. Eventually Cardinal McIntyre succeeded in having the Sacred Congregation of Religious in Rome declare the Immaculate Heart sisters to be "noncanonical" which meant they were no longer to be recognized as a religious community in the Church.

The superiors of American nuns had petitioned Rome in 1965 to give sisters a voice in the Church bodies that ruled the lives of religious women. The major superiors had met in a conference at which time Sr. Mary Luke, S.L., chairperson of the conference's executive committee and an auditor at Vatican II was quoted in the *National Catholic Reporter* on September 1, 1965:

There is a serious concern on the part of major superiors that women should have something to do with the regulations that bind them. Traditionally such regulations have been made by men. We are strongly suggesting that we have representation.

Sr. Mary William of the Immaculate Heart sisters was reported to have said:

Either we find ways to develop and encourage this forward-looking constantly converting type of person or, by default, we will, in my opinion, be foisting on the world psychological pygmies who will be a scandal to religion.[4]

At the height of the crisis over the Immaculate Heart sisters a group of clergy and superiors considered going to Rome to protest the decision that the sisters were noncanonical. Ruth was part of this group, a group that was controversial and not representative of the majority of clergy or religious. Ruth's father was very seriously ill then.

I came to see my father, who was really, really ill, and my mother. I told them I was going to go to Rome with a group of bishops, priests, and mothers general, who were going to ask the Sacred Congregation of Religious in Rome to reconsider their decision about the Immaculate Heart sisters. In the course of the conversation I said to them . . . I was leaving the following Saturday . . . and as I talked to them I recognized that I might never see them alive again. I told them that there were very, very many in my community who were very, very upset because I was taking this stand. Taking a public stand. They felt the Annunciation sisters should be kept out of it and that if their mother general went that was bringing all of them in. I knew that probably he and my mother would hear from some of these people. I knew that this would hurt and it would be better for him to hear it from me. Well, he was sitting in bed, and he looked at me and he said, "Did they ever read the story of the Good Samaritan?" A couple of days later I came back, and in the meantime the decision had been made *not* to go to Rome. When I came back to see him again, he said, "You know, your mother and I talked a long time after you left, and we want you to know that if ever you feel the necessity, and if your community will not let you do whatever you believe in, whenever you feel the necessity of starting over, like . . . this house is yours." And you know other people would be thinking in terms of shame-shame, look what you're doing to us. He also said to me, "You know I think you are going to have a hard time with Paul . . . he won't understand." They saw the Church changing and religious life changing; they backed me. They were . . . strength during those six years I was superior.

I didn't think of myself as rebellious. I had no consciousness of rebelling as a child. I don't ever really remember doing it. I left high school and three weeks later entered the convent. I don't sense a sense of rebellion . . . but . . . my father had said to me, at one time, that he didn't know how he ever kept the faith, in Ireland, because of the clericalism in the Church there. He was also like . . . really a lot involved in the labor movement in its early days here. In a strike he was warned . . . but he always cared for the underdog. I thought it would be very unnatural for me not to go to help the Immaculate Heart sisters because it would be so false . . . from the way I was raised.

When I went to visit his home place in Ireland . . . after my father died . . . they told me that before he left Ireland, when he was a young fellow, that he burned the landlord's . . . they had hedges to separate the fields, and he burned the hedges down as sort of his last bit of rebellion. So [laughing] I come from rebellious stock.

I feel a continuity . . . I do feel that I was as dedicated to my convictions twenty years ago as I am now. But they were a different set of convictions. And therefore my personality twenty years ago would have been much more involved with law . . . because that was where my ideal was. You obeyed Christ through obeying authority. And I'm sure as your values change . . . and especially if they change diametrically . . . I can remember being so upset when the sisters took the veil off in Colombia. I was Mother General and in 1965 we opened this mission in Colombia. The sisters went down to do six months training in Cuernavaca . . . with Illich.

And I had said to them before they left, because of having had the experience with the week there with Illich. He had said, you know, *give* them the *freedom*. Let them live among the people. It's not . . . they're not coming here to bring Christ to the people. The closest thing you can say they are doing is announcing to the people that He is present, that He is there. So I sent them off and said, "Now you make all your own decisions. But keep me informed." So— they were there about three months when they wrote back and said they had given their veils to some group of sisters going to Peru . . . they didn't need them in Colombia! The whole veil was like a big symbol of being a sister. It was like a whole consecration . . . cut off her locks and take the veil. It was a deeply symbolic thing for me. I was *really* torn, because I believed that there was an important principle involved there. I also believed there was *another* important principle which is that those people should be self-determining. I had told them that. So for six weeks I couldn't write to them. I was in such an ambivalent state. I guess I had enough good sense to recognize, don't pour this on them. You've asked them to do it and if you don't like what they're doing, don't pour it on them. After about six weeks, and talking with some friends, I finally got it straightened out within myself. I don't think I would *ever* get that upset about anything right now. At this point. But my absolutism then!

I took off my own veil . . .

Yeah . . . but not then. Not for . . . oh, gosh . . . for about two years.

Symbols, such as veils or a religious habit, do not obey laws of logic nor do they prove anything. They affect, even overwhelm, a person with many images which meet in meaning. A single symbol, such as a veil, can represent a multitude of things. A symbol is an image that can evoke a feeling and can be evoked by a feeling; a symbol is grasped without effort as it repeats or reenacts the familiar and points beyond itself. Symbols and symbol systems are essential; they also have grave limitations. They can express similarities, but always to the point of eliminating personal differences. A symbol can never depict the uniqueness of individuals. A symbol is static in that sense, enabling one to avoid grappling with complex reality. Tillich[5] has pointed out that symbols, "like living beings, grow and die . . . when the situation changes." Development involves the transformation and transvaluation of symbols and their systems.

Wrapped in changeless medieval garb from head to toe, the nun was perceived by herself and others as a symbol, not as a subject or a person but rather as a self-*less* object. To perceive a person as an object, no matter how "ideal" the object, is fundamentally alienating. The habit that indicated the special status of the sister was found by many to be an alienating barrier. However, removing it meant relinquishing a symbol associated with "woman" and that had identified her. Veils go with categories: virgin, bride, mother-madonna, widow. Each veiling identifies her in terms of a sexual relationship. The nun became the virgin-bride of Christ as she knelt before the bishop to recite her vows and receive her veil. Taking off that veil implied more than a change of clothing. It was an anti-hierarchic leveling act that relinquished an alienating status and called into question hierarchical forms of submission and self-effacement—Christianity's purdah.

Thus it is not difficult to see why each inch of hemline or shortening of a veil evoked warnings from Rome. A "little" modernizing of the habit was favored by Paul. Each time a sister in Ruth's order modified her habit, removed it, changed her living situation, or moved into a different type of ministry she challenged her own community and threatened the vertical structure of the church. Thus, complaints came from within and without, resulting in Ruth's being called into the chancery office of various bishops in whose areas the "offense" had occurred.

On the one hand they told us to renew; on the other hand, every step we're being stopped . . . and things like—"what's wrong with these sisters? Why won't they respond?" A lot of that is just no longer there . . . I think one of my strengths is the ability to let people be where they are. And I think . . . when I began to recognize that for some people to change, it was really doing violence to them. Then I began to recognize this must be wrong . . . the wrong approach. And with the willingness to let people be where they were, I recognized that it would be better if I were not the person who continued to put demands on them.

I made the decision not to accept reelection and the ultimate and following decision to go to St. Abraham's. I think that began the process of recognizing that *I* went through a process of self-determination and it was good for other people to go through that same process. Right now I am trusting in that process.

What I really accomplished as mother general was the slowly-formed realization that I was a self-determining person. That is the most important accomplishment . . . of my life. Those years . . . I have to ferret up . . . many people would say to me, during that time and still, "How lifegiving you have been. Do you realize how much you have done for us and how much you have freed us, to be who we want to be?" Even now they will still say to me "We not only grew within ourselves but we gave a lot of hope to the Church here." There are people who say that to me and they seem to want to *evoke* some sense of my recognizing that I have been instrumental and have effected a lot of good. I just can't be as enthusiastic in that as other people are . . . when they point out how the community was before I was mother general, and as we were during those six years. My very deep honest response was that I did not feel that. I was aware of good that happened, but I was also aware, for example, that something like between fifty to sixty sisters left the community, and I'm not sure that all of those sisters went with the idea of going *to* something and of growing. I felt very inadequate; many of them were affected by too rapid changes; subsequently several of them just made messes of their lives. I've seen people in the community . . . one sister won't even speak to me. She walks the other way when I come. I am so aware of the negative response to much that has been . . . I do not see how I have been a constructive influence for some of these people. But I have a sense of rightness to it too.

  ⁻ I think I would have found it easy to be mother general twenty years ago or fifteen years ago . . . But then . . . I had the experience of falling in love and that was more than the little falling in love I had had in high school . . . really and truly falling in love and working through it and failing in a relationship. Failing . . . I feel I failed in it. I was mother general, so I was forty-one—in there. That was after the Cursillo . . . that first year. I think I loved a person that I idealized and imagined rather than the person that really existed. I think I really learned a lot though in the sense that in that relationship I tried to get the person to change to meet my needs rather than accepting him where he was. I think he needed to be needed by many people and I was a needer. But I discovered I was not able to really stay myself because I could never be strong. I think when I was strong—now I can only tell you my feelings—I felt very put down; like he couldn't handle it when I was strong. He could handle it when I was needing him but he couldn't handle it in terms of being really reciprocal. And I think he had defined himself in terms of—that he loved me because I needed him but I don't think there would have been a relationship if my needs had not been very deep at that time.

Before that time I responded to people rather idealistically and probably more manipulatively than I do now. I feel that was one of the really good things I learned from that . . . that was . . . I guess I never loved a person enough to let them manipulate me and I saw how devastating that can be . . . like I felt very used . . . even though I have always felt that it was never intentional . . . it was just the circumstances. If the circumstances hadn't been there I doubt there would have been a relationship. But I feel it was very freeing. I feel he was very freeing, instrumental in helping me to grow and I think . . . he was oblivious of the fact it was going on. I don't think the areas in which he thought he was helping me were where he really helped me.

I couldn't keep it going on his terms which was that I be dependent and I'm not. I don't think I am a very dependent person. I think I am rather independent. [laughs] But I don't think I realized that *until* I went through this whole thing . . . because of the transference from my home where I felt very dependent to the convent where I felt very dependent. Even when I was independent in the sense of having authority I still felt very dependent, on Church structures or on people other than myself. When I was mother general there was no one to depend on in the community structure. I depended on this person and in that process fell in love.

I guess it is easier for me to take the blame, especially with regard to personal relationships. Of a relationship breaking off, it's easier to take that to myself than to blame the person I loved. I guess I still idealize the situation . . . him . . . to a certain extent. I'm still not emotionally free of it. Umpteen times I felt like I was batting my head against the brick wall. Since that time I have had some really close relationships . . . where I feel just as in love, but really *myself* in love. I didn't feel that way in that situation . . . you see I never felt picked out for Ruth, I felt picked out for mother general. It was nice for a priest to have a mother general on his string. I felt like a scalp on his . . . do you understand? I would take the initiative to move out . . . I would have to take the initiative because he would say, "It's okay . . . I can handle it." Handle the relationship . . . the psychological dependence.

I can remember three, six months, and problems when I was mother general. Every day was a problem and I remember saying am I leaning too heavily? I mistook his need and his capability of having someone need him for a mutual relationship, which it wasn't. But in the meantime, my dependence emotionally and psychologically was growing. Growing and growing and growing and I think another psychological thing was working there: I was being so hurt in community. I was being so hurt in this relationship that I was psychologically closing off hurt. You close off love and support which is there also. I think that was happening. So I ended it. I couldn't keep it going on his terms.

Given her traditional background, it is doubtful that Ruth would have thought a reciprocal relationship valuable had she not had the rich exposure outside the convent subculture, accompanied by an ongoing questioning about authority and dependency brought about by being in authority and being continually questioned. That she saw this questioning as important led her to question many of her assumptions, including the one that someone should *be* in authority in the manner it was conceived within the Church. After deciding not to accept reelection, Ruth was invited to become part of a team ministry at St. Abraham's, a working-class parish, seemingly an ideal situation.

When I got out of office I knew what I didn't want! Which was to always be the person leading. I wanted to work *with*

people and being there was really good. It was really interdependence and shared responsibility. Authority went on
very normally from one to the other. I was only there for a
few months—six—and it hit the fan. John [pastor] knew he
was going to have to be moved out.

The situation Ruth was referring to was one of a
very liberal pastor who had decided to share his position, had taken innovative positions as far as liturgy
and parish life were concerned, and also had announced his intention to marry. John was correct in his
assessment of the situation and the bishop did remove
him even though his parish opposed the removal. It is
interesting to speculate what might have occurred had
he not obeyed the bishop's order to leave. The six
months that elapsed before his removal were very important for Ruth: they opened up a new vision of
shared responsibility in community:

I did not know John as well as I would like to . . . there were
just those few months . . . but I think he had done some real
soul-searching and through that had taken some very definite stands himself. I think that enabled him to let other
people be very free. And having gone through the whole
thing I just described to you, I think I needed that . . . that
space. He really made that possible by who he was as a person. Roger, another priest, was a very sensitive person. Each
strong in his way. I didn't feel put down as a woman in *that*
situation and I think that is obvious by the fact that they invited me to live inside the rectory. I felt equal . . . oh, I think
there were times prior to that, when I was mother general,
that I felt [laughter] better than . . . after a session with
Charles [a bishop] but this was the first time that I really felt I
was accepted . . . in the Church . . . on an equal and com-
plementary basis. It was strange because it became a non-
problem . . . like why does anybody think that this . . . authority . . . is a problem. For six months and then zoooom.

"It's nice to remember Camelot!!" Ruth remarked sadly. The priest selected by the bishop to replace John had been a military chaplain and found the situation did not conform to his idea of how a parish is "run."

The whole time I was there you might call crisis time. Because I got there and the whole thing with John started, and then finished. Then Joe came . . . it takes about six months to really see and get the feel of a place, get to know people, and at that time, six months later John went and Joe came. So it was always crisis, I would say. It's taken me a while to jump/bounce back from that. Even . . . I think I've found a lot of happiness amidst all the pain at St. Abraham's. I found it very supportive and very fulfilling. Just being with people . . . being accepted in an atmosphere of openness and trust. I found it extremely strengthening, and very healing of all the hurts of those years that had gone before. I found the six years as mother general very painful years . . . and there was like . . . no reduction of it except for friendships I made with people that I never would have met except through that. They were just very, very painful . . . the personal living situation was very painful for me . . . the whole mother house atmosphere . . . and then the demands of going from house to house [convent to convent] and being chief sponge for problems and worries and decisions. In contrast to that I had more of a sense of personal affirmation from the St. Abraham's situation than I ever did from the mother general situation.

After going through that whole thing with Joe I know that I do not want to go back . . . to having someone make my decisions for me. I hope to find mutual-interdependent persons. I recognized that I had made a decision and I was not going to get pushed into the position of making the decisions for the whole group. I was going to give as much as I could. But there is no way I am going to let those people push that off on me. You know, you're a sister and . . . so they would get mad at Roger [the other priest] because he wouldn't take the initiative. It is not going to bother me any more . . . like this is all of us together and we've got to learn it. Sometimes I'll know what to do next and many times I won't. You can't rob people . . . of the pain of making decisions.

Eventually the parish polarized with Ruth and Roger and many of the people on one end, and a traditional pastor and his obedient flock on the other. One problem presented itself over and over again. Ruth wore ordinary clothes, addressed people by their given names, and had dropped titles as forms of communicating with others. She was relating to clergy and laypersons alike as equals and was quite comfortable and open. Thus, many did not perceive her as a sister or thought she ought to be "different," and told her so.

Every once in awhile in the midst of this whole crisis at St. Abraham's . . . it was really funny. I came home one night, and it had been a really harrowing day. I was sitting reading, before I went to bed, and all of a sudden I said to myself, "I wish I had a whole habit to put on." You know, like a sense of security. I'd just like to walk out to these people, and especially people like Joe, people like that, that didn't see my nun-ness because I wasn't dressed as a sister. I'd just like to prove it to them, kind of thing. But when I'm cool, and away from it, I recognize that . . . we're dealing with symbols . . . right at this point in history. We're dealing with reality. Symbols only have meaning if they are internalized. That one for me was really internalized. But for a lot of other people it just wasn't. I began to find out, after I went through that whole thing with the veil, that other people had internalized very different things from the veil. Then I recognized that the reality of my life of dedication had to become real. I don't know how to symbolize it very well . . . except . . . maybe to symbolize it by making decisions. To live alone rather than to go back to the convent. Maybe that's a symbol. I think that is sort of a symbol, living in the convent, at the present time. Later on it will lose its meaning too, when a lot of people leave all the convents and find out that they're still not dedicated. Being in a convent doesn't make you dedicated.

As the polarization of the parish deepened Ruth began to sense that *she* was indeed a symbol and that this was destructive for her and for those who perceived her as such.

I think the main reason for my leaving St. Abraham's was recognizing that I would become symbolic; that it was OK—you know, people were seeing me hanging in there and I tried to work things out. I really could have settled down there. I could have done a lot of good things. But I recognized that many people would only know me as a symbol of "this is the Church leadership" and saw me saying that's OK to something that was *opposite* to what I had come there for. That would really be very destructive for them ultimately and I would say very definitely it was becoming more and more destructive to me. I think if I had gone on compromising . . . that's another thing that has changed in my personality, I think. Through this last experience I've just said that I won't compromise what I deeply believe anymore. Before I went to St. Abraham's . . . up until that time, I would have said this isn't what I really believe is the best for me, or the best for what I believe in. *But,* I still could do good things. I would no longer do that as a result of being at St. Abraham's. I could have done that . . . I could have stayed there for four or five years more, really convinced that this whole parish was being effective. I am really convinced through this experience that the only people that are affected are those where there is a *real* give and take in your relationship. Therefore I am not putting demands upon myself anymore to relate to numbers of people—like four or five hundred families!

Ruth's decision to leave St. Abraham's came after a year and a half of trying to make the situation "work" after John had left. During this time she constantly questioned the situation talking it out with someone she trusted—frequently with Roger.

I can remember, just before I made the decision to leave, maybe a couple of weeks before, talking to Roger once and saying to him, "You know I feel a deep sense of powerlessness . . . that doesn't bother me. That's not what's bothering me. I am afraid of myself. I am afraid that I might become not only angry, but destructive. I can clearly say that I do not think Joe is doing this purposely. But there can come a point where I feel I will be so hurt that I am not sure I can continue." As we talked I think we *both* recognized that we could only transcend it with this kind of support from others. Maybe one time he would be strong and could help me, and another time I would be strong and help him.

So shortly after—a couple of weeks—I decided to leave and once I made the decision . . . I made the decision on Thursday and I was gone the following Wednesday. Once the decision was made I knew I would move quickly. I found a clash between honesty and . . . being with a person in an honest relationship. Where I would try to do that . . . it would be misunderstood or misinterpreted. My motives would be misjudged. So I guess I felt—in different ways, from different persons—de-humanized, either from their expectations of me, or their inability to be honest with me. Like I feel with Joe . . . the only way he could deal with me was by the "putting me down" kind of thing.

Ruth's decision to leave the parish was a radical one in that she was not "going somewhere" but was taking "time out" to rest and find a *self*-chosen task. During the time she was in the parish she had worked with many groups within the parish, had also continued to work with groups of women in the Cursillo setting, and was in a study group dealing with the issues of the war in Vietnam. Roger was a part of this same group, a factor which probably increased the tension between the former military chaplain and these assistants, particularly when the group decided to boycott the carrier *Enterprise* by going out in motor boats and canoes. This move elicited opposition from Ruth's immediate family—the first time her family had not affirmed her choice.

It's really strange but the only time I didn't get affirmed was when I went out to meet the *Enterprise* in a canoe, and if my father had been alive he would have! He would have understood the radical in me. My sister didn't understand, nor did my brother. My sister was really upset. I remember saying to Roger "I'm not going to tell her until after I get back." Roger said: "You'll be sorry." I knew that was true. So I told her and she got really upset but she worked through it so I think she grew through that whole process. She would not be happy to see me deal with it again because she was nervous for me physically as well as disagreeing with that kind of a tactic. Even if my father had not agreed with it, however, I think he would have believed in my doing it. He would have given me a sense that it might be foolish but there are some things we should be foolish about.

I guess my parents are the wellspring of my faith even though they both have died. Just their belief and their ability to change and adapt and be joyous and hopeful in seeing us children change and adapt. My father's affirmation of all that

I tried to do as mother general was very, very strengthening and I think has kept me on the move . . . affirming the steps I was taking because *faith is what you do with your life.* I don't think my faith is intellectualized much anymore. I would probably fail if the Pope asked me what my faith was today . . . if the Pope asked me to say . . . what do you believe about Jesus? Or what do you believe about God or heaven or hell or all the rest?

At the same time I don't conceive of or fantasize myself growing outside of the institutional Church. I don't dream that at the present time. I think of myself at the outermost limits . . . if you want to see it as a big circle. I think I am way out on the fringes . . . the margins. It seems to me that I still have a lot of space around the circle to keep looking for possibilities. I'm still thinking in terms of that. Yet, I feel very free of the authority of the Church. I'm not worried about it. If I got thrown out that wouldn't bother me, but for me to choose to go out, I wouldn't. But I won't stop being me in the process of it.

When I think in terms of what I believe the Church is, I think of a very broad Church. I think of it as wherever people are together in love. And where they knowingly are doing that in the name of Jesus, well, that is Church.

Now, when I think of institutional Church, and structures of Church, Pope, bishops, or in my community of mother general and such, I'm very free of that. I do not feel hemmed in—now that could just be at this period of my life. It seems to me that where they have put a crunch on me, I have moved out of it. After three or four experiences like that . . . in the last five years . . . I'm no longer afraid. They are not going to stop me. At present I would have to consider very deeply if they did try to stop me. I think I would still move, and still wait for them to take the responsibility of throwing me out, which I don't think they are going to take at this point. So maybe that's a calculated risk, not a real risk

. . . it's interesting, because presently I am not in a position, since I left St. Abraham's, of having to confront an authority. I don't think I'd ever put myself into the position again of feeling under authority. If I cannot find it in a shared, responsible way, then I will probably leave the group, because authority is the group's responsibility.

But that is new. Up until the last *two* years I was concerned about how I and people like me could renew the structural Church. That has shifted to how can I . . . and other people like me help to spread the Christian message regardless of structure. Yet, I think the people who would be really comfortable with where I am—for example, in my religious community—I think there are very few. Most of the people in my religious community that I identify with are still very comfortable, or are still able—I shouldn't say very comfortable—they are able, or they want something patterned after the structure of the institutional Church. Everyone else with whom I related has either left the religious lifestyle we shared or those that remain condemn what I am doing. I don't know if they are ahead of me . . . those who've left . . . I just don't sense within myself that that is the way to go.

As for faith . . . I believe in Christ . . . and having been surrounded by His love expressed primarily through my family and close friends . . . where I have literally been redeemed . . . that has made me aware of the way I must live my life . . . for others. I think my life bears that out . . . in action. I think my belief is more than a verbalized belief. Being faithful means living out that belief for others . . . sort of finding the depths within me which respond . . . but it is in terms of others . . . a combination of the two. Like the depths of who I am as a person and then responding to other people's needs with that.

Five or ten years ago decisions were . . . pretty much decisions that were made for me by the Church. You know, the structural Church. Right now I think I've moved out of that—as far as process is concerned. I think the actuality is that I have internalized many of those things. For example, abortion. Sexuality. I think the extramarital, or premarital, for me personally, is probably . . . at this point in my life I can't see myself doing it. But I think I have opened out to recognizing that other people should *not* be conditioned as *I* have been. I am much more concerned about helping people come to their *own* decisions in these matters, in a way that would both help them to grow and not be injurious to others . . . at the very least . . . not be injurious to others. That's a different value. I would still say to others what my value was. But recognizing that it is very much conditioned by the way I have lived. I'm not saying that if I were thirty years younger I would grow into the same value system that I have now. But I'm not thirty years younger.

As for my own sexuality I think I use a lot of just *normal* means. I fantasize. I masturbate at times. Ultimately, I face myself and come to decisions recognizing that I have made some life decisions . . . it's a struggle . . . that's a *big* change. This is a big change for me. It is a change that's been recent. Well, recent in the sense of the last ten years. I can remember how I came to see my body, my sexual feelings as good.

I think it all began through that same process I spoke to you earlier about. I think *all* these things were going on concomitantly. I can remember when I didn't even *think* of either masturbating or fantasizing, thought I was sinning if I did both. Then I came to a point where I would do it, but only speak to my confessor, or someone I really trusted . . . sort of . . . that idea . . . "say it's OK, father." I think I got fairly good advice in the sense that he said to me, "Don't worry, that's normal," kind of thing. But then he also said to me, "that is for two people together. It should never be done alone" [sic]. Then I went through this whole thing, and finally just made up my own mind. At this point, it's better for me to do this than to go screwing around [laugh], or to withdraw from situations or from people, or close relationships that I can't handle without some physical outlet. It was quite a few years later that I was talking to a friend and we were . . . like both in the same place sexually. I found somebody I respected in the same place and I got the feeling "that's really neat." At the same time I would not have been thrown with "Well, I don't think that is right." I am more and more trusting of my own decisions because I know I don't make them lightly. If I ever come to the point I feel I am wrong, I will say it to myself and not be afraid of that.

I made that decision about my sexuality . . . I think I was under a lot of stress and I remember wanting to talk to someone about it. But . . . I think I had probably read enough that I was intellectually prepared . . . you know, this isn't any big deal. It's something you decide through yourself. It made me surprised because of the whole religious background, and having worked through so much in making the decision to be celibate. Thought it was like "all taken care of" kind of thing. And all of a sudden "boom." Well, it's not all taken care of. It's never all taken care of!

While the issue of sexuality is not central to Ruth's development, her acceptance of her own sexuality and her decisions as to what was good for her in her own situation follow a pattern similar to other decisions: initial obedience to the traditional position; subsequent questioning with some reference to authority; and a final deciding on her own. Certainly sexual feelings are not wished away nor "settled forever" because one is single, married, or celibate. Ruth, despite previous conditioning, is no longer fearful of being a sexual being, or of having fantasies or impulses or feelings. She does not deny this aspect of her being; neither is she dominated by it.

For the future, Ruth hopes to be part of a diversified community that would live and grow together in shared responsibility. However, she does not feel any pressure to "make that happen" right now. At present she lives in an apartment with two other sisters in a working-class neighborhood. Along with Roger, several families, and single persons, Ruth is part of a nongeographic community that meets together weekly.

Ruth's development encompasses a twenty-two-year period that began when she was twenty-eight. At that time she decided to change her work, became aware that her ideal model had been doing her deciding for her and doing it badly, and was given a position of authority. This pattern of obedience, of challenging or questioning that obedience, a new awareness, and a resultant change in behavior is to be repeated over and over again. In each instance the questioning or challenge comes from *outside* her *peer* group, the sisters who had entered the community with her and were approximately her age. In this early period Ruth is frequently disillusioned with persons *in* authority, e.g., the novice mistress or subsequent superior with whom she differed, and eventually the hierarchy. Later on she rejects the use of hierarchical authority at all. Each time she is assigned a position in the community she obediently carries it out but finds there is something very wrong with the nature of the task or the belief or rule underlying it and disobeys. Sisters are not supposed to touch one another, to have friends, or to be close. One of her sisters was ill and in pain and reaching out to her—detached charity no longer fit and the rule was discarded. Along with the discarding went the concept of a transcendent God out there somewhere who was

unrelated to persons. Growth came to mean helping
one another discover inherent goodness. Ruth's next
task was to socialize the novices. When she had been a
novice, unquestioning obedience was the rule. Twenty
years later in 1962 the novices questioned her until she
realized that what she had assimilated didn't make
sense. Unable, then, to follow the rule, she groped for
ways to explain it away. Quite obviously she was *re-
socialized* by her novices as she attempted to tell them
what a good sister was like. She was able to disagree
with authority, reject rules, and allow herself to be challenged. As mother general she obediently set out to do
her work, to renew her order and the Church. The
Church of the 1960s was becoming concerned with
social issues and persons, with education and ongoing
formation. Ruth became involved with laypersons on
an equal basis in the Cursillo, attended institutes and
conferences, and became disillusioned with the hierarchy of the Church; she began looking elsewhere for direction. Illich said "give them the freedom," Ruth
obeyed, and her sisters discarded their veils—the symbol of Ruth's life of service—challenging her to examine the *meaning* of dedication. Authority and truth dissolved as she became aware of the "cumulative fantasy" called "God's Master Plan." There simply wasn't
anybody out there to tell her what to do. In the rejecting of the concept of authority she rejected the nature
of it as well. Redefining the Church in order to be in it
as she wished, she also decided not to accept any more
imposed tasks; hers will now be self chosen. Nor will
she participate in or be governed by vertical authority
as she perceives it to be destructive to her new understanding of herself. She remains both a part of and
apart from her community. There is a power in her ab-

sence from obedient conventional life. She lives without the security offered by the system. Instead she lives in new space, self chosen, self defined, and revolutionary because there is no turning back to ontological security—The Master Plan has slipped away.

There is a naive simplicity to Ruth and a capacity for surprise, a seeming unawareness of how far her journey has taken her and others. I asked her at one point how she expressed her creativity. Ruth replied, "I don't see myself as creative." I asked her about numerous instances where people around her had made their own choices, where she had not encouraged dependency and so forth. Ruth remarked, "Until you mention it I hadn't thought of that as creative. . . . I was learning so much from those experiences." For her each instance of movement "just seemed like the next obvious step to take. I didn't see that as creative or courageous . . . it was obvious. I couldn't commit myself or invest in people I didn't believe in. I see my response to circumstances as probably fearless but I hadn't thought of it as creative."

Reflecting upon Ruth's development in adult life it is obvious that the questioning is as important a challenge as the emotions and awareness that come into being in that process. Ruth perceived her vulnerability—she had based her identity on imitating a model. She did not have to become a rebel; her parents provided a firm authority that supported her in transcending it. Ruth's growth is not explicable in any linear fashion or by any one event; the process is ongoing and of a whole.

5

Productive Rebellion

RICHARD WRING

Commitment is both a choosing and inherently a narrowing down as this particular person or profession is chosen and other possible choices set aside or given up. Once chosen, the commitment remains to be lived and worked out. While culturally established role norms provide some guidance they are a constraint as well; blind conformity to them can lead into a commitment that is actually escape from the process—one becomes immersed and the career "takes over." When years of preparation and intense involvement are necessary to acquire competence, the detachment that would enable commitment to be reevaluated or cast aside is not readily available.

The same "productive rebellion" that Perry proposes as necessary for the adolescent to break free of orthodoxy and the embeddedness of family and community can also pry loose the adult who is encapsulated in a career. A style of commitment that includes "considered conformity" or "productive revolt" can lead to an awareness of embeddedness. Development may then continue as the adult affirms or chooses not to affirm a commitment made in earlier adult life.

Commitment and development are never an abstraction: they occur within a temporal and cultural

matrix. A person can choose a profession that he perceives as good—even honorable—and over time can
come to question that choice. Considered conformity,
productive rebellion, rapid culture change, and new
understanding may reveal that good and honorable
choice to be a betrayal of honor. This crisis of commitment is the experience of Richard Wring who came
to perceive his profession of career officer in the
Marine Corps as immoral.

Richard Wring, thirty-seven, an only child whose
parents were divorced when he was four, describes his
childhood in Kansas as "disturbed."

My recollection of early childhood was primarily one of
being picked upon by other kids—peers. I was an easy
mark, so to speak, without the father influence. I was not aggressive by nature and I grew up in an aggressive environment and so I was the one to be picked upon . . . this was up
or through junior high.

Richard's mother remarried when he was thirteen
and in the eighth grade. He had done very well in
grade school but "bombed ninth grade . . . tenth
wasn't much better."

I don't know what it was . . . maybe normal teenage rebelliousness with the system or whatever . . . I just didn't give a
damn about school or anything. I just wanted to raise hell. I
almost got killed one night. A best friend of mine and I were
in the ninth grade and our particular school had one of the
best basketball teams in the state and we'd gone to the state
finals . . . played teams around the area: Topeka, Leavenworth, and others. It was nothing mileage-wise but then it
was big. We were just discovering girls and got interested in
a couple of girls who lived in one of the towns we played. He

[friend] had relatives there and so we went down and spent a weekend there . . . it was an infatuation-type thing with the girls . . . and then a couple of weeks after that we played the high school. I don't know . . . just for orneriness or what it was . . . it's so ridiculous, I can't even explain it at this point, but he and I sat on the opposing side's stands and cheered against our team. What made it even worse . . . I was on the pep team . . . the whole rooting section at school all wore nice sweaters and had a big whatever it was on them. So there I sat in my nice blue and gold sweater over in the opposing team's stand. We had a crew of people who took out after us, after the game, chased us up and down alleys and around through the dark. We managed to escape them but I was scared shitless to go to school Monday morning. It's crazy! Why we did something like that? Hell, I don't know . . . I don't even know what kind of mood I was in at that time . . . during ninth and tenth grade I just felt constrained but I don't know why.

Richard's family then moved to a different area in the same city. He noticed changes at that time which he felt began before the move:

The last two years were markedly different, in that it seemed like overnight . . . I don't know whether the whole peer group grew out of that stage but all of a sudden the picking upon people went away and from that point on adolescence was enjoyable.

I think one thing is the age . . . just everyone getting to a new place . . . and too, we moved, but that wasn't a complete break. I don't know what it was . . . maybe it was to the point that all I was looking for was an excuse or a change to let me go. After I changed schools I was on the honor roll straight running. I was told at the end that the only reason I did not graduate near or at the top of my class was because of my poor grades in ninth and tenth grades.

After graduating from high school Richard took a competitive examination, received a scholarship and congressional appointment to the Naval Academy at Annapolis, and in the fall of 1956 he entered the Naval Academy.

When I graduated I had a scholarship in Chemistry to go to Kansas State University, but it paid $150. The scholarship to the Naval Academy paid everything . . . and I'd say a large percentage of those there were there for that reason. It was a good education and free—good, free, and honorable—at least it was *then*. And they had that whole first year to teach you to love the Navy—or to hate it—and I guess at the end of that year I was in love with it.

Four or five weeks into his first year at Annapolis Richard turned in at sick bay with stomach pains.

It was within the first month or so after the upper classes got back and the harassments started . . . I guess it was the harassment. I am almost positive in my mind that it was strictly psychosomatic. I had this stomach trouble and it took me a couple of days of laying there without food. They wouldn't feed me because they felt if it was something they'd have to operate on—at least that is what they said—they didn't want anything in the stomach. The longer I laid there, hungry, with nothing to do but think, the harder it dawned on me that whatever stomach trouble I had was likely psychosomatic. I was rebelling against the system and the plebe-year atmosphere at the Naval Academy. The harassment wasn't that bad . . . but in my own conscience I had always been fairly proud of the fact that I could do a good job . . . deliver a good product . . . and the system was set up to strain you, to test you. I guess it was just frustration on my part. I understand it now but I didn't then. The system was set up to make sure that you were tested beyond what you would normally do, and as they gave me things to do and I did them well, they just kept piling on more and more until . . . I had those two or three days—I forget exactly—with nothing to do but think and it finally dawned on me . . . maybe I am only capable of so much and the worst thing that can happen to me is they could kill me and I knew damn well they weren't going to do that, purposely. I looked at those people who were harassing me and it hit me that "if those bastards can make it, I know I can, so what is there to worry about?" I just said, "To hell with it. I will do the best I can and if that is not good enough then that is their problem, not mine."

So when I got out of sick bay, that is the kind of attitude I carried with me and . . . it worked . . . because basically from that time on if I didn't feel I could get up 100 percent of what they asked me, I did the best I could and if that didn't do it, well, sorry, and better luck next time.

At the time Richard was at Annapolis, church attendance on Sunday was compulsory. He began attending instructions and became "impressed with Father McCarthy, a lovely old man," and was baptized at the end of his first year at Annapolis. Prior to this time Richard had not been involved in any church—his parents were nominal Methodists.

Once I started to go to Mass I was impressed with the ritual in that I think at that point in my life—being in the militaristic atmosphere—the pomp and glory of the Church fit right in and seemed to be a match. Everything at that point seemed to fit. It was very, very meaningful.

Richard's "meaningful match" of church and the military also fit the times. In 1956, America was fighting the cold war and patriotism was a positive moral and religious value—largely unquestioned. A simple and naive patriotism prevailed as Americans perceived themselves to be the chosen people who would lead the world to freedom, a view epitomized by President Eisenhower's proclamation: "America is the mightiest power which God has yet seen fit to put upon his footstool. America is great because she is good."[1]

This view of America as a "chosen people," innately good and therefore great and destined to lead the world to freedom, is not new. The Declaration of Independence, inaugural addresses of the Presidents, addresses to Congress, and special proclamations repeat themes of deliverance, exodus, and rebirth. America has been seen from within and without[2] as having a specific meaning for the rest of the world—a people with a mission. Presidents have reiterated this theme as did Lyndon Johnson in an appeal to Congress for a strong voting-right's bill:

Above the pyramid on the great seal of the United States it says in Latin, "God has favored our undertaking" . . . it is our duty to divine His will. I cannot help but believe . . . that he really favors the undertaking that we begin here tonight.[3]

In America religious pluralism has served to give the republic a non-particularized religious dimension such that *every* President has called upon the biblical God in his inaugural address. How this religious assent is given does not matter. As in most nations, politics and government are matters of ultimate concern: religion provides the transcendent goal for our political process, legitimating and sanctifying it. A civil term, nation, is linked with a religious one, God—"One Nation under God"—a nexus with theological and sociologi-

cal implications. Sociologically, through rituals and
symbols such as inaugural ceremonies, seals, and
oaths of office, specific human behavior—assuming
the Presidency or a commission as an officer—is given
an "ultimate" meaning or direction. Theologically,
linking this civil world to transcendence enables us to
imagine what God is like and what relatedness to God
is like. This is not to deny that human good can result
from such an arrangement, such as attempts to abolish
hunger or extend justice. Nevertheless, the theological
consequences of linking human concerns to civil religion are to legitimate certain human political arrangements or domains, i.e., law, government, or the state,
as being a "natural" expression of ultimate reality.[4]
One serves God by serving the state, as John F. Kennedy declared in his inaugural address.

John F. Kennedy was inaugurated the same year
Richard Wring received his commission in the Marine
Corps. In 1960 the Church and the military's "very
meaningful fit" were just beginning to be subjected to
examination. Richard entered the Marine Corps with
"no qualms at all."

I just had no qualms at all. I wasn't really a Patton type but I
felt there was a very valid reason for the military and national defense at that particular time. I thought this was the
thing to do. Maybe I was just carrying on what I had been
conditioned to . . . but I intended to make a career of it . . . to
spend the full thirty or forty years. In fact I even intended to
go on to naval air to be a pilot . . . kind of crazy . . . I haven't
thought about it since then, but circumstances kept me out
of flight school.

I guess it is another example of my rebelliousness
against the system. When the bureaucracy takes over I just
get fed up with it. Traditionally, to go to flight school in the

Navy, the procedure was that you were screened at the Naval Academy and if you were qualified and passed the tests, both physical and written, then you were certified *there* and you were shipped right from there to Pensacola for flight training. The Marine Corps system was that you went to Quantico Basic School and while you were there you applied to be screened and if passed you were sent to Pensacola. There was dissatisfaction with that system and so with our class they were going to do it differently. They were going to let us be screened at the Academy, take all the exams, be certified and put the letter in our jackets so that once we were in and went down to Basic School we would automatically be shipped to Pensacola.

So I went through that process and was approved with the letter in my jacket saying that I'd been stamped— annointed to be a Marine pilot. They indicated that once we got to Basic School and the people came around and said "who wanted to be a pilot?" . . . we would just point out that we'd already been screened. So I went to Quantico and after a few months a guy came around and said "All of those who want to go to Pensacola. . . ." and I said "Yes, but look in my jacket. I've got that nice little letter." They said, "So you do, well, take the tests next week." I said, "Wait a minute, it's in the jacket . . . I've already gone through that stuff." Then they said, "Well, that may be true but word has come down that everyone is going to take the tests." So in effect I just flipped them a common gesture and said "Take your flight school and ram it."

The individual I said it to wasn't too high up and he took it rather good-naturedly. I got called in to see the Battalion Commander. Karla and I had gotten married and I didn't ask her about it . . . as to whether or not I should or should not do it . . . but, I think I kind of sensed . . . thinking back on it, I don't think I recognized at that time or was willing to admit it to myself . . . whether I was rationalizing to myself or protesting against the system. I think I have to admit I was affected by her feelings. When I got called in to see the Battalion Commander I just said . . . he wanted to know why since I had applied before and why wasn't I applying now and following through. I just persisted and said, "I went through all of that before and I was assured that that was going to be it and now you are backing down on that promise and I don't know what promise you are going to back down on next month." So I just said I didn't want any part of it and that was the end of it.

After completing training at Quantico, Richard spent one year at a desert Marine Base and then was assigned to the Philippines for two years as a Brig Officer.

I was responsible for a prison population of about forty-five and a staff of twenty-six, a clinical psychologist and a staff NCO. I was in charge of the brig and of training the personnel to make sure they did their jobs . . . equivalent to being a warden. I had been involved in military justice prior to that which is probably why I got the job. One of the other reasons is that the correctional system, especially the Navy correctional system, was under a lot of fire from press and members of Congress to do away with archaic practices . . . trying to be more humane. I think one of the reasons I was selected was because it was sensed that I would take a more humane point of view as far as treatment of the prisoners was concerned and interpretation of the rules. I had punishment authority . . . there were certain things I could do—withholding privileges, for instance. I could take whatever action I deemed appropriate. I could dismiss an offense, say it was unfounded or I could give him a tongue lashing, or if it was serious enough, then I could refer him to a court martial . . . but primarily . . . it was withholding privileges. I also had the authority to put the person in solitary. Back in those days I felt very comfortable with the whole thing because that was my career and that was what I had been brought up in. I can't think of any decisions that I would do differently. I had a certain amount of power and I tried to use it judiciously and fairly. I did have a brig of forty-five people and it went all the way from kids who just had too much to drink out on the town . . . to a murderer. I tried to do what was best under the circumstances to maintain order in the brig.

After two years in the Philippines, Richard was assigned to Twenty-Nine Palms, an arid desert base in California.

My obligation was up after a year at Twenty-Nine Palms. I was a Captain. We were seriously thinking about getting out and the only thing that kept us in at that point was I had applied for the Naval Post Graduate School in Monterey and was accepted and so we stayed in.

It was there that the first seeds were sown . . . even though we enjoyed P.G. [Naval Post Graduate] School. We enjoyed the two years in Monterey but we got so royally screwed when we left there that that was the deciding point as far as getting out . . . there was no question in either of our minds about going on. When I left Monterey in 1966 to go to Vietnam there was no question that I would get out but I had to serve the four years' obligation that I had picked up by going to Monterey . . . had to serve two for each one at P.G. School so that Uncle Sam got his money's worth out of my education.

Richard was enrolled in a three-year Master's Degree program, and had completed two years of the program near the top of his class. The routine papers assigning them to the third year did not arrive from the Pentagon although all but two had been recommended for the third year. The Marine Corps "wouldn't make a decision, wouldn't make a decision, and there were phone calls going back daily and we got past the time where we had to register for the next semester. The school advised us to go ahead and assume that we had been approved and select our electives." Richard and the others went ahead and registered. At the last moment, as classes were to begin, the Marine Corps announced to them that only one man, the top man, would be allowed to go on and the rest were assigned to Vietnam. From that point on Richard wanted out, stating he had been "royally screwed." Richard went to Vietnam as a communications engineering officer and joined an anti-aircraft missile battalion for two months. He then made the first move which was to take him out of the Marine Corps.

I finally told the battalion commander . . . he was a very good friend of mine . . . that I had no intention of . . . you see, he had me exactly where I was supposed to be if I wanted to be commandant of the Marine Corps some day. But I told him . . . no way . . . we had already made the decision and I was getting out so rather than waste that good billet on me, send me up to Da Nang and let me work in what I had been doing at P.G. School. So for the remainder of my tour I was up at Da Nang. It was here it began.

It was at DaNang that Richard first questioned the war itself—a questioning that would continue and deepen in the years to follow.

It started, the first seeds of it, very, very . . . very minor . . . but they were sown while I was in Vietnam. Just reading some of the material that picked up on the origins of the war and why we were there cast a few doubts, although not major ones. I got very, very upset with the way the war and the news of it were being managed.

One good example that I can relate: Karla sent me a clipping that showed this Marine carrying a young Vietnamese child all bloody and battered and the caption was "The Ravages of War: This child was damaged in a Viet Cong attack right outside the Marine base at Da Nang." Since it was right outside Da Nang she cut it out and sent it . . . and it just so happened that I knew *exactly* the incident they were referring to. The ravages of war they were talking about were the result of a poker game among the South Vietnamese right outside the gate at Da Nang. One guy was a poor loser, so he tossed a hand grenade in the middle of the crowd and one of those standing by was a little kid that didn't get away and was the one that got blasted. It was close enough outside the gate that one of the Marine sentries ran over and grabbed the kid and was carrying it back through the gate into the dispensary when the photographer took his picture. *But* in the press back here it was the ravages of war and the results of the Viet Cong and how they were mutilating poor good children.

That was . . . one of the straws . . . maybe it didn't break the camel's back but it loaded it down. I think it was . . . my whole outlook on the war . . . I can't look at any one point in time. It grew over the years.

When Richard returned from Vietnam in 1967, he was assigned as the Technical Representative working with a major aerospace corporation: Nexon Corporation. The following year, 1968, Robert Kennedy was assassinated. Richard made a decision to "become involved":

I wanted to be a social engineer . . . I guess when I really made the decision was at the time of Bobby Kennedy's assassination. I felt like a bucket of ice water had been dumped on me. I guess . . . I just decided, as a result of that, that I was going to get off my ass and go out and get involved in a community and try to do something . . . try to change the world. I had never really taken that much interest in it before. That was when I began or—I thought about going to law school then.

In 1970, his obligation fulfilled, he resigned his commission as a major in the Marine Corps and entered law school at night while working at Nexon. The aerospace industry was just beginning its downward slump and positions were difficult to find. Having worked with Nexon for three years Richard knew the management people and was offered a position as a systems engineer writing new proposals for new business.

During the period that Richard was Technical Representative and while he worked for Nexon, he and Karla belonged to a discussion group and later on to a nonprofit community which they helped to incorporate. In the discussion group, located in a very progressive parish, they met people who were involved in the Cursillo movement, Farm Worker organizing, and the Peace Movement. By this time, in 1971, both Richard and Karla had come to perceive the war as wrong and became anti-war and anti-Nixon after the Christmas bombings. Richard Wring then began to overtly question his position with Nexon.

I guess I had always questioned it, but it's been the type of thing . . . it was the only job I had at the time and I had to have a job. I guess I didn't question it so much then as maybe . . . it was the Spring of 1971 . . . that would have been the next big turning point. That was the reason . . . I guess something just awakened me as to what the hell I was involved in . . . that was the first of these Peace Conferences.

I can't remember why we got there . . . some church flyer or someone asked us. But we heard about it one way or another and went. We were surprised to see so many people from church groups and the Cursillo there.

I had never really looked at Nexon, you know, stood back and recognized from a perspective the type of things they were involved in and the impact they were having on the continued war over in Vietnam. The Ecumenical Peace Institute, mostly Quakers, I think, had a slide show that they called "The Electronic Battlefield." It's a whole slide presentation that they give on the electronic battlefield and I guess that was really the eye-opener . . . in seeing that . . . the whole slide program . . . the involvement of American Industry in the perpetuation of the war and *recognizing* and watching that . . . even though Nexon wasn't pointed at directly but . . . knowing what I know about Nexon, recognizing that they were just as deeply involved as Honeywell and some of the other companies. I didn't do anything then. Nothing, except just became frustrated and maybe got more interested in finding some way to get out of Nexon . . . to find a different job. I *was* seriously looking, but I guess that depends on your definition of serious. I didn't go to the extent of going to a head-hunting house and saying, "Here I am, go find me a job and I'll pay you a fee." What I did do was start paying a lot of attention to job offers and every time I saw something I'd fire off a résumé. That got frustrating because . . . after a while . . . there were no bites. A reflection of the times, I guess. Lack of jobs. I rationalized— said there weren't any jobs—to *stay* there. Generally, the whole time I was there I had a desire to get out of it. The job was not that distasteful . . . just the fact of being at Nexon. It ate at me.

To go back. First, I was in the Marine Corps for those ten years and I had the security of good-mother Marine Corps for that time. Then I left the Marine Corps because I wanted out . . . just wanted out and there is nothing that would change that . . . but subconsciously I guess I was still very apprehensive about the insecurity of being out. One thing after another. Nexon hired me because they were bidding on a particular job for the Marine Corps . . . I worked my tail off but the contract fell through . . . so there was a certain amount of apprehension there as to whether . . . and not being familiar enough with the industry . . . and all their hiring and firing practices. I was very apprehensive that I would be on the sidewalk within a very short time. As I look back on it I realize that I was probably the last person in the world they would have fired. But then I didn't have that confidence.

So one contract fell through and they put me to work on another proposal down in a very secure area. A special security clearance was required. I just never got in with that crew, since they were within a closed area of the plant, they were their own little community if you will . . . a kind of an outsider going in.

I got a call from this guy who had been the "honcho" for the proposal writing . . . the type of personality that grates on me. I just never could get along . . . even when I'd been in the Marines at Nexon . . . a guy I couldn't get along with at all. He called me and there was this crash thing, an opportunity to submit a revised proposal and he wanted me to work on that for a day or two. So I went in the morning and started doing what he was saying and I just couldn't agree with him and he was saying, "Do it. Reduce the man-hours. . . ." That type of thing. Well, hell, if we reduced the man-hours any more we can't do the job as we are down to bare bones. "Well, I don't care," he would say. "Reduce it— make something logical out of it."

I had a small office up there on the fourth floor. It was a risk Nexon could take and was their problem and I couldn't rationalize it in my own mind. It was just the build-up of a lot of this anxiety and all . . . I couldn't think properly and I just rebelled. I sat down with all this stuff, bare office, desk . . . just me and the four walls and started to work and I just could *not* function. I couldn't do it. . . . I found myself getting nervous and I'd go in and walk downstairs and get myself a cup of coffee and come back. I'd no sooner finish that cup of coffee than I had to have another one. I went down and got a sack of peanuts and then I came back and got about half-way . . . I remember this . . . I got about halfway through that sack of peanuts and I just had to get up and get out of there. I got up and left the building and walked. I must have walked for a good half mile. I walked around . . . I just felt I had to keep going and finally I was way down the end of the block. I guess I went all the way back up inside the plant . . . back up there and sat down again . . . I've had it . . . I've had it.

I got up and walked out of there and down to the end of the block . . . back to the doctor's office, went in and told him that I'm about ready to flip my lid or something. He did the good things of taking my blood pressure and this and that and the other and all that *crap* and called Karla—very nearly scared her out of her wits. She came down and drove me to our family doctor who gave me some tranquilizers, I guess, and told me to stay away from work for the next two days which I did. Then I went back, still taking the pills for a while . . . this was the beginning of 1971 and . . . I don't know whether I can analyze myself or not, but it was an extended period of depression . . . about a year and a half . . . crack-up or whatever you want to call it. But . . . but I have always felt that if I *had been* forced to stay there *another* hour or something they may have carried me off. I don't know . . . I just felt . . . I just had to keep moving . . . I couldn't concentrate . . . it's hard to describe . . . maybe it was a feeling . . . the whole world is closing in on me . . . or something like that. I really don't know.

It doesn't make me uncomfortable now to talk about it. But two years ago I think it would have. Even the fact that I was feeling that low all the time I didn't even talk about it . . . not even with Karla. No, not even with her. Really I just took the pills whenever I started feeling that way . . . I'd start down and I would sense it coming on and I would usually take half a pill and that was enough to knock it out of me.

As Richard related leaving his desk and walking down for coffee and back again, his speech rose in tone with increased rapidity. He experienced difficulty in remembering the sequence of events and could not recall some portions of the time at all and they "remain a blank." As he related the experience he said that it still "puzzled" him. He thought it was "unusual," that he might "be going crazy" and "that," he said, "scared the hell out of me, you know the whole two years . . . yeah . . . I thought I had cracked up . . . because if I had to stay there another hour. . . ." This experience was followed by about two years during which he did not "really feel good," a period characterized as one of ups and downs—"mostly valleys." After this episode Richard transferred over into contracts and out of proposal writing, a move which required a 10 percent pay decrease. During the next three years Richard negotiated and managed contracts for Nexon. He still remained in the highly secure area of the plant.

A year and a half later, in 1972, Richard attended the Cursillo, wondering if he ought to do so.

My particular state of mind at that time was low. In fact, I was . . . to a certain extent wondering if I should be at the Cursillo . . . because of association with leadership in the Cursillo . . . I knew what the ground rules were from the point of view that no one with a psychological problem and that, this, or the other should be going and in my own mind I almost thought I was sneaking in because I thought in the mind that I was in . . . I didn't belong there.

The whole Cursillo experience was maybe similar to that thing back in the sick bay—all of a sudden someone turned on the light and said, "Hey, what's the worse thing that can happen to you? Well, you know damn well that isn't going to happen so why worry?"

I found out other people got depressed and in that instance *not* feeling "unique" felt good. After the Cursillo experience . . . right after that I started thinking seriously about getting out of Nexon and started sending in résumés. The Cursillo reinforced the idea of getting out of Nexon . . . really getting out of there. The problem was running up against the cold reality of not being able to find a job. It didn't sway me to the point that I was ready to say, "To hell with it," chopping off completely, and then I'd go find another job.

Also, I was out of proposals and into contracts and my boss . . . well, we had a very good relationship—we were classmates at law school for four years. But I told him I wanted out—you see the problem was that I was *still* in this secure area that had required special clearances and it cost a hell of a lot of money to get people cleared and so once you're in, there has to be a good reason to get out. He and I probably had a closer relationship than any other employee-boss at Nexon. But I had a different perspective and even though I liked the people I worked with . . . the whole involvement in . . . the morality of the thing.

It became a moral issue . . . with varying degrees of intensity because of the nature of the type of spook [intelligence-gathering] activity that I was involved in. Just rubbed against my grain so I had a kind of distaste for the whole thing. I guess I was able to rationalize it because I had to or because I wasn't willing to chop it off without some place to go. The spook activity bothered me. It really did . . . I just don't like to be associated with that type of thing. I be-

lieve too much in people's civil liberties and people's right to
know what the government is doing and all this and there
were just millions and millions of dollars being spent for
things that I had a feeling the American people should know
what the money was being spent for.

I didn't feel it was immoral specifically—I guess. I don't
know if it were made public tomorrow in the newspapers—what they were doing, at least the particular programs that were going on there—that anyone would scream
immorality. It depends on your definition of immorality. But
it's the type thing . . . who was it . . . I guess it was Cordell
Hull, said something like, "Gentlemen don't read other
gentlemen's or people's mail" or something like that. Well, if
you are like the Cordell Hulls of this world then you would
be offended and maybe say it is immoral. But if you are like
the bulk of society, I guess you wouldn't be offended by that
type of thing.

While Richard's distaste for Nexon increased during this period, at the same time he was deeply involved in local government and law school. This
former involvement began when Richard returned
from Vietnam and was still in the Marine Corps.

It was after the assassination [of Robert Kennedy]. Karla saw
an ad for the Junior Chamber of Commerce. That was the
first thing I had ever joined in my life and that started the
whole thing. First thing I'd ever joined or been involved in
and they were, at least philosophically, their idea was to get
involved in people-type concerns. After I got out of the
Marine Corps I entered law school but before that I had
been President of the PTA. So when it came to running for
the school board it was a combination of things . . . one thing
being just a desire to be involved in government and politics
and the other of having a long interest in education so I was
attracted to the board.

Richard was attending law school, running for the school board, on the school board, working in a sensitive job, and coping with frustration and depression. His priorities were first, "family, then the school board, law school, and last, the job." At the time he did leave Nexon he was due to be promoted even though Nexon was at the bottom of his priorities.

I was able to get along by just putting in my eight hours. A good percentage of them . . . that is the only thing they are involved in and maybe family. Their only priority is family and job, so they can stay there from eight in the morning until six or seven and still satisfy their family. Well, I couldn't do that. I was strictly eight to five. Once five came I was out the door and I guess there were a few people who resented that but I didn't feel compelled to stay around and work after hours and I very seldom, if ever, went in on a Saturday, although that was probably the rule for the biggest percentage of people in the area I worked.

Nexon never put any pressure on me to get out of any of these things . . . my boss was in law school with me. They were not aware of my activities in peace and I don't know what their reaction would have been . . . some of the people there would have been fairly up-tight about it especially since I was in such a super-secret sensitive area security-wise . . . they maybe would have been a little up-tight. Even now, when I don't work for Nexon anymore, if I want to leave the country I have to give them thirty days' notice and that is applicable for the next two years. I had to sign a contractual agreement that I wouldn't disclose anything. The thing that comes most readily to mind is the guy who has been trying to publish this book on the hidden mechanisms and inner workings of the CIA. And the CIA brought out this contract he had signed and said he would not write or they would get an injunction to stop it being published, or have all those blank lines. I had to sign a similar-type contract before I left Nexon.

I just didn't like being continuously in a hassle and I wanted to be out of this super-secure area. That goes back to last December. That was the worst time. I missed a few days work . . . I missed a lot of days of work and most of it—and I knew it at the time—I just don't want to go in today, I'm sick. It even got to the point where . . . I guess that's when I laid down my ultimatum and said to my boss that if he didn't have me out of there . . . again, the problem was the secure area . . . I told him I would give him three months. When I gave him the ultimatum he kept talking about the light at the end of the tunnel because he knew he was leaving and I was in line for his position. He knew I wanted out anyway so he pointed out this position to me, I called the guy, and it was just a matter of agreeing to salary. I knew it would mean a cut. I was making $20,600, and the cut was to be to $18,500. I would be working for a quasi-public non-profit corporation.

Well, my boss said I was taking a $6,000 cut because I was due both for a promotion and for a 10 percent raise. He kept telling me I was looking at a $6,000-a-year cut and I was looking at it more from a bird in the hand, not worrying about the future. I had called him right away about the job and it looked as though all I had to do was come in and sign the written offer. I had had this conversation on Friday afternoon and went home. I knew it was going to mean a substantial pay cut. I told Karla that I'd found a possibility and was on a one-to-one level with the guy and there was a possibility of getting it and she said: "Fine, take it." I said, "Wait a minute, one thing it is going to require is a good cut in pay." She said, "I don't care, take it. If it's what you want and it will get you out of Nexon then take it. We'll manage, we'll work around it somehow."

Finally, in the spring of 1974, Richard Wring left Nexon. A few months later he graduated from law school. Over the years he came to perceive his work and career in a new light and to make changes. He also looked at the Church and interestingly these changes had also begun in Monterey when he was in Naval Post Graduate School.

Things really started changing in Monterey about ten years ago. It came on fairly gradually . . . it was a particular chapel, a kind of forerunner of changes that were to come in the Church . . . it was very liberal. It was our first experience with a community-type parish where we got together after Mass . . . pretty much the same people there every time. That was about the time of Vatican II and they claimed the first Mass in English was sung there. If I had to pick any one thing it would be being invited to join a discussion group . . . that being a growing thing in changing attitudes and questioning what was important and what wasn't. Now I would not be concerned with the practice . . . I'm concerned to the extent that it is a community gathering but I feel no compulsion to be there every Sunday or at all. Those times that we do go . . . it's been months now . . . we go not because we're looking forward to Jack's sermon or anything like that. It is more to be with the people . . . might as well have coffee and doughnuts.

It was about five years ago or so, in the late sixties, the Church ceased to be an authority . . . just leave the liturgy out of it completely and we'd be just as happy. I felt the institutional Church or the laws . . . I just didn't feel bound by them. The decision to have a vasectomy . . . we discussed it before we made the decision. I don't really recall that it had anything to do with morality . . . I guess it depends on your definition of morality. A no-no in the Church . . . what the church cares or doesn't care, that doesn't enter into it at all. We had pretty much decided in our own mind how much we really cared about what the Church thought on such subjects when we started using the pill ten years ago. So right or wrong . . . I don't really know that I know what is right or wrong. In any situation that comes up I have to evaluate the situation based on my own experiences and decide . . . what is right in the circumstances. It may sound trite to say there is some kind of inner morality or conscience or whatever you will, but . . . I think right and wrong depend on the situation . . . I've never studied situation ethics but that phrase pops into my mind. So if you ask me what is right or wrong I would ask what is the situation . . . what is the effect upon the people involved both directly and indirectly. Some relationships that are person-to-person have to be judged by the people in them. There are other relationships that by their nature are going to affect other people whether other people want to be affected or not . . . the goodness or badness of that relationship is in line with the situation!

There are good upstanding Catholics who would look at me today and say, "In no way." I guess I don't know what makes me a Catholic. . . . I don't really care, I guess I don't know what the label means anymore. I still call myself a Catholic because that is the institution I have been associated with. I guess that part of my rebelliousness is in looking back at *the* "Catholic Church" I think that where I am at, right now, is closer to the original Church. I don't see where anyone has a right to tell me I am or I am not at this point . . . as long as I feel that I am—that is what I care about.

Over time Richard came to change his belief system and his choice of profession. Less dramatic but as essential to his continuing development is his perception of his "personality changes."

I think I feel much more comfortable with people and in talking with people—being open and expressing myself. This kind of interview—ten years ago I would really have been up-tight about going through this. I guess it is still something I am getting over. I always had or have projected an image of being able to talk in public and maintain composure but at the same time I have found it very hard to initiate the social contact. My natural inclination would be to find the punch bowl and to stand in the corner and watch what was going on. I haven't been the kind to walk up and introduce myself—I feel that is changing. It has not changed that much yet.

I think what has changed is my ability, once the ice is broken, to open up and instead of just making small talk or telling the person what I think he wants to hear—to tell the person what I am really feeling. I think that is something that has very definitely changed. But the initiative is still not there that I have, say, in a public school board meeting.

I've given a lot of thought to the political and I've about decided that the earliest possible time that I could run for office would be 1978, more likely 1980. In the meantime, I want to get into law. Just as soon as I pass the Bar, I want to make a move, one way or another. The job I am in is not too demanding and gives me time for involvement in local issues.

This final interview with Richard took place a month after Richard had left Nexon. He noted that it had taken him "four years to get out of Nexon and whether it is a rationalization or what—it just didn't happen sooner." A somewhat detached amusement, chagrin, and quiet firmness characterized his manner and tone as he described the preceding years. A believer in the "good," he becomes disheartened and rebellious when he finds himself among the untruthful. Being aware of broken promises and untruthfulness, he acknowledged rationalizing Nexon's surveillance activities while carrying them out. The rationalization was only partially successful: depression, anxiety, and two years "of mostly valleys" accompanied the attempt.

In the historical context of the late sixties Richard perceived that he might be "steeped in wrongful ways." He had made a specific career commitment that he could no longer affirm even as he accepted the fact of having made it "unthinkingly." Affirmation of commitment takes place as one stands back, critically, and examines with a more enlightened sense. Deciding not to return but to disengage himself, Richard then began to create a new direction for himself—seemingly as an idealistic response to the assassination of Robert Kennedy, more probably to give a beginning in time to a new commitment. He then endured disillusionment without surrendering to it and went on in the belief he "might change the world a bit." With the completion of law school in sight, Richard virtually challenged himself to "stand back and recognize" his own involvement in perpetuating the war. He then judged such participation to be immoral and possessed the moral courage to act upon that judgment: to rebel, though anxious and depressed, and to take a new direction.

6

A Dissenting Pilgrim

RONALD SEAFORTH

Commitment in a relative world is a continuous and affirming experience. One constantly defines one's identity and clarifies the value of one's choices and directions, asking oneself how one is involved in the world: What is it that one cares about and invests one's energies in, and why? Questions of meaning and authenticity arise simultaneously as one has to judge what is worthwhile for oneself and what is the worthwhileness of one's moral, social, and political traditions. To be aware that one's own authenticity or truthfulness reaches beyond the self to a greater whole is to accept responsibility to question one's own direction and that of one's relationships, traditions, society. Such questioning is basic to commitment in a relative and plural universe.

A questioning voice, however, is a difficult one to understand. In the transcribing of a conversation, there is the danger that the voice will become words, data, or information one can read silently.

Personality is not a finished product. It is always undergoing change and transition. This is seen in the life history of Ronald Seaforth, and is reflected in the unfinished and open nature of his oral style. As an adolescent Ronald was concerned with living a worthwhile life; at forty-five he substantially retains this open commitment, reaching toward a higher good, not knowing quite what that looks like, just that it is there and it is partly his responsibility to bring it about.

Ronald Seaforth's early childhood was spent in the Santa Clara Valley. At eight, his parents were divorced and Ronald moved to San Francisco with his mother. Difficulties ensued which his mother recognized; she consented to Ronald's request to live with his father. Ronald returned to his father's home and entered a Jesuit preparatory high school. After "fooling around for about three years" Ronald became part of a closely-knit group of friends who met with a young philosophy instructor.

That last year in high school I began to become very serious about life and what I wanted to do. I had close friendships that were not based on being a member of the Block F society—wearing sweaters and the whole bit. We had plans to go beyond making a living—to do something worthwhile. That was the whole intent. Whatever it was to be . . . whether it was to be in teaching or writing or whatever. To do something worthwhile and that came out of church—not Church as this school or that parish but church as we understood it, the gospels we read and talked about as friends.

Ronald wanted more independence and felt "constrained" at home. He met with resistance and after finishing high school, Ronald left home "abruptly." He went to live with four other young men who had decided to try out an informal, communal religious life while they attended a nearby Jesuit university.

Those times were very insecure. I had no idea of what I wanted to do and must have changed my mind about fifteen times when I was in college. Writing was my major and everybody I worked with on the quarterly went into journalism. I was the only one who didn't. I had always said I wanted to be a husband and a father. That was what I wanted to do—that and music. I put myself through college, supported myself working at Sherman-Clay selling music and I sang on the weekends with a band. So, I paid for college. Always liked music, but once I got married in my senior year and we had a family—that's what kind of forced me into business. That seemed to be the best way to support them. Music was too uncertain.

Ronald's eight years with the Jesuits left him disenchanted with the philosophical underpinnings of his education. Graduation day arrived and Ronald decided that having fought the Jesuits "all the way, especially the last two years," it would be a sham to participate in the ceremonies. Ronald took a bus to the auditorium before the ceremonies were due to begin, went in, found his diploma in a cardboard box, took it out, and left. Married, with a child, he went to work for a large insurance company.

That was the only period I did that. In 1955–56. I worked for a large corporation for one year and almost went out of my mind. I've been independent ever since. I had done some part-time work with my father who was a broker and I decided, "Well, I'll do it on my own." I've been independent ever since and for all its uncertainty—about income—I know that I can sleep better. That's the only way I could go. I couldn't work for a large corporation. I was convinced that with most large companies you had to give up a portion of your own liberty and that was too much to ask. At least I couldn't live with that.

With a large company you would have to represent the company instead of the people you were trying to serve. I mean . . . they would be paying you to say what they wanted you to say and you'd feel an obligation to say it and I just didn't want to—I wasn't at ease with that. Being different wasn't always good. It carries with it a responsibility of knowing that you can't settle for something shallow. A relationship has to have depth to it or it doesn't mean anything. You can't buy friendship or love. You can see through—that's the trouble—all the rip-offs, all the lures that people can usually settle for. You know, the dangling carrot with the large company. I couldn't do it. So I got into my own business and it has expanded into planning, investments, retirement, and so on.

The next ten years went by and left "no time for reflection. I was too busy trying to raise a family—four children—and just paying the bills. Too busy for anything else." The group of friends Ronald had lived with during his college years had disbanded and each had moved away. Although contact was infrequent during those years Ronald had kept in touch with Jack, whom he had brought into the group. In 1963 Jack attended a Cursillo.

He got me interested at a time when it was very important to me to be kind of revitalized. I was busy with the family and the faith—it had gotten to be a pretty dull thing. I was bored with it. Until the Cursillo I was just fulfilling old obligations.

The Cursillo began to make me conscious of the community experience and going out from your family and yourself. Not just close friends. Just going out. I wasn't doing that before. It began to get me working with groups of people. I never enjoyed that before. You know, the Junior Chamber of Commerce luncheon is not exactly working with people. Or being on some stupid committee. To me that was a turn-off. It had no meaning.

The Cursillo got me to participate in more things, made me more conscious of social concerns, justice. Hell, I didn't know what a farm worker was. I mean I had worked on a ranch with Latinos and I'd seen the caste system and whole bit, but I never would have cared one iota for the farm workers, I don't think, if it hadn't been for the Cursillo. I wouldn't have gone to Delano but for the Cursillo. At Delano I recognized their plight and so I organized a parish to bring down four tons of food. At the time a very dull parish. But we were able to do it and it wouldn't have happened if I hadn't gone down there and experienced four days of understanding more of what their plight was.

"Recognizing" and "understanding their plight" again demonstrates the "shock of underdevelopment" whereby the person may be brought to a sense of personal responsibility to act. Initially motivated to act when he stayed with farm workers at Delano and saw that they lacked sufficient food, Ronald continues to work with the farm workers. During this period Dorothy Day, Cesar Chavez, and others visited the Cursillo Center, including Barbara, a Quaker and peace activist, who was later to be arrested in a Washington, D.C., sit-in. Barbara invited Ronald to a two-day meeting in 1969, sponsored by the American Friends. There he heard a young man who had fasted while stationed aboard an aircraft carrier in order to protest the war in Vietnam. He met conscientious objectors who had served time in prison as well as others who were resisting the war. Ronald continued to meet with Barbara and a group of eight who were asking, "What can we do to end the war in Vietnam?" These meetings continued for over a year.

We just kept meeting and we said, "What can we do?" I just felt the war was totally wrong and had for some time. We were headed for terrible things if we didn't stop and turn it around. The bombing triggered—wrong, totally wrong.

Like Richard Wring and Ruth McCarthy, Ronald Seaforth was drawn into the peace movement through ecumenical contacts outside institutional Roman Catholicism. In the early and middle sixties, Catholic pacifists were rare and a majority of Roman Catholics as opposed to a minority of Jews or Protestants supported President Johnson's Vietnam policy. The position of the American Catholic hierarchy was even more extreme: "In 1967, when the moderate movement called 'Negotiation Now' sent its petition to every religious leader in the country, the ratio of Episcopal and Methodist bishops to Roman Catholic bishops who signed it was about thirty to one."[1] Even though John XXIII, in the 1963 Encyclical *Pacem in Terris,* called for total pacifism in a nuclear age, the first major public statement against the Vietnam War, the 1965 "declaration of conscience" opposing the government's policy and "pledging total non-cooperation," signed by hundreds, included the names of only two Catholic priests: Daniel and Philip Berrigan.[2]

Socialized to a moral and doctrinal absolutism in an authoritarian institution, American Catholics have been noted for their conservatism, obedience, and unquestioning patriotism—the latter buttressed by the "just war" doctrine. Originating with Augustine, the "just war" doctrine emerged after Christianity became a state religion in the fourth century and has been used to justify the wars of Christianity ever since. While the "just war" doctrine is not peculiarly Catholic it may have a more secure formal status among Catholics.

Many of the Roman Catholics who did oppose the war had, like the Berrigans, first been radicalized by participation in the civil rights movement of the early sixties and its resulting ecumenism. Among those who marched to Selma, Alabama, in 1965, were a handful of men and women from the Cursillo Center, including the director of the Center. While Ronald was not among that group, he was influenced by the increasing involvement of the Center in social concerns—concerns which revealed the inexorable connection between war and racism. Ronald had thought that the war was wrong "for some time" and it eventually became "totally immoral" for him. He then began to look for an effective means of dissent.

In August or September of '71 I learned from a Quaker meeting that there was going to be a group going down to San Diego to get a straw vote from the people in the city of San Diego to stop the carrier *The Constellation—The Connie* they called it—from going to Vietnam. The vote was very simple—whether or not the carrier should go. Anybody could vote and the group that we had organized went throughout the city. I was one of the only businessmen that worked in the thing. They couldn't believe it when I showed up one day in a suit. That's the way I came off the plane.

I went down there twice and went into the streets—for the first time—to get the people to do something. Seeing the energy the young people were putting into this, and experiencing a military town, and getting a vote of over 60 percent that said the carrier should not go to Vietnam at a time when the country was saying that the war was right.

Going to San Diego was sort of an experience . . . I had already gotten the little form that you carry with you in case you are arrested: here are your rights. The group that I was working with had these forms because a lot of them had

been to certain things, riots or whatever—demonstrations
—where they felt it was important to carry this. This
form was passed around to people in case they were hassled
by the police. I'd heard all kinds of stories. I thought, "Oh,
God. . . ." You know, if I get busted? I could picture myself
going to jail—really going to jail by going down there and
working on this thing.

And yet it never happened. I never even came close to
it. Nothing ever happened to me. I kept my suit and tie on
[laughs] for protection. I was prepared for the worst and it
never happened. It seemed after that experience that the
business of not paying taxes seemed minor, although Sally,
my wife, worried about that, too.

Going to San Diego was an icebreaker for Ronald.
It did not remove all fear and anxiety but did reduce its
impact. Ronald's individual relationships with his peer
war resisters supported and influenced him. Once
Ronald got out into the streets, his old friends were not
supportive; in order to dissent actively, Ronald formed
new relationships.

I don't think Sally really could understand. She was nervous
about it, but that was what I wanted to do. I was so upset
about the war. I felt I had to get it out of my system some
way or the other. I had to do some visible thing other than
just complain and this was one visible way of getting people
to say . . . to tell the Navy that this is the way the people of
San Diego feel. "Now are you still going to send it over?"
And of course they did.

It was said that it was a flop. But out of that came
sanctuary. Eight guys jumped that ship and went to Christ's
Church—a Catholic church—and sought sanctuary. From
that came sanctuary in San Francisco. That happened after
we left San Diego. No one anticipated that, at all, that these

guys were going to run that risk. Well, they went into the brig. And once here, in San Francisco, they went into the brig. Then we got very involved in organizing sanctuary here.

I can't say how many people, including some of my closest friends, said, "That is insane." You know, to publicly say we will give sanctuary. The archbishop's chancellor wrote a nasty letter to the director of the Cursillo Center in San Francisco, saying, "Any legal fees will be your responsibility, not the archdiocese's." There was a furor over sanctuary and yet there were at least five or six Catholic churches in San Francisco who had agreed to it—as a result of that meeting we had put together with the group out of San Diego. It was a good idea but it really strained a lot of relationships. For the first time I found that I had some friends who were very upset about how far-out I had gotten. There was a lot of tension. There were some strained relationships that remained strained [at the time of this interview].

Compared with what I saw in San Diego and talking to guys who had been in prison and some who were on probation and were breaking probation by being down there— running much greater risks than I was—that makes you feel kind of like, "Hey, what are you worried about?" So I decided not to pay my taxes.

I had met Kaplan and he talked about it and kind of got me saying, "Well, why the hell should I pay taxes for war?" I'm an independent contractor; I don't have automatic deductions. So it is easier for me than for somebody who has no choice. The money is taken out of their salaries. So, what are the risks? I spent a long time talking to Kaplan about it. "Well," he said, "the biggest risk is that you can go to jail. Let's start off with that." [laughter] Then he said, "I've been doing it for ten years and I haven't gone to jail." I said, "How do you do it?" And he told me.

You simply withhold that amount which is spent for war, remembering that when they say defense they're talking about war. Defense is war. You withhold the amount which is used for that and you put the amount down that is used for other purposes. Then they bill you. I send them a third, or whatever that amount I put down is—I get the information from the War Resisters' League. They don't get the rest. I send a letter along with it saying, "The reason you're not getting the rest is because I can't, in conscience . . . ." Then eventually someone phones you and says, "Hey, you owe us . . . ." And I say, "Well, have you got my letter?" They always say, "What letter?" [laughs] I tell them I will discuss it with them when they have read my letter and I send them another copy. Then they phone and say, "You understand that we have to go to your bank. . . .?" So they go to the bank and it costs them a lot of trouble to collect it this way. They take it. That's not a criminal offense. Anybody can do that that's an independent contractor.

Of course we do the same thing for the telephone war tax and they do the same thing. When it gets around to collecting it, they call you, they threaten you, and they finally go to your bank account. I told my banker, very clearly, that I expect to pay no fees to do this. And he said, "OK. But why don't you write a check?" I told him I couldn't do it in conscience. The bank has gone along with me and they've never charged me for this. Some banks have charged people for having to go through the rigmarole. It gets very involved because they have to come in and seize your account.

This hasn't affected my business. It has bothered a few people that I've worked with. They've wondered whether it might mean an Internal Revenue agent might come into the office and that would reflect upon the whole company. I could sense that in the fellow I used to work with . . . who was very Republican and was looking forward to Spiro Agnew being the next President of the United States. He was nervous about it. I don't worry about that too much. I did in the beginning . . . the first year. I'm not worried about it any more—business or otherwise.

What did affect Ronald's business was his support of a ballot initiative favored by the Black community and subsequently passed. Ronald volunteered to be treasurer or "fiscal person" for the group. The issue was of particular concern in the Black community and Ronald's sincerity was questioned by Black leaders who noted his conservative dress and his business connections within the financial district. Eventually accepted by the Black community, Ronald was ostracized by some of his fellow businessmen who made a point of telling him that he had "lost their business because of his support of the controversial issue." Ronald remarked, quite calmly, that several "had come on rather strong over the matter. So I lost business. My final words to those people were, 'Well, screw them if that's the way they feel.' They went home each night to suburbia. They do not have to suffer the problems of the inner city."

Business-wise what is important? I could very easily gear myself toward the most profitable. I gain by recommendations to people. And sometimes I get nothing out of recommendations to people. There are so many gray areas, aren't there? You know, does it hurt somebody? The question is: Are you hurting or using somebody? That's pretty broad, but it's a guideline, I think. Are you using somebody else, or are you giving to someone else? Are you serving someone? Are you serving someone for their interests or for your own? I'm faced with that possibility. What do they want to do? Where are they? What do they want to accomplish? Financially—I'm talking in terms of business. In terms of counseling people—that would be the same thing. What do you want to do in life?

People can be on the brink and you may not realize it. Terrible decisions, or terrible changes, or tremendous changes in their lives. You have to be sensitive to that. And I *haven't* always been. If they come to you for advice—that's a terrible responsibility. I used to think that it was *great* to be able to give advice; now I don't look forward to giving advice to anybody about their life. Their money—that's easy—compared to their life. The two are tied up . . . you have to be in tune with people you deal with.

I've known one . . . if the guy would only say: "I'm scared to death because I've got crippling arthritis and I'm only forty-eight, and I may lose my family." But instead he's saying, "I've only got $150,000. How long will it last?" You know he is scared to death about it, but he won't say that. I try to say, "Look, you are fortunate, you can. . . ." But that doesn't matter. So I asked him if he was walking a lot and if he felt any better. I didn't do any business with him. I almost did quite a bit of business, but I ended up not doing any with him and then I thought, "Well, so what. To hell with it. Maybe I can be healing." He lost his job, has a very up-tight wife. She's like a wound-up coil, scared. I'm more able to help him than I can her. He can't express his fear, but he knows that I care about him getting better. You can do that for someone, be healing. So I didn't do any business— you're still working with people . . . creating. I think I have been dreaming about this more in the last six months than ever before. I suppose because I question what I should do with my life. I have for all my life.

I was going to be a writer and a philosopher. Yet here I am in the business community, the last thing I thought I was going to do. Yet it seems to be the thing that I'm most effective at doing. I've been able to work with groups while I'm doing this, so that one does not necessarily preclude the other. Or eliminate the other. What keeps coming to me is that I am most high when I am working with a group, whether I am with a group trying to record a song or whether I'm working with a group of people trying to get an assemblyman elected. I'd like it to be more and more of that.

I'm not on a salary. I'm on commissions which means you have to scratch almost all the time. I'd like to get away from that. Not more security. No, not that, but I'd like to have the income without scratching for it. [laughter] I'm working on that. I mean it has to be legitimate, worthwhile. My whole thing would crumble if I owned a brothel or something. I'm talking about legitimately, whether it be consulting work for three months out of the year. I could conceive of that. I don't know what it's going to be. I keep dreaming of working with people.

I thought of myself as a member of the business community a lot more in the beginning than I do now. Yet I am a part of it. I've been moved by people in the business community. People I've known through business by their honesty and willingness to take the lumps, when there were other ways—short cuts—that they could have taken that they didn't. To me that's a sign of the sacred. That's sacred. I think you see it all around you where there are people making great, great sacrifices to maintain their integrity. That's sacred, where there is hope.

I feel there is hope in the Church that is happening—the new Church, that's coming. And that's here to some extent. It's evolving, I feel like I'm very much a part of that. I think there is much more possibility of freeing your own turf than there is of doing something on a national level—say in government. I can't forget Ford was for the war. I can't forget that he was always pro-Vietnam. But he's an improvement. Of course, Charlie Brown would look like an improvement after what we had. [Interviews took place a month following Nixon's resignation.] We went through a tremendous crisis and are still in it. The Constitution—it's beautiful. The Declaration of Independence—great. But the government—it's too big, too remote from the people. I'll work for certain candidates—individuals that I believe could be an improvement—but I can't get excited about the government.

I'm directly involved in the Church that's happening. I want to be one of the people that is very directly involved in selecting a bishop for this diocese when this guy dies or retires. I think there is more hope here. The spirit can work through the Church but I don't know what the spirit can do with the government. With an individual, sure. But I don't trust most governments. Or politicians.

In this day and age doing it right is comparable to sainthood. You're risking all kinds of things. The risk I think you are constantly faced with is losing yourself. Losing your own identity and starting to believe the adulation, you know, your organization, what they're saying and what's written about you. That seems true for all the politicians I know. And the time away from your spouse is a marriage breaker. I don't know that I'd be willing to take that risk. I could see it more on a local level than a national one.

I'm just more politically aware than I was ten or fifteen years ago. I used to think that you had to find the right answer. Now I know that's . . . I *don't* know that this is the best form of government. I really don't know. I've never lived in any other circumstances. I'm sure of this—that the government isn't meant to stay the same as it was. It's got to go through the process of change like everything else. What that means I don't know.

Look at marriage—the changes—Sally and I are nowhere near the two people we were the day we got married. We've both gone through certain things with our own parents. Not caring what they think, whether they are dead or alive. I think they can affect you from the grave, almost as much as if they're alive. I think we have broken the ties of our parents, which is part of the process of growing closer and making our own decisions. I think many people go through life never breaking that relationship with their parents. Therefore they don't begin to realize who they are. I think that's very important. I never would have thought of that when I was first married. I mean I knew I wanted to live away from home, but I didn't realize the significance of that. You may *think* that just because you move away, that distance is your independence, your freedom and your liberation. But, by God, it may mean nothing more than you're not going to see them as much. They're still running your life. They can still run your life if you love them. An occasional phone call, a letter. There can be a lot of ways of doing it. You can care very much about what they think, and it's very natural, I think, that you should care, but it's not the way you grow up. We had to break that.

There was a point we came to. Well, we had time to reflect, for one thing. Before, I was just too busy, and then we started to try to communicate. We reached a kind of crisis at the point of trying to communicate. It's like getting over the peak, so that you can climb the larger one. We had to get over that first one. And you get to the point of "Are we going to get over this? Are we going to make it or not?" We got to that point a couple of years ago. I was forty-one . . . forty-two. It took two to three years. It was very difficult. It was very painful, critical. Much more so than our relationship with our children because it was the center of the whole thing. And we both knew it. The relationship we had, well, broke. That's a good way of putting it. That's been falling away ever since. We've been better able to express ourselves with each other than we ever have before. It's almost like a whole new start since that breaking. A whole new thing. Like going away for the weekend which we just did—something that never would have happened ten years ago. Sally drove—she's learned to drive now.

We share a lot more. She has more time to do a lot of
things I would like to do. So we share a lot of that. Especially
in the last few years she's been much more interested in the
business world. I've worked with a lot of widows and retired
people, and I knew that if a woman isolates herself, or just
leaves it all up to the husband, she is really vulnerable.
There was a time when Sally didn't even handle the household account, going way back in our marriage, and that
wasn't good. I would see women who were separated or divorced or widowed suddenly faced with trying to balance
things. So gradually I put more and more on and she was
agreeable to taking more of it and then finally it got to the
point where she's now very interested in all different areas of
finance. She would be self-sufficient if she had a large
amount of capital, which would come from insurance in my
case.

Sally has been freeing. She has a gift of healing
wounds. And I get wounded on Montgomery Street. Have
frequently. It's as much of a jungle as the whole arena of
politics. It has some hard knocks. I have been hurt . . .
people that I have done work with have been very disap-
pointing. You come home bleeding a little bit. And it doesn't
seem to change. So Sally, in that respect, is great, in understanding and support. But there has to be more than the
family. You have to go out beyond our relationship, to other
people.

People who are able to laugh, in spite of the insanity
around us. That's absolutely essential . . . that you have
some friends, people in transition, people on pilgrimage.
That's what makes us feel close to them. They're not phony;
they're not caught up in the system; their lives are changing
. . . in some cases are changing radically, but they are doing
what they want to do. Creative. Independent. Revitalizing.

Ron attempts to be realistic about himself and his
world as he holds to his ideals of care and justice. He is

able to laugh at much of the insanity but experiences despair, futility, and outrage on occasion:

If I get angry enough I talk to an attorney. [laughs] Almost sued somebody. Never sued anybody in my life, but I came close to it. I had made a verbal agreement that I should have gotten in writing, and they went back on the agreement. I have had that experience twice—it won't happen any more. That's one way your anger can be taken care of—legally. I play paddle ball about three times a week. Hit a ball around the wall. That helps.

Then . . . well, I go to the ocean. That's another way of coping. I go to the ocean frequently. The ocean is very meaningful to me; it blesses me. I go to the ocean and I jump in! Frequently—sun or not. And it's freezing, but it's revitalizing to me. Because, by God, I know, all of a sudden it's a question of almost freezing to death and moving in the water. All of a sudden I'm back to the very basic and out of my head and into life. And then—the sun. Laying in the sun can be very therapeutic. And then always a book . . . eventually it gets to reading. But the ocean means a great deal. Tremendously peace-giving; it blesses you.

Ronald is a giver to society. He acknowledges evil as an ingredient in the world. The little wrongs that he can attend to he will—not because he has a jurist's response to injustice, but because there is an obvious wrong and somebody has to take care of it.

Ronald does not have clear, ordered, and logical reasons for many of his choices. It was exceedingly difficult to tie down his *meaning* of good or worthwhile. "Areas are gray, aren't they? Does it hurt someone?" Abstract principles are not concrete moral rules. Hence, what is at a high level of moral development may appear fuzzy or irritatingly imprecise. Judgments underlying concrete behavior, such as refusal to pay his income tax, take on, for Ronald, a self-evident aspect. At the same time he notes, "It is easy for me because I am an independent contractor." Similar reasons are given for time away from work to participate in a stockholders' meeting. On one occasion he gathered a group of people together and flew to a stockholders' meeting in Minneapolis to protest Honeywell's involvement in war-related research and manufacturing. He said that while they were few in number, they were heard. But "to no avail." Ronald does not demand that others go and do likewise.

He continues to make commitments that lead to action. These commitments give a further focus to his life. He is open to the insecurity of his own direction. He does not have a clear plan for the future; nor is he frightened by it. He has maintained integrity and essential continuities in his life and relationships while giving them effective new "worthwhile" direction. His life pattern appears to emerge piecemeal rather than from some coherent life plan. It is a commitment to commitment, but also a sequential acting upon commitment, even when risky and difficult to do. It is working through the consequences so that his life and relationships increasingly, cumulatively, are in accord with his emergent core values.

7

Crisis and Conversion

ROBERT DUNCAN

Although conversion is described by those who experience it as moral and ethical development—a metanoia or turn of heart and mind toward what is perceived as more worthwhile—it is not commonly viewed as moral development. As skills of relative thought are acquired, one discovers pluralism in religious meaning. One ceases looking for the truth, either in a metaphysical absolute or in the sense of one religion being "true" and others in error. Religious commitment then becomes a unique relationship to a truth one cannot possess. The person calls herself or himself religious despite the fact that the existence of God cannot be confirmed.[1]

Conversion is both an abrupt and a gradual *process*. It requires the capacity to recognize ultimate differences—other people are rooted and grounded in religious belief different from one's own—and this, in turn, can lead to new self-understanding. If conversion is understood as process rather than a discrete event it then becomes a life commitment to find out for oneself and in oneself both what and how one thinks, believes, and loves. Robert Duncan perceives himself to be called to this uncertain process; for him it is the *meaning* of his conversion.

123

Robert Duncan, a middle son in a family of three boys, was born in Colorado and lived there until his family moved during his last year of grammar school. The move was a "break" and "loss of belongingness, of being part of the Duncan clan." After the move he spent more time with peers than with family, noting both "rebellious and resentful feelings" at being "taken away" from Colorado at a time when he "was just getting comfortable." Settled in a large city in Arizona Bob's interests in study "evaporated" although he maintained a B average throughout high school without effort and embarked upon a brief career with two gangs: one climbed the local mountains; the other "verged on thuggery with occasional stealing." During his senior year in high school, Bob fell in love, "deeply, intensely, and I had a sense of loyalty to her and to loving her." At this time his father's small brokerage business declined and the family moved to Texas. Letters went back and forth and after two months Bob had earned sufficient money to return:

She wasn't where I was. That was really bad for me. She broke it. I moved, but she broke it. I can remember walking home from seeing her. I had hitchhiked up from Texas. I stayed there for two weeks—she wasn't where I was. She broke it and that crushed me. I decided I was not going to live. I remember wanting to jump off the bridge—we didn't have a high bridge! [laughs] I was very suicidal in terms of wanting—but I never did anything. I stayed there for a little while. I didn't have a job so I went back to Texas and volunteered to be drafted. I thought I'd go into the Army—I thought I'd be killed in the war but the war was over and I was discharged as everyone was being let out.

Bob then worked as a roustabout in the Texas oil fields, "ten hours a day, seven days a week at ninety cents an hour." After six months he was in "fantastic physical shape." He also recognized that he wanted to go to college.

I followed my father and brothers. I never thought about it. And it didn't bother me either. I thought *that* was good. It wasn't a bad decision; I had a good education. I started in pre-law—it was a good background for business and I wanted to be a salesman. I had always sold things and had taken care of my own money since I was thirteen. My Dad was a salesman and I knew I was going to be a salesman. Then I tried economics and took writing courses and was attracted to it. I kept on taking literature and writing and clashed with my father in my junior year because I had decided to become an English major . . . I was surprised I did so well [honors]; I worked, but I didn't have to work as hard as Sue did. She just killed herself—of course she was in pre-med.

Bob and Sue met in their second year of college and decided to marry when both were juniors. After graduation both worked for six months before they were married: Sue as a cytologist for a drug firm and Bob as a salesman for a meat-packing firm. She was the "right" woman to marry.

I had a kind of ambivalence about my relationship with Sue. I felt that there were other girls that would be more fun to play with—Sue would be in this double-standard concept I had of girls. She was the fantastic woman to be married to and to live with, but she wasn't really a playmate. I wasn't thinking of playmate in the sense that you say "playmate" now. I was thinking that she wasn't all that much fun in some ways—although we did enjoy the things we did and we worked and studied together.

Bob set aside writing. He recalls, "It just wasn't thought of as it wasn't an economic thing." Looking back upon his choice he finds it "unthinking, an honest choice, but a completely un-thought-out thing." He didn't have the "courage" to think about writing, had made several contacts with an insurance firm, and was to be hired after he took their tests.

I took the tests—some psychological tests—answering like I thought a salesman would. I failed it flat out. I couldn't pass it and they wouldn't hire me. Attitudinally and long-range that was a blow. To be told I wouldn't be happy as a salesman—that was the way he told me. I took it as a fantastic blow—I was in this very unsure state anyway and that lasted some years. I don't know that it ever did resolve itself.

For the following two years Bob and Sue lived in Middletown, Pennsylvania, and Bob began his affiliation with a church—"for social reasons. Sue loved to sing and we had no social contacts. She joined the choir in the Presbyterian Church and I went to their Wednesday-night potlucks. So when she went in to sing, I thought—well, I'll go in and sing with her. The only reason we were involved was because we liked to sing. I didn't know anything that was going on in the church."

Social needs, not "ultimate concern," brought Bob to attend church—without belonging to it. Members of a congregation are there to legitimate themselves, and the congregation exists to legitimate the conduct of its members. To the sociologist, the congregation is a visible manifestation of religion whose function is to create social solidarity. This social solidarity is best accomplished unencumbered with content; contentless faith does not conflict with the overarching religion in the United States—Democracy. A contentless faith fills social needs without undue challenge. It may also, however, enable the individual to come to believe in herself or himself, or to perceive that as a possibility.

Theologians may deplore the contentless faith that has emerged from American pluralism, describing it thus:

A God without wrath brings men without sin into a kingdom without judgment through the ministrations of a Christ without a cross.[2]

This lament, attributed to H. Richard Niebuhr, is within a tradition in Judaism and Christianity that insists there are prophetic religions whose purpose is to stir people out of their complacency. Niebuhr's symbolism, however, appears more fundamentalist than liberal in the seventies, more likely to lead to exclusivism and legalism than to social commitment. A religion can stir people out of complacency only when it encourages social involvement. This it does by providing a base of shared common meaning out of which people may operate.

Moving to Denver, Bob and Sue switched denominations, again for social reasons—Sue's family was involved in an Episcopal mission. "It was fairly close to where we lived and we thought we'd sing with them. So we went down there and did that. I couldn't figure out what the hell was going on—in terms of the service. So we just sang for four years, were very conscientious, very regular, and gave money—but I couldn't buy any of it intellectually." Sue's father was an executive in an international food corporation and her family was located in Denver. After six months of working with Sue's cousin in a brokerage firm, Bob decided the "situation was a loser."

I was making money. But the family influences were gross. It was not intellectually stimulating, but it seemed obvious to me I couldn't sell out for the economics of it—I *was* making money. We took a drive one night—after another clash with family—and I said it was crazy and we ought not to live this way. The next morning I walked in and told Sue's cousin that I had solved our problem: "I'm not going to work for you!" [laughs] So we were in Colorado, buying a house and Sue was five months pregnant and I had no contacts there. The furor with the family—both her family there and mine in Indiana. In their eyes I was totally irresponsible—giving up a job like that.

Bob "walked in off the street" and obtained a position with American Machines, a multi-national manufacturer of data-processing equipment. After being hired he was again given psychological tests:

. . . that was terrifying. One was an aptitude test of some sort and the other an achievement test and then some—would you rather pick pansies or roses. I don't know what they were, but I took them thinking, "Oh, hell, I'm not going to figure it out. Just do it." So I did very well and had great mechanical skills. I was enthused about going into sales— and I still had a few scars from not knowing whether I'd be a good salesman or not. American Machines—in terms of finding career, stimulation, and challenge—it was fascinating. I had significant aptitudes and I was very good. . . .

During this period in Denver, Bob became a national sales leader in the company, obtaining the largest purchasing order, to date, in the company. A

back operation to repair a disc "slowed" him somewhat. Then Bob was burned in a plant accident and
spent a week in the hospital.

An Episcopal priest came to visit me. We talked and both
knew and respected each other. Later on, after I was back at
work—he never pushed me at all—I said I'd like to be a
Christian if I could do it without checking my brains at the
door. I thought it would be very nice, you know, but if I really believed in everything you Christians talk about I would
have to give myself fully, which for me meant the whole
thing. So I asked him if he would let me be baptized even
though I didn't believe in the divinity of Christ and the rest.
. . . He told me that that was the way I would begin. A wise
man. So shortly after I became a member of the Episcopal
Church on those terms. No *fraud* on my part and no believing what I didn't believe—but a willingness to commit.

Bob, Sue, and their two children were baptized
and confirmed in the Episcopal Church shortly before
Bob was promoted to manage the entire Alaska division of his company. He was twenty-nine years old.

I was sent to Alaska because I had the technical skills and
didn't have to have a lot of support personally. They threw
me in way over my head. I bled. But I kept going and in four
years I had more than doubled the revenue with a slight increase in staff. I was involved—I had this intensity in terms of
involving myself in what I am committed to—in the community chest and school board because it was part of my
work—a portion of my job. It was part of my job to be involved and I was very involved. I was a lay reader and Sue
and I did musicals in the mission parish.

We were there about two years when I was invited to
lunch with Will, an Episcopal priest I had worked with. I
couldn't figure out why he asked me to lunch. After we
finished he said, "I don't know what your reaction to this is

going to be." So I said, "Ask me and find out." He said, "Have you ever considered becoming a priest?" I said, "God, I never considered it!"

But I also recognized what my concepts were when I'd committed to this thing in the first place. I really did begin to believe. I didn't know how I was believing but I knew I believed something significant was happening. That night I went home and stood in the doorway; Sue was over in the kitchen. I said, "You'll never guess what Will wanted to talk to me about this afternoon." She just turned and said, "Will wanted you to go into the priesthood." They hadn't talked—but she knew. That was an added leavening— a minor spooky experience.

For two years Bob alternated between accepting or rejecting the invitation. At thirty-two he was in the top 10 percent in income in the industry, accumulating stock, and doing work he thoroughly enjoyed. Bob wrote letters to men who had gone into the priesthood from different careers "and all these men were having regrets about it." He couldn't decide. He knew he was going to be successful in the corporate structure; he also knew he was "going to pay a price and there were limitations" to what he was doing.

I was very effective and I liked what I did—but I could see . . . it gnawed at me from the back of my mind and from the back of everything. I finally decided I couldn't make that decision in Alaska so I wangled a promotion to the Bay Area—close to a seminary in case I wanted to make the move. And, too, I thought if I got back in the heart and center of things business-wise I would be able to make a better decision about the seminary.

It was about two years. I spent a lot of time with top executives and taught middle-management and coordinated management people from manufacturing, systems, and re-

search. I brought things together! I did it well. I began to see
which way it was going to take me and I wanted to go with it.
I went to a sales meeting I had set up and heard the president of American Machines: "You men, as I have, have dedicated your lives to American Machines." And I knew—I
hadn't dedicated my life to the company. Oh, pragmatically
I had. It was the reason I was successful because I really had
given my life to American Machines Company. No hard feelings about that, but I realized that wasn't the whole of life.

That meeting had been on the back of my mind. Then I
put on a convention—the leadership role. The speeches and
the rah-rah was going on and I said—I was driving home
from that—and I said, "Oh, shit, you know, this isn't where
I'm going to live." So I didn't even go home; I drove to see
Dave [priest] at St. Anselm's and said, "Dave, what am I
going to have to do to become a priest?" I was thirty-five.

The question in its context and content resembles
that of the rich young man in Matthew (19:16–22).
The question has little to do with assent to propositions
or articles of belief. It is one of meaning, or the lack of
it. In this instance religion is functional as it delivers one
from meaninglessness. Bob's decision to enter the
priesthood did "deliver" him from a four-year struggle
to decide; it did not represent a turning away from a
sinful self or a life of wrongdoing. There was something
wrong—not with Bob—but with where he stood;
neither guilt, blame, nor self-condemnation were evident. Bob's "What must I do? . . ." suggests James's
"faith-state," that "may hold a minimum of intellectual
content. It may be a mere vague enthusiasm, a sense
of great and wondrous things in the air."[3]

I had never read a book of the Bible; I had never read any
theological books. I wasn't interested in that type—I could
care less about that. I said I would give it a year and see what

would happen in a year's time. At the seminary, I really got caught up in it. It was fascinating. It was intellectually stimulating and intellectually fascinating.

When I left American Machines a lot of people thought I was a little courageous, which is another synonym for stupid, I think. Other people wouldn't even talk to me. Didn't know, didn't understand what I was doing. But American Machines wrote an article on me.

Then I was in the seminary for three years. I had always said—when he asked me if I could consider being a priest— that I had enough money and stock that I could, by going to the wall, support myself and my family for three years. I didn't work except at books—except during the summer months. The first year as a cabinetmaker; the second summer, I don't know, I worked around the house. Then I studied. And I studied. I just said, "This is my only time to get this and I've got to go all the way into it." Again I did. I commuted and spent the week in the seminary and the weekend at home. Some of my seminary professors have been significant influences for me—one New Testament scholar who affirmed my stance and justified it with academic skills—the integration of the academic and the experience was a freeing process.

At the end of his first year in the seminary Bob "decided to see what the Romans were doing" and spent the weekend at a Cursillo.

I had just gotten through with my year's seminary experience. So I just thought that the Catholic Church was a pile of crap. But David asked me if I'd talk to the people in my parish about the Cursillo. I said, "Sure." So I went to see what the Romans were doing. I knew that I could learn from that experience and I was open to a learning experience. So that's why I was on that Cursillo. It was a very good experience. We did all those silly things, but at the human level it was pretty real. It put a lot of academic pieces, a lot of the intellectual things that I had and a lot of things that were my own—deciding to be where I was—it put those things together in a package, which was really a very honestly-experienced community which had Christianity *in* community.

The "Romans" were undergoing "a positive new orientation in regard to other Christian churches, in regard to the Jews and the great world religions, in regard to the secular world altogether, and thus in every respect also a new orientation . . . to what had . . . been her own traditional structure."[4] In these optimistic words theologian Hans Küng described the turning point of the Roman Church that began under John XXIII, the first pope ever to pray *with* other Christians. In 1964, the year Bob began his involvement with the Romans, and shortly before Vatican II closed, the mutual excommunication that had separated the Eastern and Western Churches since 1054 was simultaneously revoked, in Rome and in Constantinople. Ecumenical conversations may generate friendship and make evident the limitations of one's own point of view. Praying with others, particularly when there are no words to convey commitment, is unsettling. If the unity of all is valued, then parochial notions of a "chosen people" are shattered; there isn't anyone to annihilate nor to convert, and social responsibilities take precedence as knowledge—theological and other—is perceived to be in the process of development.

The ecumenical direction of the Romans was undertaken in "obedience" to the directives of Vatican II to the Church to renew and reform herself. No longer was the world divided between right and wrong. According to Authority some absolutes could now be doubted, and the possibility of thinking about one's own thinking and theoretically reflecting upon one's religious experience (doing theology) arose.

The Roman Catholics in the Bay Area Cursillo[5] brought to their ecumenical encounter an experiential and epistemological innocence; the Anglicans (later followed by other Protestants, Jews, and nonbelievers) brought interfaith experience with other Christians and Jews, and opinions—sometimes rudely put, as by Bob Duncan—that the Catholic Church had little to bring to any such encounter, but an epistemology that included the possibility of error. In cognitive terms, disequilibrium and inner conflict arose—a necessary condition for change. However, the disequilibrium was not experienced by all—many returned to their homes and local churches having had a "good experience with good people from *other* denominations." For some, a benevolent dualism appeared to result. For others, the challenge impacted; unlike the laboratory, life does not moderate its impact; the variables resist control. Encounter with those who have been judged—in the past—as "other" are now perceived to be ultimately concerned, but differently so. It is not possible to "go home" after one has experienced both a "separation rite"[6] and an initiation:

The Cursillo was an initiation in a community awareness, but I involved myself most—in the process—it wasn't just the weekend. The weekend began it. Then two weeks later I had a pain and swelling in a testicle—it was a Friday, and I went to the doctor and he told me it was probably malignant. He was quite concerned—he wasn't saying that in two weeks we'll operate, but, "I can't operate on you this afternoon; I don't think I have to, but on Monday morning I will."

I had buried a friend in Alaska with this so I thought I was going to die. On Sunday night John [Anglican priest] and others were going to have a communion service at the hospital—a private sort of thing. Danny [Roman priest] drove down from the city—this is the man who had never been involved, never even seen a non-Roman in a church-type thing and he brought others who had been on that Cursillo with me and they were there while the rest of us were having this little Anglican communion service.

That was Sunday. The next day they operated and affirmed the fact that I had cancer, told me I would be in the hospital for a week and that I would then probably have cobalt therapy in two weeks. The cancer was contained and they ran special tests and didn't find anything. By *Wednesday* I was out of the hospital and back in classes in the seminary the following Monday; that afternoon I started the cobalt therapy.

I decided that attitudinally, I would fly with this whole experience and be as involved in it as I could. I gave myself as completely as I could to the whole. And the payoff was unbelievable, in terms of, if you give yourself fully, you will be paid fully. All of these things were confirmed in human experience. Not for intellectual reasons, but because it worked. This was affirmation for me in a very significant way, almost in ultimate terms—of the fact, you know, dare to risk and fully giving yourself—this is the way to live.

I pretty much knew that cancer—after I began the cobalt treatment—was not going to be a problem for me. I knew I was not going to be killed by that. I had the feeling that I was right-on—that I was dealing with stuff that was radically significant in terms of human experience. I was involved to the hilt with it and I knew I was more important; I had a sense of calling.

James notes that in the extremes of crisis "the self that consciously *is* can do nothing . . . the more literally lost you are, the more literally you are the very being . . . already saved." Fundamental to the mystery of religious experience is "the satisfaction found in absolute surrender," surrender to "the larger power." "Fling yourself upon God's providence without . . . reserve . . . —only when the sacrifice is reckless and ruthless will the higher safety really arrive." The "higher safety" is a state of "assurance" rather than the "faith-state." "Dull submission is left far behind, and a mood of welcome" ensues as "Religion in its strong and fully developed manifestations . . . never is felt as a yoke."[7] New vitalities and new energies come into being and the impossible seems possible.

I gave myself completely—I had a sense of calling and also of being able to be of service to people and live a different life, be a priest in a place, do a good thing in the ministry and in the church organization. I knew I could do all those things—fairly well, responsively.

But what was happening to me through the Cursillo experience is that I became—I was an embryonic Christian. You know, really annoying Christian in terms of the conversion experience. I really had a feeling that I had a handle on things and that others—I was beginning to see that I knew more about community than the people that were teaching me in the seminary. The grounding of my Christian background was in the light of the Cursillo experience because I did not have a background of people telling me things. What I had was real and it was beyond what anybody was teaching as Roman Catholicism or Episcopalianism. All of my

Christian *experience* that is meaningful is transdenominational and humanly real, affirming of risking.

I had a real sense of community from the Cursillo and from the seminary. From that kind of Cursillo support, I could go to a place that was a desert-land, a cultural desert-land, Trinity Church, and still have a sense of community and be a priest there. I did that for three and a half years. That was the principality of my institutional experience. I was very fortunate to be able to move through that so quickly and not have to worry about it. Because I will never do that—obviously.

I started at Trinity Church by trying to make the decision to be a Christian in a place where they could use this. [Trinity was located in a wealthy and prestigious area in the foothills of the Bay Area.] I had three thrusts of my ministry: the Cursillo as a leader and running part of the organization—which they gave me time to do; I was involved in the Black community through the organization that I was influential in beginning; and I worked with youth—a free spirit—and we worked effectively at it.

There were some really freaky conservative people from another church; they were trying to halt the Blacks and they were using this organization—these wealthy whites. When that became so obvious, that they had to be able to keep the Blacks where they were and that that was their motivation, I had to clash with them. I couldn't support that so I got out of the organization. Through the years, as I became, as I tested what my experience was against the reality of the Church I was in, I realized that the Episcopal Church is a culture. It's not a religion, unless a culture is a religion. But what I was involved in was not something which was trying to perpetuate a culture; it was trying to create a human experience, which was different and exciting and renewing and all of this. There was radical need for it. But I also found myself ultimately in radical conflict there—even though I had quite a bit of freedom. It just became evident that I couldn't maintain my integrity and my thrusts staying there, without killing myself—I was at some very significant levels. I also couldn't stay there and do my thing without killing some other people at their level. I don't think that that would be too bad. I think there would be some theology involved—about resurrection, death and resurrection for them—but, that's my simple interpretation of that and when it became evident that I couldn't do that, I had to leave.

Bob left Trinity and invested himself in a "free-lance" ministry for the next two and a half years, continuing his Cursillo involvement and work with youth. Feeling "overworked and overextended," Bob sought counseling. The particular therapist, a clinical psychologist, did not unilaterally counsel married couples; thus, Bob and Sue were in group-marriage-counseling. For Sue it was "extremely destructive" although Bob did not "see it at the time."

Separate interviews with Sue suggest that the counseling experience remains to be worked out. Sue perceived the experience as devastating.

I wasn't measuring up to their [clinical psychologist and his co-therapist wife] model of a woman. He had Bob convinced of what I should be like. I wasn't . . . I never would be that and I knew according to them I should leave Bob because I would never measure up and I didn't want to live without Bob. My whole world was falling because all of a sudden you are not a success at anything. It was devastating. His [therapist's] comment to Bob—Bob said it had been very destructive to me—was that it wouldn't have been destructive if it hadn't been true! I didn't measure up: I was bored with theology and I loved my music. I loved Bob but I could never satisfy him in all areas. I was the one who was wrong. I could not win. Bob wanted to stay with it and I said that was the end of the counseling because I knew that no way was I going to get rid of anything, except my self-confidence and more weight—I was emaciated. Those kinds of scars are the hardest to heal. The experience was bad for me because Bob, of all people, really accepted me. All of a sudden I felt that he didn't. It was as though my whole life had been a failure. You know, that was rough to live with. A lot of the magic that we had before was destroyed. It took me a long time—almost two years—to build, for us to build this up again. I remember Bob looking at me and saying, "When in the hell are we going to get over the ——— experience?" And you know, you do, in little bits and pieces.

Counseling gave Bob a "ticket into another economic path." While he pursued his free-lance ministry for four years he obtained a marriage-and-family-counseling license.

You have a sense of being on to something that is beyond any denomination. It is exciting if you have a sense of the spirit of your world and you are there and it is significant. When you bet on those possibilities and they're not happening, and you don't have an area for deciding for yourself— that's where I have been for the past two years. I knew I wasn't just going to be a marriage counselor—that was the way I would back out of ministry. Do some responsible things with people, while I was having other things happen. And the other things are not going to happen. Then you think, "God, where am I?" You know, in this mix, and I was nowhere.

I had this loyalty of being involved in something—right down to the end. It wasn't going to happen. I said, "Oh, shit. I'm forty-five years old and I don't want to do this again." Then you get to the point where you say, "I think it's more responsible to wrap it up."

Rather than do a half death by selling out, it is probably more responsible to use a theological position and just tear the whole thing. I got to the point—which way would you do it? Jump off the bridge? Of course the family knows the consequences of your depression, responsibility starts getting kind of weary. You want to say, screw the whole thing. You go through the fit of petulance, instead of through positive decision. You think death would be a better approach. But you don't make decisions from petulance—I make them from reasoned, for the most part, from reasoned—and I had worked it out so I could make it a reasoned position for suicide. Here I am nowhere and you know it isn't working [Bob's reference here is to any regrouping or social change within church communities] and I'll be honest to myself and to my God and wrap it up. It doesn't make sense to go on.

A chronic failure of one's system of interpretation, one's explanatory principles, or one's abilities to construe one's world raises a doubt as to whether or not the beliefs one held about the world are workable. The "givenness" of one's world is no longer evident. One wonders if one's beliefs are applicable in the world. If they fail in application and comprehensibility a deep disquiet and despair may result. In this light, Geertz recalls that "Lord Russell once remarked that although the problem of the existence of God had never bothered him, the ambiguity of certain mathematical axioms had threatened to unhinge his mind."[8] Bob's mind did not become "unhinged" nor did he attempt suicide; however, during this period he accidentally chopped off the first two joints of his left forefinger while doing some cabinetmaking. It was a clean cut and healed promptly.
Over a period of several months Bob came to

realize that he did not want to end his life even though his work was not "hopeful."

I was involved in qualitative ministry and all our measures are quantitative: how many, how much, how often—not what or how? So this hopeful thing is not happening. When you make that kind of a statement you are thinking in quantitative terms. I have seen significant growth in people in our community; I've seen significant growth in people in my counseling. The things that I've invested myself in are not going to happen. I say, "How long can I test something?" How long can you commit to something before you find out that this is not the time and place for you any more. I was trying to push the river and it wasn't happening. So I said, "All right, now I have done what I can here but maybe it is time for me to move to another situation where I really can do something and where I am making my own choices. I will not have lost anything I have done here. I will still work with people, so maybe this is the time to go out someplace and maintain the contact and let some of this germinate. I don't write off anything that I have done." I'm not sure moving to northern California to a ranch and doing some counseling is going to get me apart from where I have been—make me more capable of dealing with where I have been.

Decisions . . . you have to decide right or the goodness of a decision. A decision which gives value to myself and another person at a personal level, that's right. A decision which is devaluing to myself or another person is wrong. That's simplistic. All of my choices give value to the human. I think my choices right and wrong are—I draw a dichotomy between the personal and the legal, the law—to give value to another person is another way of saying to love. Love in the best sense. And I guess . . . not to decide, I think it is wrong. To avoid or evade decision is almost by definition wrong. Because you're always confronted by situations—

moments—which demand decision, *beyond* the obvious. For me personally, if I, experientially, when I'm not deciding or not involved in a process of deciding, then I feel like hell—depressions and everything else.

Knowing a decision gives value to the person. Thinking about the *deciding* of Jesus . . . I don't model myself, or model my deciding on a fairly understood *model* of Jesus, but on Jesus as a man who decided for a person. That's not scripture text, that type usage. I mean talking about the whole complicated person of Jesus as opposed to the Bible quotes. And to know the person of Jesus, you have to be involved in the extended period of time. Your testing and decidings. It's involved with the creative possibilities which are my givens. I have to be responsible for my creative possibilities. And so I can only create a portion by my decisions; I can't create the environment—completely—in which I'm deciding. I can't word this well. There are adult consequences of adult decisions—not child feelings of making you feel good inside—but of feeling like you are with it—with yourself again, in the process of deciding. I have to work it on several levels and talk about the areas. So if we're talking about growth, that would be different for you than for me as well as the deciding process.

Having successfully evolved his own religious belief, Bob's stance might be termed an enlightened one. He shed old vestments and was able to listen to his own internal demands for change. Within his own denomination Bob remained marginal and even though his free-lance ministry was approved by his bishop it was not accepted by his fellow Anglican priests who remained within their parishes and seminaries while Bob decided to be both self-supporting and a minister. He faces and questions his own feelings about things with searching honesty, a habit that—at times—

brought about despair that he did not hide or repress. He left the Church as institution and organization; he did not leave the ministry which he perceived as service.

The conversion process encompassed fourteen years of Bob Duncan's life—the years between thirty-one and forty-five. Remarkably little is known about this period of life. However, conversion is frequently experienced in these years. Bob is attempting to keep on taking his conversion seriously—but in the context of a changing perception of religion and community. For the time being this may mean the absence of community. In speaking about the beauty of the land in northern California Bob termed it "filled with glory and magnificence, but I have another concomitant awareness that it really isn't mine, but that it is mine to use for a while . . ."

There remain the questions as to whether or not the religious experience is genuine or possible or true or real or an illusion. These questions will remain, unless one assumes an attitude of absolute disbelief or fundamentalist disbelief. Fundamentalism, of either sort, avoids insight and the constructing of meaning as well as *encounter* with one's social reality. The priest or minister's *role* is peculiarly susceptible to a fundamentalist interpretation. He is a "certified" person around whom the community gathers. The temptation is to remain safely within the congregation. Rather than confronting or challenging the congregation, or entertaining doubts raised outside the system, one identifies with the system, thinking one has made a decision of faith. Berger points out that any total identification with a role enables one to avoid ecstasy in the original meaning of the word: "standing outside oneself."

What all experiences of ecstasy—sudden insight, hor-
ror, joy, awe, desolation—have in common "is breaking through the routine, everyday, taken-for-granted
course of our life. Society functions to prevent this
breakthrough . . . its fictions are designed for this purpose."[9] The vision provided by an ecstatic experience
can take one outside the system and confront one with
what suddenly appears to be an inauthentic situation
just as readily as it can convert one to a system or belief.

Tracing this dialectical process of insight and conversion in the life of Bob Duncan might begin with his
intense and "fundamentalist" commitment to American Machines and subsequent recognition that he had
"given his life to American Machines." Moving away
from culturally sanctioned achievement and success,
Bob then began a career within a particular religious
denomination only to find that "all his Christian experience that was meaningful was transdenominational
and related to social concerns." Committed to a religious pluralism and social concern, he then attempted
a free-lance ministry and concluded that his role as
priest, whether inside or outside the institution, evaded
making his own choices. In this instance conversion
has been a process of moral, ethical, cognitive, interpersonal, affective development with its ecstatic edges
intact and mysterious.

8
"It all came crashing in on me"

DAVID HENRY SMITH

It has been said, Camus tells us, that "great ideas come into the world as gently as doves. Perhaps then, if we listen attentively, we shall hear, amid the uproar . . . a faint flutter of wings, the gentle stirring of life and hope." We may find hope "awakened, revived, nourished, by . . . individuals whose deeds and works" set aside barriers to freedom and negate "the crudest implications of history."[1]

The person who carries hope in today's world seeks to avoid pessimistically believing in a crude pluralism—a world "made up of a lot of eaches," or optimistically believing in transcendental absolutes—a world of benign wholeness where the salvation of all is inevitable. Midway between these extremes is a position of "meliorism"—less a doctrine than an attitude of hopefulness.[2] It is a perspective, a possibility which can become a probability if people believe they have the power to better their world. This position sees human experience as open-ended and *potentially* melioristic—capable of betterment—yet is aware that human progress is not inevitable. Specifically, this position considers that even though Christianity originated with a particular revelation—Christ—that revelation and its interpretation are no longer fixed, inevitable, and

145

static. They are subject to ongoing development and interpretation by *persons* situated in a particular culture.

If religion is both an orientation to reality and a social construct, and if the dominant theme in the humanities, arts, and sciences is one of critical relativism and pluralism, then theology—reflection upon religious experience—will reflect that pluralism. Thus the conversion experience of the second half of the twentieth century may be both an event and a process, a reconciliation of opposites yielding a melioristic pluralism. People experiencing such a conversion will be willing to live with uncertain possibilities and will be willing to pay for the realization of ideals they believe in and hope for.

The life history to be interpreted here is an especially pure case of such conversion. I take it up because by virtue of its extremeness it yields profound information. My position is one of a critical relativism. I am not suggesting that one religion is better than another or that none is better than any; rather, I think each should be evaluated as it relates to the individual and common good. I think an arbitrary dismissal of religion as "ideology" begs the question. It evades the difficulty of interpreting other "varieties of human nature" and making clear their *social* meaning.

David Henry Smith, a fifty-three-year-old bachelor, lives in a dimly-lit room on the top floor of an old church gymnasium. Candles, pictures, stacks of books, cases of books, papers, shabby furniture are in view and the sound of Mozart fills the room. A warm and affectionate man, a bit rotund, David is quite comfortable with his living arrangement and at ease with himself and his poverty. He obtains his food with honoraria and remarked that if he got down to his last quarter he hoped he had the good sense to spend it on a flower! David is a Roman Catholic Christian and at the same time fully aware of how often and with what diversity the "Popes, people, and clergy have fornicated with the Emperor," to the "oppression and dehumanization of all."

David remembers his childhood and adolescence as happy while he "preached sermons from the roof of the house." Religion was always important to him; from childhood he imagined he would be a minister. His parents were Methodists and his mother was quite dismayed when he told her he wanted to become a Roman Catholic. His father was somewhat "amused" and wondered if she thought he would become a Baptist since they had sent him to a Jesuit high school "to take advantage of the curriculum." At sixteen, David became an Anglican as this was acceptable to his parents. Continuing on at a Jesuit University, he became a Roman Catholic at nineteen. Becoming a Catholic meant becoming a priest for David and after graduation he entered the Roman Catholic Seminary.

The seminary was a very lonesome place, partly because I had always gotten along with my family—even though we disagreed on religion, it never seemed to disable us of our love of one another. The seminary is like the training ground of any ideological, totalitarian viewpoint—and I'm not sure that all totalitarians don't emulate the Catholic Church. The Church has probably been more successful at turning out its cadre, until perhaps Chairman Mao—who seems to be more successful in a more humanizing way, from what I hear from people who have been there. The seminary begrudged you of your name. You were to be a function of the Church and the reward was lifelong honor, prestige, and power, within the structure. And I can't say that the seminary ever

promised you a bishopric if you knuckled under; on the contrary, the thrust was that you should never aspire, but serve
the people and the Church will tell you how to serve the
people—that is the only way to serve them. To serve them
differently is to betray the Church and people.

Questioning the environment of the seminary
along with the reading of "indexed"[3] liberal theologians and non-Thomistic philosophers led David into
conflict with the faculty; at the same time he became
quite ill with migraine headaches. The rector of the
seminary questioned his interest in art, music, and
ballet, and thought "my interests varied from the interests a priest should have." David's confessor[4] couldn't
understand what that had to do "with anything since
the Church had always been a patroness of the arts
and hopefully the clergy would go on doing so." However, the rector did not agree and "thought I should
not become a priest." At this time David was within a
few months of ordination and was twenty-five. Leaving
the seminary he applied to the Jesuits and was accepted by the order. During the six-month period between application and admittance, David decided he
did not want to become either a priest or a Jesuit. He
thought he didn't "need *certification* to serve." He
then began a teaching career, first at a Jesuit high
school and then as a regular member of the university
faculty. From this position he began an adult education
department and ran it successfully until a change in
administration ended the program. David resigned in
protest and went into a business he had inherited. The
business was a small management consultant firm and
was willed to him by a friend who thought he might do
well in that work. David was in his mid-thirties as he

began to do executive growth appraisal for companies on a contract basis. Under David's leadership, the firm flourished; ultimately, David did not:

We were hired to evaluate and select executives who were to be groomed for accelerated advancement. We succeeded.

I was president, chairman, and majority stockholder. I remember, toward the end, wondering if I could take the time, because of overhead and salaries, to go through the half-hour or so it would take to do this for this man—and that was what was tearing me up.

I had businessmen break down and cry in my office. One I remember, toward the end, told me his wife would leave him if he moved again. She wasn't going to go again. The great mobility of the American corporate executive! Loyalty to the company says you go where they send you. After two or three moves, the executive would be confronted with a wife who wouldn't move—who was fed up with moving. Well, this man was devastated because his wife said she would leave him. He was at the top as a troubleshooter which meant that he had moved from place to place throughout the United States. He broke down and began crying; he was nearly fifty and I was thirty-five. I remember thinking that my time was worth three hundred a day and could I take the half-hour or so to go ahead with him—and deciding to do it.

So I said, "When you leave this office and go downstairs—now, I'd like you to answer this question without thinking. Quick." And he said, "All right." I said, "You get off the elevator in the lobby and someone says: 'Who are you?' What would you say?" He said, "Well, I'm the vice-president in charge of sales for. . . ." and he gave the name of his company. I said, "That's strange, I'd say that I was David Henry Smith!" And he said, "Well, he didn't ask me my name." I said, "I asked you who you *are;* I didn't ask you what do you do. Just let me say this and then I'm going to have to go on to the next appointment: You go home, and you think about your answer to that question. Then reflect upon this. Evidently, some eighteen years ago, a woman called you by name and took you to be her husband—and sometime, recently, she woke up with the vice-president in charge of sales and she doesn't feel any obligation to him at all. Because she didn't marry him!"

Two weeks later he came back and said he had found his name and did not have to leave his company nor move. That was exciting. Fascinating. But then I saw this kid in the garage. Maybe I was, as Paul says, preaching the gospel to others and myself becoming a castaway. I began to realize—it all crashed in on me one whole day.

David Henry Smith perceived this "one whole day" to be a principal "turning" in his life. Mandelbaum writes that "A turning may occur through a single event or experience, a *turning point,* or it may be a gradual shift." Turnings suggest transitions and changing states of mind over the life span; some may be normative and ascribed, while others appear to be improvised. However, such "improvisation" is patterned within the society. "A person's own view of the watersheds . . . may not exactly coincide with the significant turnings that an observer may notice, but that view may nonetheless be important [in directing a person's life] . . . each provides an index to the person's conduct after the turning."[5]

David's life—after this "turning"—changed direction in response to what he perceived to be a conversion experience and also in response to social factors: it occurred in the early years of the civil-rights movement. David's earlier participation in religious institu-

tions socialized him to Christianity; at the same time it
enabled him to note the discrepancy between his values and his behavior. As he says, "it all came crashing
in on me in one whole day." However, an observer or
interviewer would interject a, "Yes, but. . . ." One
understands that such an event has a "landmark"
quality to it, but one does not know why "this time" is
more important and so utterly different than previous
times.

"This time" or "Kairos"—"fulfilled time," a "right
moment"—emphasizes the unique as opposed to
"Chronos—the continual flux of time measurable." Intrinsic to Kairos is its emergent quality in which all dimensions of being participate, from which new orienta-
tions are experienced with new clarity. Kairos is not
measurable time; it thus escapes simple location in
time, but must be "placed" by the person in order to
be interpreted. What coalesced in a "point of time" is
then perceived as having occurred in that "moment"
or day.[6]

Religious conversion has generally been perceived as an event located in time. Indeed, the converted one frequently gives a specific day, time, and
place to the conversion "event," as did Augustine in
his *Confessions*. However, "an analysis of Augustine's
writings immediately after the date of his conversion
(A.D. 386) [suggests] that the account he gives in the
Confessions is premature. The crisis in the garden
marked a definite conversion from his former life, but it
was to neo-platonic spiritualism and only a halfway
stage toward Christianity. The latter he appears not
fully and radically to have embraced until four years
more had passed."[7]

Insight, conversion, paradigm shift all have this

aspect of Kairos—"the moment when"—of being unique time and are remembered as the moment when the shift was apprehended by the person; these moments are inexplicable and impossible to place.[8]

To return to David's "day":

I've never forgotten that day. I had played the *whole game* the way you had to play it and I had a current-year Cadillac in the garage downstairs, and when I wanted to leave, the secretary phoned down and my car was ready. I enjoyed it; I thought it was great.

That day I drove into the garage and the black kid that was supposed to take my car was talking to another kid. I was late to an appointment. I got absolutely furious. Enraged! I thought of walking over to the manager and having the kid fired. I remember glaring at him. So I hit the air outside the garage and the whole thing crashed in on me. It never occurred to me what he was talking about. The person he was talking to *couldn't* have told him his mother or brother had died. Or anything. It had not crossed my mind that something was keeping him over there and from parking my car like he always had.

It dawned on me that I wasn't playing a game anymore—the *game* had become more real than my own *values.* A few weeks later I sold my share of the business. I got out of it. By that time I was so sick—the whole thing had gotten to me. Later, the doctor thought I had mononucleosis, but at the time he didn't know. I was very sick; I used to get up and sit on the side of my bed for an hour or so and listen to the coffeepot perk and want to be able to get up and not be able to.

David's father died during this year and he stayed with his mother for a few months but found that "impossible." During the next two years, David lived alone part of the time and with close friends, Bob and Judith, for several months. While noting his own commitment to a celibate life as fitting his "commitment to serve," David often stated the importance of his friends: "When you don't marry, your friendships tend to mean a lot more to you, I think, than if you do marry. I could be wrong. I never have married so I don't know. Sometimes things do not pan out and you feel treachery; you don't want to lose friends, but have to reach out to others . . . I think friends hold me together. I kind of like what Buber said of Kierkegaard: " 'I don't say that Kierkegaard does not have a right to sit alone. On his rock. The single one. But I bid no one to join him!' " David's friend, Bob, was enthusiastically involved in the Cursillo and after much urging, David participated in one and "didn't like it."

I didn't like the one I made at all. In the first place there were sixty-five people and it was old church, that was 1962. I got to know the director of the Cursillo Center and worked with him on farm-worker problems—then I went down to North Beach . . . it was bothering me that I didn't have any third-world people. Let's just call it that. In those days, I knew no black people. There wasn't a black person in the world that could say that he or she was my friend. I didn't know brown people. I didn't know anybody that wasn't white middle class. So I moved to North Beach and lived in the cheapest hotel I could find. I kept the same room for the four years I stayed there. I spent most of my time in that room. It took six months before anybody would talk to me, because they all thought I was the fuzz—spying on them. Little by little, it eased up and I made friends. I got very well acquainted with lots of people who lived there—the very young and old. The maid in the hotel, Lily, was a remarkable woman, a very devout Baptist, who had murdered her husband and spent

seven or eight years in prison for manslaughter. I didn't
know all the particulars of that, but I had long since come to
the conclusion that he must have needed killing—I couldn't
imagine her doing anything really wrong. The fact that she
was convicted of manslaughter indicated that it was probably self-defense. If she had been white, she would have gotten off. Anyway, she ran the hotel—didn't own it, but ran it.
That was an enriching experience I hold: meeting people
who were unlike any I had ever met. I met the night people
and the numbers people.

James writes of the extremes of religious experience which "has always, for a time at least, driven him
who had it into the wilderness, often the literal wilderness out of doors, where the Buddha, Jesus,
Mohammed, St. Francis, George Fox, and so many
others had to go."[9] David did not fast, nor sit in hollow
trees; he felt himself called into the wilderness of North
Beach and any accompanying asceticism had more to
do with a simplicity of living in order to merge into the
environment than with self-mortification. He interprets
his choice of a sleazy, run-down old hotel in North
Beach—in contrast to his former life of luxury—as arising from a sudden recognition that there were people
who were *not* white-middle-class and he did not know
one he could "call by name." He then set out to find
friends in a world whose existence was now manifest to
him. Reflection upon his experience and his continuing
interest in education also resulted in David's reappear-
ance in the classroom:

At the same time I had met Sister Anne who was at the university in an Urban Life Institute and she asked me to take
her place while she was on vacation, which I did. It was the
new careers program and two thirds of the students were

black and the rest Chicanos. Only one white in the class. They were recruited off the street with federal funding. So I taught her class for those few days and as a result the students got together and told me that they wanted me on the faculty. I didn't want to go back because I had sworn, when I was there before, that I wouldn't return until the previous president was removed. But I went up there and taught for three years in the new careers program.

It was amazing how the four years in North Beach and those three years dovetailed. I didn't know how to teach a class of third-world people; I knew better than to try; so I moved into the class situation and I told them I didn't know how to teach them. I felt that the first couple of months I would like them to tell me *who* they were and how they wanted teaching to be conducted in that class, what they were there for. For two months they did, and I let it alone until they told me that they wanted me to start teaching. Then I started and I had a much better idea of how to go about it. From then on it went very well. I suppose that was the most educational experience I have ever had in my life. I learned more. They tell me they learned a lot—so there I was, living in North Beach in that hotel, working on Cursillos, and teaching at the university and the whole thing psychologically jelled. I think I turned into an entirely different person.

The hang-ups began breaking; I became much more open to almost any thought without fear. Then getting into community organizing—it was like a pressure cooker to do all that. It would either make you or break you and I suppose because I have some very good friends—I don't think anyone could do it alone. I'm sure of it. You—the blacks taught me—don't shed culture and you can't become transcultural if you lose your footing in your own culture; you deepen the notion that it is yours. You shed your superiority. You shed the chauvinisms but you don't shed the culture.

The blacks taught me that; they didn't want me to stop being a white Westerner who loved Mozart. I was assaulted on all sides with the clash of culture: white middle class, Filipino, Spanish Cursillos, farm workers. It became impossible to sustain my previous outlook: I either had to become something that I already had the intelligence to reject and that was a complete chauvinist and to say that the white-middle-class society was what God had in mind when he made man. Well, that wasn't possible. I couldn't agree with that. It just all collapsed.

When it all collapsed—the old structure—for me it was happily a healthy transition. I never suffered a period of total demolition where I was at. One thing led into another and I knew everything was collapsing but it was not a painful thing when it happened. It was confusing at times. I found it terribly exciting—assaulted on all sides by the clash of cultures and teaching blacks—so I had to recognize our morals aren't everybody's morals. They aren't morals at all. What is moral?

I got pushed back to scriptural notions of justice, which has nothing to do with courts. It began to dawn on me— justice has nothing to do with courts of law; it has nothing to do with crime, recrimination and punishment. It has to do with every man getting his due—which is oversimplified but a good place to start.

If Western morals aren't morals; if they are Western customs and not morals—Western conventions. If they work with us and don't work elsewhere and they don't have divine sanction—once you rob them, deprive them of divine sanction—then you start saying: Well, is anything wrong in the absolute sense? I had to use scripture to find some hints and I found that justice had to do with this process of de-divinizing local customs. I realized that humanity does mean something and the humanness of a human being does mean something and it is real but it varies in its flowering in the world.

But underlying that is a reality that must not be deprived of its opportunity to exist; one of the things that deprives it is divinizing local culture so that instead of serving the human being, it dominates. That has to go. Society has to look and we as individuals dealing with one another have to be liberating influences to say, "Yes, it is good to be who you are." No one can tell you who that is but you. You must quest for the answer and maybe fail in finding it, or in your experiment with it. It is not for me to sit in judgment *on* you when you fail but rather to help you reassemble your efforts to make another attempt and to tell you that I am not threatened by your liberty.

It is not the business of society or the law to control human behavior to make *one* group of us safe. It is the business of society to make it possible for us to find out who we are. That's justice! Whenever that doesn't exist and one group structures things to protect itself from the other—then God's justice is defeated and he cries out against the oppressor: "Leave offering me your sacrifices until you stop that oppression and take care of the poor" and the poor—that is anyone who doesn't have the power to make a decision for his own future and carry it out. Any society that makes it more difficult for one group than for another is an unjust society.

So I sort of started there and drew morals out from there. You end up with not too many morals—not too many things are right and wrong. Oppression is wrong—it's funny. You get very liberal with some things your society takes very seriously: you can't get excited about nudism on a public beach or a lot of things more serious than that. You can't get excited because there is room to disagree and agree.

You get almost absolutist about certain things. I remember blowing up at one group that said there were two sides to the farm workers. You do not oppress farm workers, not if you are going to call yourself a Christian or a human being. It is not lawful to do that and that is the condition of

human existence—that you don't do it and there is no room
to disagree. But that doesn't mean that the farm workers are
entitled to ignore the plight of the small grower. It is not in
their interest to ignore it.

David remains committed to an absolute in the
context of a relative world. He has moved from a
dualistic perspective to one entertaining relativism.
While the ecstasy of the "faith state" has enabled the
converted to change direction, to face about—as
David did—such a metanoia takes on meaning as it
becomes the criteria for choice and decision. The re-
structuring is revolutionary, both abrupt and gradual,
which makes it difficult to capture as a "strategy of
growth." It involves emotional maturation and a more
encompassing identity.

David recalls that time with awe and pride and
some surprise. His description of the early sixties is fla-
vored with "an astringent relish" and humor; a sense
of deliverance and the reality of the unseen over-
arches his retelling of his demolition. Mozart plays
softly in the background while David speaks of "being
in the hands of the living God" and very much in the
"hands of the university administrators!" He was
highly critical of the administration's lack of effort to
find any local funding to support the program for
minorities once federal funding ended. David could
not understand the university's reluctance to "grasp its
role in the urban crisis."

An urban university within the Jesuit tradition of the liberal
arts should certainly be expected to grasp its potential role.
Nevertheless, our experience during the past year would
suggest that there is either no awareness within the univer-

sity of the crisis and polarization in our city and our society, or there is no concern or interest in that crisis or there is no understanding of the historical role of the Church before such a crisis. It is as though we exist at Main and First Streets to preserve our own existence as it has been from the beginning—and whatever exists around us exists worthily or unworthily in direct proportion to the extent to which it will sustain us in existence as we have been from our beginning.

With apparent frustration and sadness, David went on:

It could have been a breakthrough toward relevance for the university. Turning the children of recent immigrants into patriotic Americans without costing them their faith—or at least their cultural commitment to the Roman Catholic tradition—is no longer an urgent and widespread need of Church and secular society. Survival once may have depended upon meeting a basic need of second-class citizens, catering to their prejudices and fanning their fears. Today this strategy translates into catering to the interests of the status quo, ignoring the demands and justified outrage of the many while fostering a groundless euphoric preoccupation with the inconsequential. Indulging and surrendering to this kind of myopic miscalculation of priorities in today's *living* society leads to the madness which pronounces anything with roots in the humus of humanity to be "peripheral to the central concern of the educational process."

Warming to his subject, David's voice rose as he stated:

No doubt these same trustees of academic continuity and the apostolic succession of the classroom would have seen the Sermon on the Mount as peripheral to the central and all-important ceremony and commerce of the Temple and

[as] the annoying but always-to-be-considered machinations of the Roman Occupation. After all, who can waste his
academic prowess and privileged clerical status upon that
rabble and their itinerant preacher.

David's "Urban Life Institute" was dropped from
the curriculum in early 1972. An interesting and pro-
vocative speaker, David continued to lecture for community and service groups and to give courses in the
more progressive Roman Catholic parishes of the
archdiocese. An unremitting critic of Christianity in
general, and Roman Catholicism most particularly, he
remains committed to challenging it from within. How
David defines "within" is as interesting as how he
speaks of the God he perceives to be central and im-
manent in his life—and in the life of the "Christian
community." David doesn't think there is any community, Christian or otherwise, in evidence, and believes it to be the task of the Christian to try both to find
one and build one.

Community, community, community! As I said at a lecture
the other evening. Always talking about this favorite subject
as if it existed somewhere! Communities are made up of responsible individuals or they are not communities: they are
collectives, people propping each other up, dehumanizing
one another in a continual underscoring of the poverty of
everybody in it, isolating their members from the rest of humanity in a conspiracy of fear. A community gives as it re-
ceives, shares, is over-rich and its leaders are hardly noticed,
do not have disciples, and when they are gone the people
say, "We did it ourselves. . . ." I am very bothered by communes and gurus.

Gurus foster dependency and infantilism—probably for
the best reasons, as parents sometimes do: fear of injury and

dangerous things. In the old days, the Church could grab someone like Hitler, before he flowered, and shove him into a monastery where he was told to do what the abbot said. If they could convince him of that, well, society was spared his machinations. But society was also deprived of an inexcusable lot of great people who turned into lackeys in a monastery. I suppose some of the great ones flowered anyway: Bernard of Clairvaux, Francis of Assisi, Thérèse. But we don't know that there weren't greater ones that we lost in the process. I don't like the process. But I think that you cannot either structure society large or small *without* taking into account the danger of the individual running amok. With successive awareness of explosions in him that he doesn't know how to personalize, they do nothing but inflate the ego, and then all of a sudden he announces that he is God. And follow me! I think we live in an age when that is happening, not just in the universal way, like Hitler, but in thousands of little local communities. Communes—where the people live on a farm and think their leader is god. And they are all living well—in one I am thinking of—except he is the only one who has dreams. That is abhorrent to me, that these people should live in the shadow of this one person. The disciples don't graduate!

Community? It doesn't exist. It seems strange that we've repeated the Lord's prayer for two thousand years, and never asked what it means. It is a search for meaning: We say "Our Father." Now he didn't say "My Father." He said, "Our Father." At least that is the interpretation we have. That implies at least two things—maybe several others: It implies Jesus's father and mine or it implies the whole community's father. Or both. What do I mean when *I* say "Our Father"? I have to decide what I mean by it or I'm just mouthing things. When I say it—personally, I have difficulty getting overexcited about God as father. I always feel that I had a father. He died and I buried him. I don't need another. But other people find this a very persuasive and important element in their religious faith. I don't. I much prefer to think of a lover, an eternal challenger, demanding that I be myself and not anybody else. A lovers' quarrel that goes on all the time. I say, "Yes," and I get the feeling that I am being moved. It doesn't happen unless you want it to. I wanted it to.

Yet it is a fearful thing to fall into the hands of the living God. [laughs] I don't particularly like what goes on all the time. If God talks me into what I'm going to do—I don't know whether or not it was God or not. A year or more later I may know. But at the moment I neither know nor care whether it is he or she [laughs] who is wholly other or part of me. That I'm not in touch with. Either one is trustworthy. It makes little practical difference where it comes from. I sometimes recognize that that was beyond even my own depths, as magnificent as they are! [laughs] But this was something that came from—you feel loved. And being loved is feeling different from loving yourself: both are absolutely necessary. At a later moment I sense that that love came from a love that didn't originate from me: that is the greatest moment of all.

. . . The idea of God as pure spirit isn't buyable to me; it wasn't enough for God *either,* as it was God's notion to get mixed up with flesh. The whole genius of Christianity and the reason I am a Christian is because it deals with the flesh and divinizes it. What I have resolved in my mind is that Christ is not male. Whether you're taking it as a myth or reality, he was a good Jewish boy. He didn't marry. Now good Jewish boys got married. [laughter] So either he wasn't good or he wasn't Jewish or he wasn't a boy. One of the Coptic Christian legends refers to Jesus as a moon friend. Where is the female? The Church is forever trying to turn the female element into spirit; won't deal with androgyny. If there were no God there would still be Christianity because it teaches incarnation: Word made flesh. I don't know whether God is in the making, or whether theologians and philosophers who would like to play with ideas of eternity as distinguished from time can bail us out—there are problems with saying that God is in the making and not here yet, maybe never. I think it is *our* business to raise one another from the dead; I think that is what human existence is all about—in raising one another from the dead, in those little ways until we learn to do it on the whole.

To me it is a healthy concept of God. I can't buy most of what I hear about God. The God I hear about isn't real to me. I think the only God that is real is the one that you fight with and you never quite know if that is another part of yourself—wholly or holy other. I think Jung was right when he said he couldn't be accused of atheism because: "I tell you that everything you attribute to God is true of you." There is a legend that God was struggling with some ineffable and indescribable experiment about himself and there was an accident. He exploded and his glory exploded. He became flesh, to repair the damage. We are simply God repairing the damage, not remembering who we are. Of course that is an agonizing process—analogies and allegories limp and cripple around. I like that one. I'm wrestling with it. Why should I work it out for you? I don't know the answer. I choose to wrestle with it. As Camus said, "What really makes the difference between human beings . . . is their choices." [laughs]

David weaves facts and ideals together and it is not at all clear if it is possible to separate which is which. His youthful conversion is imitative; his later one of the nature of the "twice born." One might even say he was "thrice born" and ask if this is not the meaning of conversion in this instance? Conversion is not commonly thought of as conversion to pluralism; it appears to be so in this instance as David is open to a Word spoken between persons and between cultures.

How does this conversion differ from any commitment made in the context of a relative world? Perhaps it is commitment to ongoing conversion, a commitment to the transforming, elaborating, and refining of one's concepts. It is the embodiment of one's concepts in one's own life as the "Word made flesh." Thus, meaning is no longer static and conceptual; conversion is not a specific and simply interpreted religious tradition; rather, a continuing deciding for and deciding to.

Religion is not a watertight compartment in David's head; it is his fundamental orientation toward reality. Setting aside his very occasional participation in religious ritual, one might observe very little difference between his behavior and that of a secular humanist.

David frequently quotes Camus's statement to the Dominican Monastery of Latour-Maubourg, in 1948, that was subsequently published in *Resistance, Rebellion, and Death* and titled, "The Unbeliever and Christians." Setting aside "lay pharisism" whereby the person believes "Christianity to be an easy thing" and then demands more of the Christian, from this external perspective, than one asks of oneself, Camus went on to declare he did not possess any absolute truth and therefore, he did not presuppose Christian truth to be "illusory"; rather he could not accept it. Finally, he stated "I shall not try to change anything that I think or anything that you think (insofar as I can judge of it) in order to reach a reconciliation that would be agreeable to all." To do so would reduce "dialogue" that the "world needs." Both silence and falsehood Camus felt to be the opposite of the dialogue that is possible between people. Camus thought the world needed Christians who remained so and considered the duty of the

Christian and the unbeliever to be the same: that of interceding "everywhere and ceaselessly for children" and persons faced with evil, not the defense of absolute values.[10]

David's search of the scriptures, out of which came his idea of justice, was not confined to the Bible: it included any and all "primary religious utterances." He included those of the Christian as well as the unbeliever since they, too, spoke both of commitment and a fundamental orientation to the world and oneself.

9

The Way of the Mystic

ANNE SIENNA

Love God and do as you will. This saying, attributed to Augustine, is symbolic and part of cultural patterns of religious belief. The meaning given to the saying can orient one fundamentally to reality and define the real; the connotation given the saying is subject to historical tradition and thus to interpretive change. It has an ineffable and noetic quality; it is both inexplicable and a way of knowing to the religious person—a special manner of perceiving truth, as well as a way of living it. It is the way of the mystic.

Mysticism in our time is *seemingly* rampant, but in actuality I think it is exceedingly rare. Since mysticism is an extreme expression of religion it deserves interest; at the same time, its "otherness" breaks open, and places in the open, a world one cannot understand. If one regards every guru as a mystic one can either follow or dismiss the guru without necessarily encountering mysticism. A second possibility is to regard mysticism with a pervasive belittling hostility that cannot be bothered to understand and avoids any critical evaluation of mysticism's *meaning*, now as well as in the past.

Meaning is a dominant concept of our time. The crisis of our time is not one of faith but of culture, and culture *is* meaning. The distinctions between philosophy and theology are vanishing as both become existential and historical and ask about persons, not in some abstract, pure state of nature, but as the person is in the here and now. We live in a world of meaning. When the symbols that have carried meaning become empty vehicles or objects, one can ignore the obvious and attempt to live in the past; one can also decide all is false and find everything meaningless. Setting out on an expedition to hunt for the falseness of all can wreck one's self and convictions. To find meaning one must construct and rebuild, filling oneself with what is true, letting the false fall away.

This reflection on the importance of meaning is quite lucid; it is also extremely rational and as James reminds us, "I do not yet say that it is *better* that the subconscious and non-rational should hold primacy in the religious realm. I confine myself to simply pointing out that they do hold it as a matter of fact."[1]

A mystic is one who has experienced the reality of the unseen and has the temerity to take both love and God seriously and strangely lightheartedly. Anne Sienna is a mystic by that definition; however, she has come to construe her fundamental orientation to reality in a different context and with changed content. During the 1960s the teaching of religion was updated. Many discovered that religion was not simple conformity to what had been learned, but rather was a challenge of justice, love, and honesty in the world. What happened to those who suddenly confronted such radical religion? They saw the official Church publicly disciplining members for action that had grown out of a new understanding of the Gospel. They saw the Church decrying its members. One had to go elsewhere. For Anne this period encompassed three

years; she then left her religious order, while remaining
a mystic. This text is her interpretation of the experience of herself and her God. Though I understand, I
do not stand within her understanding.

Anne Sienna, thirty-three, is slight, lively, with a
childlike sense of wonder that belies her abilities as a
teacher and administrator in parochial schools and in
the Colombian orphanage where she now works.
Anne entered the convent at eighteen, obtained a
teaching credential and was assigned to the Bay Area,
where she taught first grade, participated in the Cursillo
movement, designed stained-glass windows, and
learned sign language in order to work with poor, deaf,
black children as a summer volunteer counselor. At
ease with children, Anne is shy and quiet with adults;
she speaks very softly; there are long, long pauses—
some lasting many minutes—which occurred in this
interview and are not evident in the text, but helped to
create it. The silences appeared to be gathering times
for Anne as she interpreted her experiences. "If you
can wait . . . I think . . . I'll be able to talk. It is easy to
talk about things. . . . What is in the heart . . . *the* things
that matter . . . well, they're not things! It may take me
a long time . . . but I'll try."

In 1969 Anne was assigned to a Los Angeles
bilingual parochial school as teacher and principal.
After a few months of very structured and isolated
convent life, Anne moved into a small house with four
other nuns; at the same time she entered a Master's
Degree program in a large university. She was twenty-
seven.

That was . . . a decisive . . . there was a time, I think, that I
did make some major changes in my value system. And it

happened . . . and would probably be bound up with the fact that I made a decision that was *mine*. It put me in a situation where I was mine . . . first to live outside the convent . . . I was in a situation that was mine, and so then I . . . faced me! I threw away things that weren't mine. They were mine, but they weren't mine, because I . . . picked them, and that happened when I was about twenty-seven years old. My values shifted. I threw away some, and kept some, and I also examined my belief in God.

I read—I can't remember his name, but he said, "He who has a will to meaning can bear," or "He who has a why to live for. . . ." Well, he definitely didn't believe in God, and he wrote a lot about that. . . .

I was sure of certain things. When I grew up, of course, there was an outline for the ideal person. I always wanted to do the right thing—no, not right but good. I always wanted to do the right thing. That came from others and was bound up with goodwill. I always wanted to do what others wanted—the good thing. And I always wanted to do the best thing and be the best person. So, and so, being goodwilled, if someone gave me the map for that I would try real hard to do it. Of course, the map at that time would be given by parents, school, Church, and early religious life for me. So outside things . . . interpreted my morality . . . and that had to do with external things. Yes, like you could judge yourself by how many times you didn't do this or you did do this—*thing!* . . .

It's hard to think of actual times, when you stopped thinking as a child and thought as an adult. I don't think you ever really stop being one and then another. What helped me to grow up, when I was little—if I try to think of what it was—it seems the grown-up times were when I would have to cope with my little living situations, which were little but they would be little difficult things then. I had to make decisions—my Mom and Dad worked and I was alone with my brother—and I had to make little decisions that seemed to make me feel grown-up.

I remember feeling different . . . and I don't think that felt good. I can't remember exactly when feeling different became feeling unique . . . which was then something special . . . to feel . . . for me . . . an appreciation of myself as something special. I do now like myself very much, and my uniqueness. I appreciate it. I don't remember when all that happened. But I think for me there was a time when I converted feeling different into feeling special . . . *especially* different.

I felt sure of certain things—of course, there's lots of things I'm still not sure of . . . but I was sure of certain things that I was told I should be sure of and I didn't want to even . . . I just threw them away. It's hard to remember; I think maybe I felt it was time to have some convictions and to know why I had them. That may have happened because I was in a situation where everybody had all kinds of different convictions and thoughts and beliefs, about all kinds of different things. That was in the Master's Program at the university.

It seemed to be one way to settle the confusion, for me, . . . to know why I had certain convictions and . . . why I didn't. Perhaps a way of relieving some anxiety about some of the things I believe was to examine them and to not anymore just live by certain things without having made them my own, and knowing *why* I did.

Some dying . . . in a sense of decreasing of identification with certain things—that way of life I had had. It's scary and you don't know if it's right and you don't know if you're losing . . . letting something go that you're . . . that you shouldn't be. You wonder if it's your fault. Some things . . . that you don't identify with anymore, some things that maybe you were told, or taught were good . . . you find yourself slipping away from that. At first, you don't know what to do. You get angry with yourself. I have done that! I have done that with my religious way of life—ways I had identified with. The traditional ways . . . less and less I identified with that and less and less with some of the people in it. That's dying . . . and a rebirth, in a way: in the *way* that I feel is better but, I feel, also, it's hard.

I like what is happening to me, but . . . it's difficult. Because you feel yourself moving away from something and you wonder: can you maintain yourself . . . within that . . . something that you're identifying with less and less. Whether it be in ways that really matter or not . . . just simple things— like dress, for example, in a religious group. But this can carry . . . you can carry it over into all other areas: there *is* an acceptable way—of dress, or whatever—or a way that others would think acceptable. Well, I don't do that. I have my own feelings about that and . . . it's difficult to carry out my way of thinking. But I didn't care what others thought. It causes a little tension. And that carries over into lots of other situations!

I feel that, again and again . . . if it's being used for good or not harming—but questioning—it's all right. Dress is a little thing . . . you're not identifying with what they wore—the habit. You want to identify . . . but you cannot any more. And you wonder if something good has slipped away. It doesn't *seem* good anymore . . . you think about it . . . but you don't know. Like the religious values I grew up having because someone gave them to me. Then came the time . . . it was time to look at them and rearrange them, and drop off some of them. The ones that I kept became extremely meaningful, because they were *mine*. I became very simple in regard to rules and things. All those little things . . . the idea of sin. It's just a very simple matter to me now. It happens . . . whatever it is . . . I don't call it sin . . . when we break the love with another. Or we hurt the loving relation-

ship that should be. I don't worry . . . about anything . . .
other than that. At one time I did. Because I learned it was
wrong to do this, or that, or whatever. And I look at other
people in the same way now. I see very little wrong with very
many, many things—only that we hurt or harm someone.
I've learned . . . to value *attitude* more than the carrying out
of something—a rule. I've learned . . . to value attitude to
determine the wrongness of something. It's how your heart
feels . . . that determines the wrongness or rightness of
something. It has nothing to do with—it really is "How does
my heart feel about my God?" It's not measured in things I
do so much . . . though they are sometimes important. It's
more my attitude about morality, about being good.

So there is a big difference now. It didn't happen very
slowly . . . when it happened. Yes, I guess it did. No, it was
all in that time when I was about twenty-seven. Now I just try
to be as honest as I can be—about what I do. And to always
try to . . . to not hurt or harm another. And to be true to
myself—as I possibly can, because then I will be as true to
others as I possibly can. And to God.

Then there was Patrick. . . . I met him at the university. I
. . . just loved him . . . we made love . . . it just happened . . .
he wanted me to spend the weekend with him. I didn't—I
don't know why. Maybe I was scared. I didn't see him again.
That was hard. I wrote once, but I never heard. That's probably the area where I learned that it's bad and therefore
most difficult to talk about—not the morality thing—but the
need for sexuality in my life. I see very little as bad. But I do
see some bad. Sexual relationships, I feel, are not so good
when they prevent growth, when they turn inward, and become extremely selfish. That would happen . . . when the
adventure, or whatever, would be purely self-satisfying, and
not so much of *anything* else. I don't even really think that
that's bad. But it doesn't enhance, and in that sense is not
good. Then there is the other person in the relationship—
always. How much is he or she being used. Filling a need.

. . . I have masturbated; I have had relationships with other women and men. I mention masturbating because . . . I have a greater understanding of that as fitting . . . making sense perhaps . . . than I did. It is not wrong. Wrong—I don't like to talk about wrong—actually—wrong. I'm just trying to express the change of attitudes. It has to do with the relationship . . . not with the rules I've learned.

There can be harm. There is harm. It's hard to answer because I believe that no one can make us do anything, and I also believe that we are the only ones who can *do*—whatever. In a way, I see myself as very much related to other beings, and I see my choices affecting other beings, having an effect, either for good or bad. In that way, I touch their lives. But I never think of myself in control of another's life, or having power over it. Yet I do feel that I have a definite effect on others.

The source before . . . for everything . . . there was a source before—for my beliefs and it was conditioned. I was conditioned. Now I'm more myself . . . with myself . . . and with my God. It's my interpretation of life and Jesus. He's not so different from before for me. But others had interpreted Him, not Him, but His laws, for me. He was always a real person to me . . . very real . . . a very real part of me . . . and of life. A vital person to me . . . and the change has been more in my interpretation of His message. It now seems very simple. It's to love and to be truly human. Then He will be extremely alive for me and for others.

I don't know what God is to me. I once wrote a poem about a force that pulls in, and pulls out . . . and it is always something that pulls me in, and pulls me out. And it is real. It is as an end. I meet. Everywhere I go. In . . . and out. And all times and all places and all ways. And all situations. There are places for me, of course, . . . where I feel that presence with more ease. Those are times, I think, when I'm closely in touch with nature. Though I have a constant sense of His presence at all times and all places . . . I do feel very near . . . when I'm alone . . . and in free, peaceful, serene places. The opposite is true too. I also feel that presence, when my thoughts turn toward something more than persons—at times when I see lots of people . . . *really* suffering. I can't understand or comprehend, or there doesn't seem to be any sense to . . . people who are lonely . . . inequality, and there is no sense to it and I wonder if . . . if there is a time when it can happen. Good can happen.

Evil. Why is so-and-so without . . . born in an environment with no hope. Part of that, I would think—I now think, of course—that would be the Christian message. I don't know . . . but . . . I think there is—in me—there is a pull from somewhere, someone. Aside from this . . . this thing that I can't explain . . . this pull . . . to someone, there would be enough sense in the Christian message for me, because people are extremely important to me, or . . . not just important, but life *is* people, and it seems to me that the Christian message is one of people and of loving them, and they, in turn, are loving. Now of course this is what it means to *me*. That makes me a Christian. A decision and . . . I think it has to be made over and over again. A belief in people. A faithfulness to people. A response to life. And a belief in life, which of course, God is forever present and working . . . alive. That would be my faithfulness . . . a moving . . . an awareness, or a responsibility to move and not just to be pleased with thinking "church" is "something," but always being in search of it. Or creating it . . . of thinking that it is always a little bit more than it is. Or people . . . we can always be a little more than what we are. This has all changed—those things, observing rituals—that has changed.

There are lots and lots of things that nourish now. There's a center, I believe. A source and essence of our being that pushes us out, and I would call that God. But then . . . this source and center is in so many things and people, too. All kinds of things go back and forth . . . are more in touch with that center, which is also self, too. The more in touch, then, we are with that . . . I think that is what we are meant to be and do. That center. Finding that center. Most often, the center is most in touch with God. So the closer we come to that, the closer we are with God—with reality.

I suppose . . . once I called it prayer. When it happens at different times, and different places . . . it's felt most when I can try to center all of myself . . . on the center. That's hard. That would be real communion. And that's hard . . . I want to do that more than I do. Then of course there is a presence at the center and we can find that in ourselves and with others. The real prayer—what real prayer is to me is very difficult and it takes a lot of work . . . getting in touch with the very essence of being. That kind of prayer is all bound up with everything else we've talked about. It's bound up with one's authenticity, because I believe it comes from that center . . . and so it is extremely vital for me. I have to be careful not to let that slide away . . . slip away . . . because our world, my world, doesn't lend itself to . . . to keeping deeply in touch with one's center. It is a hard thing—for me.

I have to often rethink it. Bring it alive again. And of course it's funny, but . . . it's that pulling in. You can't get too far away, because you keep coming back. And coming back. And coming back. It's like a conversation with a friend—if you don't keep in touch, you lose touch. It happens. It can happen. And all kinds of ways help me to get in touch . . . people . . . meditation . . . thinking, just being. There are all kinds of ways to get in touch with God. I think of them all as prayer. I don't think of one as richer than all the rest, when one really tries to center on God and truly get in touch with that. You have to find those times, make those times. They don't just happen. But they do! The more real you become—they do!

One thought I always . . . I keep . . . we have that power to bring alive that center in other people. I once heard a story about a prisoner or prisoners—or a number of

people—maybe they are dead because no one has brought
them to life and we have that power to touch and bring alive
that center in others. I think someone once said, "To love
another is to bid them to live and invite them to grow." I
think that is very true . . . and it just happens over and over
again. I see in people that once someone begins to love
them or believe in them, they just start doing so many good
things. Changes start happening. In that sense, that center
has to have a lot or power.

I don't know if others would interpret this in this way. I
don't see any models. I don't like to speak of being
progressive—as if others aren't. I wouldn't know that. But I
do think there are others who might interpret Church or
whatever it is, as I do. And there are many others who
wouldn't. Not in the religious community, any more, at least
for me. Others, outside . . . put me in touch with that center
. . . it would be the people that I would know . . . that I would
feel are most in touch with themselves. They are usually just
my warm simple friends . . . whose values are not complicated . . . and just loving.

When I resigned from being the principal, I didn't know
what I would do next . . . not at all. To some people, that
would be *stupid*. "You mean you're doing that and you
don't have anything else in mind?" But things happen; they
take shape and direction. We have to do our part, too. I've
had to try to do . . . but things do work out, generally. Not
always.

With decisions—like that one, to resign and leave—in
my life . . . I've never worried too much, because directions
seem to take place . . . if you are just trying to be as faithful
as can be . . . to that day . . . or that moment. Each little
moment becomes a little clearer. If I can just be patient, if I
can just be patient, but at the same time, try to work out and
into the different life situations . . . they just take their shape.
The hardest thing for me, in the last five years, is being able

to be patient with life, to allow it to take its direction and to be able to just move with it, slowly and peacefully. Sometimes, it isn't slow! And at the same time not to be avoiding it. To be making decisions, but to be peacefully making them and allowing life and all to show . . . to have its part in showing directions and ways. To allow that to be happening and not escaping . . . or using that thinking—that it will just happen—as an escape from doing something. It's not placid or stagnant but waiting and moving.

They do take shape . . . you can look back. I never really think of these things as accomplishments . . . but I guess I think of lots of things as accomplishments—not just something I *did*. Other things are accomplishments—just getting through things and coming out with renewed enthusiasm, or determination, or even just with *hope*. I think of accomplishments as things I've tried my best at, and given my best to. I feel good about them . . . sometimes they don't work out . . . Then there would be concrete things . . . they would be things I have made the choice about myself and have managed to carry out and get through. Which might be simple things like completing a Master's, or . . . creative tasks . . . starting them and doing them and producing something worthwhile. But I don't really think of that too often—the accomplishments in the sense of a concrete thing. I think more about accomplishments as being not giving up and continuing to search, or struggle, or work towards things. Little things.

Anne speaks of "little things" with originality and a paradoxical simplicity. She is aware of her own process of growing and seems always to have trusted in that process: earlier it was a given; now there isn't any model or map, but only a sense of the divine as a unifying force in her life.

She does not make a clear distinction between being a child and an adult as *she* does not think people ever stop being one and then the other. Loevinger refers to this "dialectical aspect" of development: "the most mature people are in some way more like children than are people of intermediate . . . level." Is the "openness to experience" retained from childhood into adulthood by some adults, or lost and then regained? Further, is this child-like openness a "consequence of attaining a high . . . level, or is it associated with [a] high . . . level because it is a condition that happens to favor . . . growth?"[2] Anne appears to have maintained this openness to experience coupled with an increasingly differentiated awareness of her own being in the world.

Feeling unique and alone, both as a child and upon her return to Los Angeles at twenty-seven, Anne took possession of her uniqueness and as she says, "I converted feeling different into feeling special." This occurred during her encounters with the university and with extreme religious conservatism. In converting differentness into specialness, Anne's tolerance for ambiguity is evident as she experienced loss of identity and questioned the process as she experienced it— moving away from a perceived good and not knowing whether or not something good was slipping away. She puts it so simply: "I made a decision that was mine . . . that put me in a situation where I faced me! I made things mine." She came to cherish herself out of her decidings and questionings, lovings, and dyings. Anne is immediately present to her experience as she is to her emotions and rich inner life. Absent from her interpretation of her "growing" is any sense of compulsive striving or failure or bitterness. She does not deny the pain of the process, but retains those fruits of the ripened religious life: saintliness.

10
Self Creation

____

MELANIE ROBERTS

Critical thought is commonly thought of in terms of mastery: one acquires the conceptual *tools* to take up a problem, to consider it from various perspectives, and ultimately to find the answer. We have come to "consider thinking in terms of mastery. Thought becomes technological, shaped to the requirements of concepts and ideas that will give control over objects and experience. Thinking is no longer a matter of open responsiveness to the world but of restless efforts to master it; it does not conserve and act as guardian of the riches of the earth, but exhausts the world in trying to restructure it to man's purpose."[1]

This striving for *dominion* evades understanding or interpretation and is yet another dimension of the poverty that results from a single-minded fascination with technology. Agreeing with Weber that we are "suspended in webs of significance"[2] we ourselves have spun, an analysis of those webs—culture—is a quest in search of meaning. It is an explication or unfolding that one desires, not an explanation.

Meaning is not to be found in an objectification of a person's subjectivity. It is a disclosure that invites further disclosure. One enters into a *thinking* dialogue with a life history and as a result sorts out the significant meanings to be found therein. Meaning evades precise conceptualization; it is process.

Understanding requires interpretation as well as discovery of our own position within a particular tradition. As Wittgenstein[3] observed: "We do not *understand* the people. (And not because of not knowing what they are saying to themselves.) We cannot find our feet with them."

Melanie Roberts's self-chosen task is a questioning dialogue that opens out a selfhood of her own in which she stands—she finds her feet as she speaks *with*, not to, herself and others. Heidegger made clear the interrelatedness of questioning one's understanding, one's time, and one's being in that time:

Only as a questioning, historical being does man come to himself; only as such is he a self. Man's selfhood means this: he must transform the being that discloses itself to him into history and bring himself to stand in it.[4]

Melanie Roberts, thirty, is tall and slender. She has an open-eyed gaze that is alert, warm, and reflects an active intellect. Her responses are quick, intense, complex, and spontaneous. Her tone, gestures, and expressions fit what she is saying and make evident the varied significance of its context. At one point Melanie spoke of feeling "garroted" and wept; another time her words tumbled out in pleasure and excitement as she described her recent growth and reflected back upon the timidity and shyness that characterized her childhood, adolescence, and early adulthood.

. . . my need to be good and not to stand out. I was good as a child. There was a kind of fear . . . of my parents' wrath or anger or whatever. I didn't want to do anything wrong. I do not remember being afraid, because I was so good and studied so hard and got good grades . . . I knew if I did something I wasn't supposed to do my parents were going to get angry. I guess that came from watching my sisters—I have four sisters and three brothers; I was second and have an older sister—they got into trouble and *I* did not.

Adolescence was excruciating. It was just awful. [laughs] All my fears were intensified. None of the boys would want to take me out—that whole awful scene and sex was really a problem because I didn't know too much about it and I was afraid to ask and didn't know who to ask. It took me several years to find out what sex was all about. The whole time was one of terrible feelings of uneasiness and fear. I felt I couldn't do anything right as far as relationships were concerned. It wasn't only sex; I was afraid to get really close to anyone, to open myself up, because I was so timid and if you don't have any confidence you are afraid—like there isn't going to be anything in there, in me. You have nothing to offer.

Then there were the high grades; I had scholarships for high school and the university.[5] That was achievement, but that is different from being close to someone. It alienates you from a lot of people and there is jealousy. I always did well and people would say how good I was and I didn't *feel* good as far as *inside*—I felt different, that *I* was different and I wasn't comfortable with that.

At the university there was the unique situation: most of the women were brighter than the men as they had higher entrance requirements for the women—at least a B average if you were a woman. With the men it was a C and also depended on sports and other activities. It is hard to explain. . . . There were higher expectations for the women yet you weren't—you might achieve more or be smarter [in class] and the men felt inferior. At that time I didn't think that was a good thing—to be brighter than a man. I wasn't comfortable with that until a few years ago—after I was out of the university. I gradually realized that I was an intelligent woman and that was a good thing. *I liked it!*

I had some philosophy courses that were crucial. I don't know what would have happened without them. Perhaps I would have grown some other way. He [Jesuit professor of philosophy] wouldn't let us alone. He forced it: "Come on; wake up; look at what you can do!" That kind of thing. He tied it into philosophy and a theology of self-appropriation of the knower and decision making. I had some of that parent-child attitude toward him and so it got hammered in: "Make your own decisions." Of course now that is like saying two plus two equals four; *then* it was a beginning—an evolutionary beginning. And it was just in philosophy and theology . . . I did not consciously think of myself as deciding. I was still concerned with doing the right thing and never sticking out or doing anything unconventional. I was supporting myself, working, and organizing projects at a home for girls—nice, *safe* things. Even the social concerns I had then, and before that in high school, were nice, safe little things, and I did them but I wasn't committed to them. I did them because that was what you were supposed to do. You were supposed to do good things.

That continued—actually my adolescence didn't end until I was about twenty-six. I didn't think like an adult when I got married! Falling in love was exhilarating. I met Allen at the end of my first year in college and in my sophomore year we were engaged and he graduated then.

I toyed with—what if I had to support myself? Just toyed with it. I went to college to learn; I thought it would be a growth experience. I had the *idea* of a career in mind but I didn't know what yet, but I didn't have to . . . also, I didn't have to decide that right then. I would find out as I went along and then I met Allen and I was going to marry him and he had a very good job . . . so it just wasn't a question. I never had to face the question: What was I going to do? Never had to face it; it just wasn't a question somehow. Then at the end of my junior year we were married and I never thought about it after that. I don't know why.

I loved Allen and I liked being with him, but the sex part was hell. It was such a tense thing—I still had the idea then that what we were doing was wrong and we weren't even having intercourse until the last few months before we were married, just heavy petting. My emotions told me to go ahead and do this because it was a good thing—but my mind was saying: "No, no. That's sinful." I loved him and the anguish and guilt were hell and then I was pregnant two months before we were to be married.

It was a nightmare. I had to go home to Southern California and I felt I had to tell my parents. I never thought about not telling them. I thought I had to. I was sick; it was finals; I thought of killing myself. It was an obsession. How was I going to tell my parents I had done this terrible thing . . . that I thought was a terrible thing.

I *never* even *thought* of how *hard* it is going to be to finish school and to be married and have a little baby. All I could think about was how terribly disappointed my parents would be. I never thought about an abortion, never even thought about it. But I thought about killing myself and that would have killed the baby, too, but *not* an abortion. I thought about pills, but I didn't have any and I didn't know where to get any; I thought about cutting my wrists and I was afraid to do that.

I got off the plane and my mother knew instantly that something was wrong and I told her; I didn't tell my father. We were married in July and Janey was born in January. When she was two weeks old a friend came over and baby-sat while I went to classes. When she was three weeks old I took her over to the dorm I had lived in and each quarter we'd look at our schedules and see who could baby-sit while I went to classes. She was a happy, smiling baby and the girls loved her which was really good for me. I graduated that June, in 1968. I said, "I'm going to finish." There was never any question about that. I was happy to finish. I felt I had accomplished so much just to get the degree after I had Janey.

We were aware of the population problem and decided not to have any more children. I knew—from working at the girls' home—that there were a lot of children who were classified "hard to adopt" and that meant they had a medical problem or, believe it or not, *any* child over six months old was classified as "hard to adopt." I was concerned with doing what was good and worthwhile so we thought of adopting another child instead of having one and adopted Tommy about a year after I had graduated. He had a stomach blockage when he was born and had had surgery but still vomited and had diarrhea and was very sick when we got him at nine months. That whole period . . . I have an image of myself standing in front of the sink and Tommy climbing up the back of my legs—learning to stand up—and sinking his fingernails into my legs; I remember shrieking once. I was tired, tired, and didn't feel well. I didn't have much energy and couldn't understand—I felt bad about myself.

I loved Allen and I felt that I wasn't accommodating myself to him; I thought I was supposed to *make* him happy and I didn't think I was. I felt inadequate; I was tired. I didn't feel that way so much in college; it wasn't that big; I had two jobs and was busy, busy, working fifteen hours a week and setting up the volunteers and Allen and I used to fight because sometimes I was too tired from working and studying and I didn't want to do anything with him and I didn't. But I didn't feel I had to, but after—as a wife—I did.

I felt controlled by Allen although I don't think he consciously did it. I would depend upon him to be home and he would be an hour or several hours late. I had a rigid sense of time from school and because I had always been taught to be punctual and it was like a great *unknown* if something happened to him. I was afraid he would die and leave me alone and I couldn't possibly figure out what I could do— here I had these little babies—and I didn't have many friends. There wasn't anyone I could go to and depend on so I figured, if something happened to Allen, I am lost.

I was neurotic. My needs were neurotic and I didn't know . . . I would be filled with anxiety and fear and he couldn't understand why it was important to me to need to know he was all right and when he would be coming home. I wasn't so concerned with him just getting hurt—if he was fixable! [laughs]

Slater commented upon the striking contrast of the occupation of full-time housewife and mother to the premarital life of a woman, "especially if she is a college graduate. In college she was typically embedded in active group life with constant emotional and intellectual stimulation. College life is in this sense an urban life. Marriage typically eliminates much of this way of life for her, and her children deliver the coup de grace. Her only significant relationships tend to be with her husband who, however, is absent most of the day. Most of her social and emotional needs must be satisfied by her children, who are hardly adequate to the task."[6]

I am not suggesting that all newly married women experience the privatized household as isolating, nor that young mothers experience themselves as deeply dependent as Melanie did. However, marriage does introduce "profound discontinuities into the lives of women"; some women may welcome such abrupt change while others may experience such discontinuity as a series of "shocks" and wonder why they are unable—in Melanie's words—"to accommodate" themselves, never raising the possibility that the "way the social world is organized may have something to do with their plight."[7]

Melanie continues:

I was a married woman with two children and still my parents' child. I had that excessive need to do what other people felt I should do. It was almost like a physical thing overcoming me. I wasn't going to say or do anything that wasn't correct—it was ridiculous. I couldn't talk about the things that were bothering me and I couldn't express myself—feelings were bottled-up, bottled-up. I wouldn't let myself really cry; I would find some little place where I could cry; I would sort of squeeze out a few—you know—bitter tears, and then try to keep them in. Except if I read a sad novel or saw a sad film then I would weep—gushers! [laughs]

In 1970 Melanie had been married three years; Allen had become manufacturing manager of a large corporation and was attending graduate school part-time. At this time they bought a home in a very liberal parish and became involved in a weekly discussion group that ultimately broke away from the parish to form a nongeographic community. The majority of the group had been involved in the Cursillo; eventually all participated. Shortly after Melanie and Allen moved, Melanie's teen-age cousin, Elaine, became pregnant and it was made clear to her she could not remain at home. There were other possibilities for her—Melanie's third-generation Irish-English family is spread out over California and Arizona—but Melanie and

Allen "looked about the best." Elaine stayed with Melanie and Allen for eight months and gave her baby up for adoption.

After we did that we talked about the possibility of doing that again. There was a crucial need for foster homes and so I said, "Why don't we just start doing this?" And we did. There were so many teen-age girls who were pregnant and who had no place to go and I believed abortion was wrong—for me. I always felt others should have the right to make that decision to have an abortion. It just wasn't for me; that got me into foster care for pregnant teen-age girls who wanted to have their baby.

Melanie's first foster daughter ran away after a week; the second stayed for five months and then married the father of the child; Isabel, a bilingual, pregnant, fifteen-year-old was brought to the Roberts's home where she remained for the next two years. During this time Melanie examined her own beliefs and values as she was forced—through interaction and commitment—to attempt to understand the beliefs and values of the Spanish-speaking culture, and the magnitude and complexity of the social problem she was attempting to mitigate.

The need was so great; I tried doing some active recruiting. I was singularly unsuccessful in finding anyone else to take these girls, which I can understand because it is asking a lot—but somewhere out there there are people who would be suitable to this work just as there are people who are suitable to helping out the farm workers and picketing and such—which I am not. It is as though people are afraid to even *consider* doing this. I get the impression that they think everything has to be resolved at once; that you have to know how you are going to handle it before you take it on, which isn't the way it works. I didn't know exactly what I was doing when I took it on—I went through terrible anxieties and questionings: Am I really doing this right? And—what *is* the best thing? In handling situations as they came up I would wonder if I was doing what was best for her in *her* situation because I had never come up against situations like this before. What is the best thing for everybody—and you don't know! Well, I just had to say that this seems best, or the last time this came up I thought that was the best way to do it and I really don't think that anymore, so let's go with this—and of course, always asking her what she thought, and that was a one-way conversation because, for so long, I got *no* response. It's not like you have to be rock-sure and super-confident. In fact that may be one of the worst things you could do—to be inflexible, to have your rules all set out. That is what Allen and I did in the beginning with Janey and Tommy.

I was young and inexperienced and we had all these things left over from our parents—of what's right and what's wrong. Even if you have worked out in your mind that you are not going to take outside rules and are going to do your own thinking—those old things keep coming back.

I finally stopped myself, asked myself: "If you think it is important to raise kids—and I do, obviously—then you had better do some serious thinking about how you are going to do it and take your daily situations and look at them and dissect them and say, 'What really happened here? What is the central issue?'" Was I just over-reacting; had I had it; was I out of patience? Was I confused and then *seized* on something as being the reason why—"no, you can't do this or that?" And that being just stupid because it isn't any reason at all. You want to know what the real thing behind it is—what are basic values that you want to tell your children about—keeping in mind that as they grow older and older they are going to be gradually rebelling against those values, but you have to transmit *some* kind of values and what are those going to be?

What is really important to you? What are those non-allowables going to be? And finding time and again that I had to sit down with Tommy and say, "That is not acceptable here. You may not hurt people nor take their things . . . because hurting people or stealing is not allowed here." This presupposes that you have thought out what the non-allowables are—that you have thought them through beforehand by going through those situations time and again and having to make a decision: is this important or not?

To me—having other people in the house—you are going to have values that you insist upon in your house. The main value that I see us working with is consideration for other people. I do not insist that my kids love each other; I think that is unrealistic. They may grow up loving each other and they may not. I don't insist that all the people in the house love each other. But if we are going to live together we have to make that our prime concern—to be considerate of one another, to be sensitive to one another, to think—how is this affecting other people in the house?

It took me a *long, long* time to say to myself, "Let's think this through in the same way I think other things through. Let's think through the whole parent-child relationship in the way I am thinking about getting my head together as a woman—the way I am thinking through my being." It's been a fairly recent thing that I have felt in control of myself and control of myself in situations. Power over my life. *My* power over my life.

There were so many situations—particularly with the kids—where I thought, "My God, I am powerless," and it would get to the point where it was a power struggle, which is stupid because no one wins and everybody loses. I wanted to avoid those things. I wanted to have power over my own life and I wanted to be able to think it through so that I didn't feel powerless with these little kids or with Isabel—so that I didn't have this feeling that this little kid is out to get me! [laughs] I knew in my head it wasn't true but I felt like I was being persecuted and so I had to think, how am I going to get out of that box, because that obviously is a box. And then, of course, Allen has very different ideas and different feelings about the way—I kept asking him why he felt this child or Isabel had to do this or that? I started challenging him and asking him why he felt the way he did? Why was it important for him? I'd ask him, "Can we look at this situation and see why you feel this is necessary?" And he didn't like that; he didn't want to do it.

We didn't communicate for most of our marriage; now we are able to talk. I keep talking, and if he makes a generalization or if he says he believes this or that, I want to know why—and it isn't cussedness, but this is my getting to know this man that I have been living with all this time and thought I knew and didn't. This is only since I have been changing—as long as I was in that relationship where Allen was the protector and I was the dependent I didn't—I'm just learning to do that challenging with Allen now. As soon as I became a strong person, independent, Allen felt—was afraid that we were going in opposite directions and we would come to points along the way where this would happen. I never felt that this is it! But I remember thinking that, wow! there is that emotional void. We may have to live with that for a few days but something is going to have to start again.

You can't continue in that emotional void: you live like that for a few days and you have got that knot in the pit of your stomach the whole time and then you say, "Well, hey, what are we going to do about this? Can we find some way of getting out of it?" A lot of times the thing that you thought you were standing up for or holding on to, that wasn't the issue at all—it was something different.

It's a power struggle and I think that is pretty common although you call it all kinds of different names. You have to realize it is a power struggle and both sides have to let go— otherwise. . . . I guess that is what you let go of—control, controlling the other. Then you don't feel helpless any longer. You get *angry* but you *don't feel hopeless* or that feeling of despair . . . because there is communication—you can talk.

Isabel had been with the Roberts family for three or four months; Melanie was studying Spanish and she had come to accept that there was no guarantee that what she was doing was going to work out with Isabel. She was in the process of "getting [her] head together and things were going well," when she experienced what was later diagnosed as a hyperactive thyroid condition, that subsided after a few weeks.

At first I didn't know it was a physical condition and I thought I was going crazy and I couldn't figure out why because I thought things were going well. I felt like I couldn't cope any more; I couldn't face situations, day by day; I felt hassled and I couldn't get a handle on it. I didn't know it was physical and that it would pass—to think you are going crazy is a very frightening thing because when that is happening you can't look ahead and say, "Well, I won't always be crazy." [laughs]

I had that feeling of anxiety and not being able to cope, some screaming crying and—I couldn't face the smallest thing. I can't handle that. Take it away. Unable to make any decision and wandering around the house and being very restless and getting up and sitting down and not being able to concentrate on anything, not being able to think but just feeling oppressed by all these little tiny details. Wanting out of here—you know—I want to get out of here, I just can't cope with it anymore, and thinking the thread holding us together is so thin—sometimes I wonder if I have to give up everything (Allen, kids. . .) to survive, not to be suffocated, to be me and I don't know. I thought of committing myself to get out of it because I felt that—like I need help. I've got to get out of it. How am I going to get out and so I thought, "Do I really want to commit myself to a mental hospital?" I didn't want to. I was afraid to. But I thought I might have to. I really thought I was going crazy—I'm going to have to do something. Then fortunately—this was a short time of a week or ten days—I found out it was a thyroid condition and there are things they can do for that. So I arranged to take the kids to someone's house each morning and that was helpful and I just spent time listening to music and reading the *Pedagogy of the Oppressed* and not really seeing the words; reading books on Eucharistic theology and *The Non-Violent Cross*.

I didn't finish the books until the children went back to school and Isabel had had her baby, Jacob. Then I was OK and very careful with my diet. Thinking, thinking. After doing some reading I remember saying to John [priest] that I didn't think it mattered who said the magic words and his hair stood on end. He felt you had to have this official stamp or whatever, otherwise you couldn't celebrate this Eucharist feast in a meaningful way. I felt that as long as *that* idea was there it wasn't Eucharist. There wasn't a real sharing and so, for me, the meaning of Eucharist was largely lost. I didn't know what I believed at that . . . and I thought about how our very existence exploits the hungry person in the world. I could know that up here—in my head—but until you get into that and say, "Hey, I am using too much of everything and what am I going to do about it and how is this affecting others?" Before, that was just an interesting idea.

Now, I ask, do I really need that? There are all levels of needing and so how are you going to handle that? That's definitely going to make a change about what you eat and trying to handle the fact that Allen is a meat eater and that other people live in the house, too, and they may find your ideas interesting but after all, they have to live there too. So I have to consider that other people are thinking in different ways; that what I'm thinking may make them uneasy.

With Isabel—for example—we would both be uneasy about each other and so for a while the *only* experience we had in common was being ill-at-ease-with-one-another! [laughter] That's it. That's the extent of your experience together and you can't do anything about it but let it be until it works itself out. Then you don't feel that way any more.

I find myself, now, with my foster daughter, being able to relate to her because I am more sure of myself. We can speak more freely; I can look at a situation and know that it is not going to hurt me if she is irresponsible, but what *is* important is that she make decisions that put her in control of her own life. I think of how she is now and wonder if that is ever going to be possible for her. She is sixteen and plays the game of "tell me what to do so I can rebel against it." Not too much now because I hardly give her anything to rebel against. I try to give it back to her, "You decide what time you would like to get home and providing it is not totally unacceptable, OK, that is the time. Stick to it; that is your decision. If you want control of what time you come home you have to be here when you say you will be here." The alternative to that is that I will say, "This is your time. Be here, or you will be grounded for a week and I don't think you want that."

Of course, grounding her when she has a baby is ridiculous but you are trying to get her to be responsible for herself and there is the added problem that she *does* have to come home at night because she is on probation. So you keep asking her—even though she says that it doesn't matter. It may take one hundred times of me telling her she does matter—you are important to me—before she will begin to say to herself, "Maybe that is true."

Of course you make mistakes. Nothing can happen unless you can drop your defenses and say, "I'm sorry," and realize that this is growth. To say I've done a terrible thing doesn't lessen you—you are not that terrible thing—but that you are capable of doing it; that you have done it; then you say, "I've done it." I never, never could say that before the last couple of years because I felt so bad about myself that to admit a mistake was just saying, "Yes, I really am this bad." Proof I was bad. I just couldn't say I made a mistake. I couldn't get angry—except with Allen and then it was incoherent, crying. Or I would be meek and agree. Allen felt he couldn't express his anger because I would cry. Now he does.

I really feel strongly that my old self is dead because the old self was all exterior-oriented and being driven—being driven by my fears of doing the right thing and living up to everyone else's expectations. It was a death and it was miserable and now this is a different person and I feel very strongly that that person that used to be me is just no longer there. So I definitely see myself as having been reborn again. Some of that began in college, but that has really only happened in the last couple of years—probably since the Cursillo [November 1972] although the Cursillo itself didn't make much difference in my life. Probably after the Cursillo I began to be comfortable with affection. I don't think I was comfortable with that before—except with Allen. It's only in the last couple of years that I have begun to express my feelings or to realize how good that felt. Paying attention to my feelings, I began to learn about myself. Before—because I always had the feelings and I experienced—all the time I was growing up—a physical feeling, and this goes back to the story of the canary.

There is a story I read a few months ago of a woman who liked to sing and her husband—it was some tiny farm village—told her to shut up and she stopped singing. Years later she got a canary—I don't remember where—and the canary sang. Then one morning she got up and the canary's neck had been twisted and broken and it was dead. Then her husband was found hanging, dead, and there was a trial . . . what was important was the choking. And I had this physical feeling of choking on the feelings because they were there and would not come out. I couldn't make them come out.

My mother used to get angry at me because things would happen at school, school-wide accomplishments and I wouldn't tell her. It was because I was embarrassed. I mean I was proud of that and I was embarrassed at the recognition and even felt I didn't deserve it. I just could not come home and say I felt so good today because this and this and this happened. It was like I had to keep it inside. I couldn't let it come out that I felt so good or that I felt so miserable. I might give sort of a hint, just the barest hint that things weren't going too well but I couldn't say it.

Now my feelings are a means of insight; they are a part of my whole self. If they are integrated into your whole self then they are a means of insight into yourself besides being such enjoyable things. If you find yourself reacting, [that is] you have the same feelings in similar situations a lot of times—and especially if the feeling doesn't fit the thought or situation. If there doesn't seem to be integration then you will say, well, what about that? When you are integrated it's such a tremendous experience—your good feelings anyway. I wouldn't say, groove on pain or anything. But your feelings come first in a lot of situations. In fact usually—most of the time I'd say they do and then you find your mind reacting to the feeling—you can feel yourself in that situation and can see yourself and get in touch with yourself when you go back over it and that is a real method of getting in touch with yourself and of integrating yourself.

. . . That story of the canary is really morbid; I want to make a sculpture of it that does not seem morbid but just says this is happening or this did happen—this strangulation of the individual in so many ways, willful or non-willful. Many times it is an unperceptive kind of thing that people are doing one to the other and they don't realize how they are garroting each other. But they are. Just the way that bird is garroted or its neck wrung. Somehow it is necessary we become aware that we are doing it.

. . . I don't feel that I am being garroted now because I won't let myself be. I just feel that for so many years I was powerless and now I see people around me gaining the power to be themselves and that is exhilarating. . . I have a clear idea in my mind of what the metal sculpture is going to look like. A freeing way to express my anger, although I don't feel anger is a driving force in my life. I do see the need for this sculpture to be a powerful statement. Always before I would be concerned with, is this pleasing or beautiful? For a long time I just did *copies* of things, didn't let myself go and make something. Well, never mind that it is not going to be beautiful; it is frightening, not ugly, but esthetically powerful, because that is where I am. I never will let myself be garroted again. [weeps]

Something else that ties in with that. Allen and I were talking over the telephone and it finally hit me that we don't have the same goals. All this time, I thought we are different and the differences are causing us problems and how are we going to work that out? We *are* in different places and he felt we weren't going in the same direction. That was the first time I said, "Hey, you're right. We aren't!" We aren't going in opposite directions, though. That was a neat thing to realize—a freeing thing. We can say we are two neat people. I am unique and he is unique and he has been feeling inferior and—several months ago—I realized that he is basically a conservative person. At least right now. He realized it and I think that now we have gotten to a place where we can say, "OK, that is where we are and let's live where we are and we don't have to spend our energy trying to get together philosophically."

We have to try to figure out if we are going to be able to live together and be tolerant and open enough of each other to say, "Hey, you really are a beautiful person and I really want to live with you and this means I will accept you as you are in this minute and that may be very hard. . . ." So that what we have in common is joy in our own being, otherwise we will garrote each other.

There are many things that we disagree about and where he doesn't understand—especially with Isabel. This was something I was doing—Allen supported me—but, you know, emotionally or whatever it was not something leaning against his brain. Like a crying baby, a fussy baby is.

He is willing to let me do what I think is right. He thinks I am absolutely wrong but he says, "I will support you and help you anyway." So there is goodwill. Allen thinks it is better now but he is fearful of the future because I am not dependent; I am *very* independent. I hear his fear and I can't fix it. All I can say is that I hear your fear and I really love you. That's all I can say. I am still going to do the things I am doing. That was, you know, for *me*, maturity.

My fear was, well, OK, I'm a good wife but what if he meets somebody who is more exciting, more beautiful, more this, more that—all those things that don't quite count! Well, now you see, I don't feel the need to be physically beautiful in that sense of "model-type" beauty. If he should happen to leave me for some woman because she is more beautiful, I would say, "Oh, poor you! You are the loser." It would be traumatic—obviously—but I wouldn't feel that was diminishing to me. Because I know I am a good person and lovable and good for him and so if he were to make that choice . . . that idea of glamor, being a *decoration*. My excitement for my husband has nothing to do with how I look—I mean if I looked like death warmed over every day or something like that or just physically a wreck—I can't see doing that. But those cliches of making yourself beautiful to be sure he walks in the door that night—I don't feel I have to make myself beautiful so everybody can see that this man has a beautiful woman out to dinner. That used to be a big thing with him—not that I had to do it but he enjoyed that.

Now I think, well, fuck it. We're going out to dinner and we are going to enjoy each other's company and if someone says that that man has an attractive wife or companion or whatever, well, so what! It adds absolutely nothing to the evening; it means absolutely nothing; it's meaningless, absolutely meaningless.

Allen thinks I am being rebellious—making myself unattractive. I am not trying to make myself unattractive. My attractiveness is not in superficial beauty. My body is *my* body and my hair is natural and it is not—I could never accept my naturally curly hair when I was growing up. Everybody had straight long hair and here I was with this frizzy hair and cowlicks around my face. Now I like it and it makes my life easier; I enjoy it.

It was important for me to go through that, not as some badge of women's liberation but to try it out to see if it is authentically me or if I am merely being rebellious. Not that there is something wrong with being rebellious but if that is all that is there it is not a very authentic action.

I don't have that fear of losing everything; I don't have any guarantee of permanence either. I am aware that we are working on our problems and there are a lot of them.

And a lot of tensions—it is not as if we are going to be going along great like this and one day I am going to say to him, "Well, that's it. I'm walking out." It deteriorates over a long period of time and we know after three or four days if we are not attentive to each other—if we are really not communicating. You feel it right away and you say, "Hey, we really have been taking each other for granted or however you want to put it, so let's get together and have a glass of wine and sit down and be together." But there is that fear. Mentioning the fear helps. I don't try to ignore it because the fear is there, but I am confident that the fear will go away and the relationship will not end. Or if it does we will have plenty of advance warning and it will not be like—oh, there it is. But, for a while, every time I talk about a new idea that seems radical or different to him he is probably going to think—"Oh, dear, is this. . . ?"

Interviews with Allen at the same time disclose his perception of their relationship.

How has it changed? Totally. In nine years, it has changed totally. From one of someone being very dependent on me, and me being very sure of myself so far as the marriage went, to one of almost total lack of dependence on me as far as I can interpret it. I have doubts that I didn't have before—whether it will last indefinitely. The doubt doesn't bother me any more. I'm happy with where we are, and happy to keep trying to make it better . . . I'm beginning to get that way—that I don't need to control. I feel very sad in some ways because it's like watching a butterfly. You really enjoy watching a butterfly, but if you try to catch it, particularly with your bare hands, and hold it, usually, you know . . . you'll kill it. But if you don't catch it the butterfly almost always flies away—eventually. It will flitter around, today, for minutes or hours, but eventually it goes into the yard next door, or across the river, or whatever.

You can't catch it . . . that takes out a lot of the joy of watching the butterfly . . . number one. Number two, it . . . like I said, it very often kills it. So catching it is not a practical solution to the problem. These are only very recent thoughts. I'm saddened by them, and I'm comfortable with them. Maybe I can work through to where I can find another simile that would be more positive.

For now, I am comfortable with my direction in life. I was struggling with this whole idea of Melanie becoming so confident in her position . . . or not her position, but her decision-making. She feels very good with it, . . . I was trying hard to keep up, in the same direction, and then I thought about it . . . certain elements of our growth are in different directions. It's something I'm concerned about and I want to work on, but I'm not concerned about figuring a solution.

Allen's business had always involved intermittent travel. A decision to close a large subsidiary in the Bay Area meant regular, weekly trips to Los Angeles lasting three to four days, for a period of eight months. Melanie realized that she and Allen had spent a lot of time together without "being together."

We were together without being present to each other. That worked out for me on the same pattern as my beginning to think about being with the kids. My being aware—okay, we're spending time together. It's quantity time, not quality time. We weren't letting all the other crap go, saying it's not important—look at the time we have together! If we choose the time, then let's do something or talk to each other— something meaningful. And not worry about not being together a whole lot—in a superficial sense. That has worked out. Or it is working out.

There is the separation and at first I didn't like it—being alone at night. Now I do like it—I sleep in the middle of the bed! [laughs] And I enjoy being by myself although I miss the everydayness of being with Allen. There is some tension when we come back together again. I mean you don't come back again and "instant rapport." It doesn't take a long time; it takes the consciousness of each person saying, "We've been apart for a few days; let's be quiet with each other for a while; sit down and talk or whatever." Experience each other. That is particularly true . . . before we make love or anything. I mean there is no way . . . he's going to come home from a business trip or something and we're just going to hop in the sack. Forget it! [laughs] I mean, this is like servicing each other. I'm not going to do that; I used to do that because of my inability to say, "Well, this just isn't right for me."

And Allen is experiencing this need for some time together before we make love. That used to be a big problem. We weren't taking the time. I was feeling I wasn't meeting his sexual needs and of his saying that to me. And yet his not wanting to pressure me, sort of. It was all screwed up. [much laughter] But the whole sexual thing has taken care of itself, more or less, as we realize we have to nurture our relationship.

The whole relaxation of the sexual situation is new. We can enjoy being with one another, caressing one another and that need to see a goal is gone. It's like experiencing one another more. In a more whole way. A lot of times that will end up in intercourse. But if it doesn't it doesn't matter. It's not like we are thinking of gratifying each other's needs or servicing each other. We used to joke about that. But it applied and we knew it applied. That isn't true anymore because it doesn't have to be. And Allen is finding inhibitions— before I thought I was the inhibited one. I was the one who had all those inhibitions. And he didn't. So now it's different; we're both aware of them.

The whole relaxation of the sexual thing—well, I not only had a problem sexually, but also I had a problem with affection. With somebody expressing affection for me and me being comfortable with that. Obviously if I'm not comfortable with Allen expressing affection for me, I'm not going to be comfortable going to bed with him. [chuckles] And that's just when I began to feel better about myself as being a special person. As I began to get more comfortable with my body, freer with my sexuality, then that came out, of course, in lovemaking. The nervousness and tension that used to make me just not be able to let go and enjoy—that's gone.

I didn't let myself have sexual feelings before—once you're married, that's it! I wouldn't even let myself feel any attraction for others because I didn't think that was what you were supposed to do. Only for your husband type of thing. I don't feel that way anymore. I've had one opportunity where I could have pursued a relationship. It might have been sexual but I didn't want to do that because I didn't want to complicate my life just then. There were enough problems to work on or out and I just thought, "Well, I don't want to do that right now." I care for that person and I can handle my feelings—the sexual aspect of it without it being a real problem. I am just experiencing myself as a sexual person and enjoying that. I did not have that experience before. I remember—I have sexual feelings toward my children. They are very attractive. I don't remember feeling that way so much when they were babies. I felt sexually aroused while nursing Janey—somewhat—I think what happened with that was I refused to recognize that as a sexual feeling; it was very pleasant to nurse her. I thought, isn't this a pleasant feeling. I didn't recognize that as a sexual feeling and that's okay. Of course, this is all hindsight.

It is important to remember with Isabel; I was just as unconscious and immature as she is. She was talking to me about her sexual relationship with the baby's father. I want to say look, this is the way it ought to be, or this is what you should be doing or not doing. She is not able to make choices yet, so it is important for me to carry the insight through and ask her what is important for her when she talks about his "macho" trip and for me to understand that she has to work that out for herself, like everything else. I can be a helper, guider, challenger, director or whatever but she will create for herself—a self-creation. I will be a stimulating, challenging person and probably without me she wouldn't have done what she has but it is really up to her. She may just go right back into that environment because that is what most of her friends are in. It doesn't have any horizons and there is nothing I can do about that.

If Isabel were to become pregnant again—and that is what she sees her friends doing—I would *not* now encourage her to carry the baby and especially not to keep it. Of course, you have to recognize her right to make those choices—but they weren't choices for her. I have thought about that—it isn't like a moral ground as far as abortion goes. It has to do with concern for life and my becoming more conscious of life and the interrelatedness of life and the whole connectedness of the universe. If I were raped and became pregnant I would have an abortion with no qualms. If I loved someone and got pregnant—Allen's had a vasectomy so that's not an issue—if I loved someone, I don't know. I would probably have an abortion now. A year ago I didn't feel that way. There is a dichotomy here. One life is just as sacred as another life? And this one—the rape one—you can flush down the toilet and the other one you have to think about. There is a real conflict there. I am very aware of not having worked out all those feelings. If you are raped, and you get rid of that life, if you want to call it life, you don't have any qualms. There isn't any *one right answer;* that's difficult.

It's also interesting how exhilarated you feel once you get out of that bag where things have to be a certain way. I've come to a point where I don't think anything has to be a certain way. I don't think that the ideas I have today are necessarily the ones I will have a year from now. I feel like I can accept a lot of new and different ideas without rejecting them—at least I can entertain them and see what I think about them without being threatened by them. I don't feel threatened by things anymore. If someone wants to live in a completely different way from me, well, that's all right and maybe they have something I could learn from them.

A good example of that is homosexuality—that was something that—not only didn't I understand it but I thought that's something that just must be wrong because that's weird. That's just strange and it must be wrong! I can accept that now and understand how some people relate to the person of the same sex, sexually. If that is their choice, then fine, that is their choice. I do *not* want to be away from that person, get away from them. I can accept them as someone I might want to know and be friends with rather than being fearful of them because they are different in a sexual way.

Whether something is good or bad really depends on its effect upon other people. What are the results or consequences or whatever of this action. What is going to happen if I do this? What is going to happen if I do that? Of course, you may not know and you make mistakes and you can learn from them. I could never admit I made a mistake before—that meant *I* was bad, a bad person. Now, if I make a mistake, I make a mistake and I correct that. That doesn't mean I am not aware of other people or the group I am in. I am very aware of where other people are: I challenge with humor because I don't want to hurt. Often I just keep thinking, thinking by myself. Then I get that good feeling that I am freeing myself.

One of the things that has been happening—and I can't put a particular time . . . the last two or three years—is the tremendous letting go of, I call it conventionality. Just a tremendous letting go and not worrying about what is proper or conventional and having a real sense of freedom there. Like giving a party and doing what I wanted to do. Or taking tambourines to the farmworkers' dance and dancing with them. It was neat, you know, and not thinking, well, do people think I am showing off, or making a fool of myself. Just dancing.

You're willing to put yourself in a position where people might say, "Tsk, tsk, the house is dirty," or "She is painting her living-room wall. She must be out of her mind." [laughs] Not that you are out to shock people because I usually try to be *very* conscious of where the group is and if I said something outrageous it would be because I had misjudged the group, not because I was unperceptive and uncaring—not because I wasn't caring, or wasn't thinking or that I felt the need to drop some bombshell on the group for whatever.

I do try to challenge people but in a way that is non-threatening. Because if I really threaten and they close up then what good is that? That isn't going to accomplish anything. It could be that when I am speaking to people I don't know well and I am talking very quietly about my ideas, they are horrified. But if they don't tell me, "My God, that horrifies me," I'll never know.

I am much less apt to let things slide by now—if I see subtle oppression—I would say to the person, "Well, it really seems to me that this is what is happening and I am uncomfortable with that—that really makes me angry." But I think it is necessary to avoid saying, "You are doing this or that." Projecting. It's hard because you want to say, "You son-of-a-bitch." That accomplishes nothing.

With a problem it's the pattern . . . seems to be one of . . . first the confusion of something you know, or I am aware that I am . . . I am uneasy. It is in myself or in relation to another person and I am aware that something is not right here. I'm blocking something or there's just that feeling of awkwardness, confusion and uneasiness. I begin to think about that. I think about that until I get some insight. It's not an obsession like I think of it day and night. But I will think about it when I have the time . . . it's really like an unfolding. There is a confusion or the awkwardness. If it's with another person, a lot of times, I will express the awkwardness and say, you know, I'm feeling really awkward or I'm feeling confused or there's something here that I'm not working out. You can get to the point where you realize what is going on. But a lot of times it takes me several days, or maybe longer. Sometimes things may stretch out over months or years. But usually, for the initial insight, it's several days. Of course I've got input from other people, but I've really done it and I'm proud of myself for having done it. Like the Cursillo didn't . . . it was a good experience; I enjoyed it. What had more of an effect was the people in the various communities. After getting into the community I felt there were people I could depend upon besides just talking about your feelings. I felt I could depend upon Elaine because she was peaceful when I needed; Ann because she listened to me and we had some thoughts that were alike; and Janet because she was joyful. I guess Ellen because she doesn't let me be comfortable with where I am and because I can say anything to her. That was probably my first real positive experience where I was sure I could do that.

I attended Sunday Mass and the Thursday morning Mass with other women [a group of eight to twelve women who met in one another's homes on Thursday morning with a priest]. Being with the Thursday morning group was important—it was small and intimate and helpful. Then I began to feel uneasy with the process of those groups. I didn't exactly know what was going on and I thought about it—about processes and groups and people's needs and I came to the insight that the priest was taking responsibility for the group and if anything was going to happen in that group—growth-wise—I don't know how to state it, but it was going to have to be shattering and it was going to have to involve people saying, "Hey, I'm responsible, too." To withdraw the crutch would probably create chaos and it would have risked the group and the group might have disintegrated. But if it didn't take that risk, nothing was going to happen.

Coming to that insight—that it wasn't going to work— that nothing was going to happen and sticking with that for a while longer until I was sure; then it made no sense and I said it didn't make sense to me anymore—to be involved in that liturgy. That was freeing, but then you have to ask yourself about some kind of stability—you can't float with the wind! You need some kind of anchors. I have to be anchored in myself, but I don't want to be a hermit either! There have to be relationships, but they don't always have to be, I guess, the same relationships. Having experienced the pain of letting go of an anchor in a relationship, I am now beginning to understand and to build anchors in relationship. Not in *one* because then it's a crutch.

I could see myself coming to the place where I would say, "This is a dead thing, and it doesn't make any sense to do it anymore." That was scary. It definitely wasn't meaningful for me and they wanted to keep it the same. What do you do? Take the risk of saying these really scary things? Then trying to get new imagery and realizing that may not be possible. And coming back to *zero* meaning.

A year ago I went home to visit my parents with Allen and the kids at Easter and we went to Mass. It was like watching this slice of my past—as a child. This slice of my past that suddenly had no meaning at all—it was like going to a play. And I thought, this is like Disneyland. The old imagery is there and trying to get new imagery and isn't imagery a very *human* thing—mine and yours—and your talking about something that *isn't* human, if it is there at all. There was that whole thing to reckon with and to think about. Whether or not there is anything transcendent; is there a consciousness in the universe. I wasn't sure what that was or how it was working itself out and the old ideas were going. It was necessary for me to believe that death wasn't the end even though it would have been hard for me to say exactly what that would be like, but I needed to believe that death was not the end. I thought, I won't let go of that until I don't really need it.

About six months later I didn't need it! I said, "Hey, I

don't believe any of that anymore." I just realized it and it
felt good. If this is the only life I have, I have to preserve . . .
myself and remain open. I don't have that feeling of that
binding link to the universe. I feel strong.

So what am I aiming for? Can I say right now what I am
aiming for? I want to get to a point where my work is a valuable thing and I want to work out that problem of money
because it is important to be self-supporting. The goal is to
be self-supporting, self-expressing, and self-creating and
through that to have the independence that comes with
being self-supporting. But that isn't the goal itself—the
money isn't. Rethinking a lot of things, really checking why
do I feel this way? Why do I think this way? Where do I want
to go from here and what do I want to do? Where do I start?
Do I want to stick with this sculpture? Do I want to do a lot of
that or in a more practical way—to start a small business?

. . . I have directions that I want to go in. One of them is
to keep the evolutionary process going and that has to be a
conscious thing. Not in the sense that you think, my God, I
am not being evolutionary, or I haven't been evolutionary
for a month or whatever but that you are always looking . . .
what is interesting, challenging? I don't feel . . . I'm not worried about coming to the end of my evolutionary process . . .
and it's not like some huge circle that gets bigger and bigger.
I have a picture in my mind of going round and round but
up and up and out and out—just an ongoing process. I don't
feel any need right now to accomplish a life's work. I think
that will probably come . . . that I will want to . . . not for the
sake of having something live after me, but I will want to say
. . . to have a concrete expression of my life, in the sense that
there will be sculptures that are really just an embodiment of
me and my ideas.

Creativity means that to me, making something out of
yourself that is really an expression of you. I feel myself as
being creative when I'm thinking a new thought, a new in-

sight that I just keep thinking for a while. Sometimes when I make things I feel that way—but they are still too planned. I like abstract things—paintings and abstract sculpture rather than figures or set things. But photographs, too, especially the ones that evoke a mood or feeling and you *don't* recognize just what it is, some kind of object or lines. It's hard to say. . . . I like to look out the window; I like to see the trees and sky. . . . The other day there was the bluest sky and so many cloud formations—free flowing and light. Things that lift you up. . . . I like seashells and cliffs—the ocean . . . hills in the distance and rivers when they are cold and crashing down—not just flowing—going really fast, white water . . . especially if you can see the rocks in the bottom. I like paper sculpture kind of things and metal if they are beautiful to me. And I like books, especially books that are new; I don't like to mark them; I don't know why. I like the sunset; I like the sunrise even better—when you are up in the morning and no one is up. Once in a while I do that—walk alone in the early morning when it is cool to see the sun come up.

Willed or unwilled, shyness and rebelliousness are modes of nonconforming behavior attributed to adolescence and young adulthood. While the latter is more dramatic—it is apparent the rebel isn't conforming—the nonconformity of the shy young person is often a painful and nonarticulated inner experience of differentness.

It is not possible to know whether Melanie's involvement with the problems of the pregnant, teen-age girl, who did not perceive abortion to be an alternative and who wished to keep her baby, grew out of altruism—a sense of social responsibility—or an identification with her own earlier experience. What we can know is that this undertaking revolutionized Melanie's thinking as her beliefs, identity, perception of roles, and role expectations were brought into relief and called into question. The world became both interesting and complex for her! A challenge.

Melanie was perturbed by her feelings of helplessness as a parent and foster parent. It is in the context of her interactions with her two children and her foster daughter that she experienced power over her own life for the first time. At the same time, she experienced "maturity for me" as she moved out of an entrenched dependency on her husband, a move not without risk and pain. Melanie does not point to any single event or person as a "turning" but rather described the *outcome* of a process that remains mysterious.

Melanie's acceptance of challenge and her decision to question the preconceived order of things is evident in her interactions within the little communities of which she was a member. The little communities became Melanie's peer groups, perhaps her first experience of close friendship with women. Her questioning ultimately took her beyond the accepted common meaning of that group; it then seemed quite natural for her to leave it.

For a woman marriage and career *may* be taken as synonymous; for a man they are separate and distinct commitments requiring different emotional and intellectual capacities. Melanie's career—albeit an amateur one—does not appear to begin until she takes on the challenge of foster parent, a career that is encouraged by her peers although not understood. Her career is not an accomplishment in the sense that one masters a problem, rather it is a way of thinking, an interpretation of her moving as well as her "standing" in her world. It *is* uniquely her own, but of common importance in that the focus of her thinking—her dialogue with herself—is upon understanding herself and others as they interact. This dialogue that she is now able to articulate may have had its beginnings as she "obediently" learned to decide in her philosophy classes. Many years were to pass, however, before the dialogue could become external as well as internal. It was finally when Melanie was challenged by Isabel that her timidity fell away. It was at this time, when Melanie had to defend her foster daughter and her own changing values and beliefs before Allen and the little communities, that the dialogue assumed its full importance in her life and within her self.

11
Beyond the Culture of Poverty

The life history of Maria Garcia begins with her account of the hunger and misery that accompanied her life as the child of poor Spanish-speaking migrant farm workers. Shifted from school to school—four moves in fifth grade made long division a mystery for several years—education became a series of humiliations so bitter that events are forgotten and she left: "It didn't work out." Once more the conviction of her inadequacy was reinforced.

In such an environment life is restricted to a narrow present and the culturally transmitted solution is a vague wish that somehow the misery will end and life will be better for one's children, as Maria's mother wished. For oneself there is little hope of anything better. Poverty does not envision its own end: the poor, educationally disadvantaged person dreams of escape but lacks access to cognitive and interpersonal skills that would make a degree of self-determination possible.

Poverty is a self-sustaining vicious circle. It lacks hope: In Maria's words, "There was nothing I could hold on to with joy." It is easy to understand why poverty persists for individuals and families as it carries a defensive fatalism. To hope is to be disappointed. Fatalism is at least a tenable posture toward a life situation that would otherwise be insupportable. Initial steps out of such hopelessness and failure are so difficult and uncertain that backsliding is certain. This is what is meant by being locked in as M. Brewster Smith puts it.[1] One is bound by a social environment and conforms, thus repeating the pattern depicted in this excerpt from *Child of the Dark*, the Diary of Carolina Maria de Jesus, a Brazilian slum dweller:

I began to have a bitter taste in my mouth. I thought: is there no end to the bitterness of life. I think that when I was born I was marked by fate to go hungry. I filled one sack of paper. When I entered Paulo Guimarães Street, a woman gave me some newspapers. They were clean and I went to the junk yard picking up everything that I found. Steel, tin, coal, everything serves the *favelado* [slum dweller]. Leon weighed the paper and I got six cruzeiros.

I wanted to save the money to buy beans but I couldn't because my stomach was screaming and torturing me.

I decided to do something about it and bought a bread roll. What a surprising effect food has on our organisms. Before I ate, I saw the sky, the trees, and the birds all yellow, but after I ate, everything was normal to my eyes.

Food in the stomach is like fuel in the machines. I was able to work better. My body stopped weighing me down. I started to walk faster. I had the feeling that I was gliding in space. I started to smile as if I was witnessing a beautiful play. And will there ever be a drama more beautiful than that of eating. I felt that I was eating for the first time in my life.[2]

Maria Garcia broke out of the fatalism and hopelessness of poverty and over a period of thirty years attained a high degree of autonomy. It is tempting to read her life history searching for the "factors" that would explain how she overcame such obstacles. Such reductionism, however, may distort the person, may turn her into an "object" of study. It is also tempting to see this life history as an instance of "breakthrough." This is a useful perspective and a comfortable one, but it risks losing the person and thus failing to learn from Maria the meaning of her life. To meet Maria is an invitation to stand in our own poverty and recognize its implications as she has done.

Maria Garcia, a vibrant, energetic, Mexican-American woman, was born forty-four years ago to Spanish-speaking parents in the abysmal poverty of a migrant-farm-worker's camp in California's San Joaquin Valley. Maria does not remember how many schools she attended before she quit at the end of seventh grade, "to go to work in the lettuce fields," recalling that "school didn't work out for some reason or another and so I went to work full-time."

I had been working out in the fields since I was a baby. Picking prunes and picking cotton. I picked cotton in Firebaugh—the men had these great big long canvas things and we had these little flour sacks that we would dump into my mother's bigger one. That's hard work.

We were so poor. My mother was not the strong type of woman . . . couldn't handle situations. We had two stepfathers, the whole bit, the whole dreary mess so there is nothing I can find there to hang onto with any joy. We were always moving around. Hungry. Always hungry; near starving. We were eight plus my mother, seven girls and one boy: There were three older sisters born—I think the last one of them was born in Monterey, on Cannery Row, in a shack. Then my mother married my father and the four of us—

three girls and a boy—were born. After that there was another stepfather and I have one sister from that. So I was the seventh of all my sisters and brother.

We were always moving. My father left but lived nearby. My mother used to make a big thing when he would come to see us and bring food. Seldom had enough to eat. My father used to give my mother twenty-five dollars a month; I remember that. I remember the Depression and standing in line for food. For a while my father worked in a restaurant; sometimes he would bring food. My mother was a good cook and she would ask for soup bones. I remember people would give us vegetables from the fields and she used to get spinach and she would cook the greens and give them to us; the next day she would cook the little tails—she would wrap them in egg and give them to us. She would find ways . . .

I never had a home life—my mom was not stable—you never knew what to expect: one day she'd hit us and the next day she would let us get away with it—she had the old Mexican ways. She didn't speak English, only Spanish. We [sisters and brother] spoke both English and Spanish. I didn't talk to my mother that often—most often to my sisters and brother.

I went to live with my dad when I was twelve; the welfare sent me. They felt I'd be better off with him. So for two years I lived with my dad off and on until I was fifteen . . . half the time I was seeing my mom, though. My mom stressed education; she didn't want us to quit school. We all did. [None of Maria's siblings completed high school; four completed elementary education.] That was why she was on welfare all those years—because we stayed in school.

I was fourteen when I quit school. I quit because I went to work in the lettuce fields—it was more tempting to have all that money. To have food, clothes. My father never took

our money. That was when [at fourteen] I was picked up for
street fighting. I was forty before I could say that; I was so
ashamed of it. I had to hide it from everyone.

I was in trouble; I was more stubborn than the rest [sis-
ters and brother]; I argued with everybody. My father used
to say, "What do I care what the people say?" We had to
make decisions with him; he never told us you can't do this
or that. If I wanted to stay with a girlfriend I would ask him
and he would say, "If you want to." And off I would go. He
never made the decision; he made us make it. It is rare. I
always felt he didn't like us because he didn't make these
decisions for us—tell us what we had to do. He had a steady
job; he could have contributed more. We never felt bitter
towards him. There was no joy, nothing stable.

I can remember my life turning at seventeen when I
came up to Mountain View to live with my sister. Then my
life started to change. I lived with my oldest sister—she was
married and had a family. I married—I was seventeen—a
dumb eighteen-year-old with no goals. That was annulled
after a month. Then I worked at the cannery and I met Juan
[Maria's future husband] and my sister told me I had to look
nice and wear the right color—act like a woman—to get
money off of Juan if I wanted to. Of course, I don't see that
way anymore. She was good for me then. I needed somebody to show me. Juan was the brother of a friend I met in
the cannery. We got married when I was nineteen.

Like Maria's parents, Juan had been born in
Mexico and had come to the United States as an adolescent to find work. Juan had finished the third grade
in Mexico, speaks fluent Spanish and English but has
some difficulty with both written languages. After a few
years of work in seasonal industry, Juan began working at an auto-assembly plant and remains there. Marriage was another change for Maria.

I see myself as a child and growing up in a life of desperation and I saw life change. It changed when I went to my father's and I wasn't happy but it was a change. It changed when I married Juan—but mainly I remember my life turning at seventeen when I went to my sister's. Then my children— Juan and I were married three years before Juanito was born. I was careful and only one of my six children came too close and that was because Juan said to me—after Juanito was born—that it had taken three years and I wouldn't get pregnant that quick. I thought I would but I went along with him. After that, they were all planned. My baby [the last of six] is seven and the oldest, twenty. They are the most important to me—it should be marriage but it wasn't. I guess having my babies. Nursing my babies. To me that was the most exciting thing. That's one of the things I can remember with joy, tenderness. It is really something to have that baby start searching for the nipple—because I breast-fed.

I was working most of those years. In the cannery and the Church. I joined the Legion of Mary. We were getting all those instructions and I looked around me and I thought to myself that all these women are so good and what the hell am I doing here—always my connotation of women working in the Church was that they had been virgin-marys. Here I had been married before and even though it had been annulled I looked back into my life. I was so poor and I worried that if they knew all that—I was so insecure I used to think, "You have no business here." But it started to change. It started with the Legion and then as I worked with the Cursillo and more and more through the years. The people that I was working with [in the Spanish Cursillo and a Spanish-speaking parish]—I realized . . . what the heck? They accept me as I am. They don't care who I am or what I have done; they accept me just as I am. I didn't feel they were better than me, I guess because I started to like myself more, I started to think of myself more. I really didn't care what they thought of me—not that I didn't care but that it didn't affect me. It wasn't a particular time because it came gradually. It did not happen overnight. It came gradually, just like being what I was came gradually; where I am now has gradually come through the process of things. I like to get involved; I like to see changes. I feel different about myself—from being involved, I guess.

Maria has been involved in the Spanish Cursillo from its inception in the early 1960s. A natural leader, Maria was the "Rectora" (lay director) of many Cursillos and came to be involved in La Raza,[3] a group concerned with the economically and educationally disadvantaged Mexican-American. At the same time, she was selected to be one of several laypersons who were to be trained for leadership roles in team-ministries. Maria remained with the group throughout its training over four years. When the list of those to be recognized for such roles was to be sent to the Bishop, Maria was told the list would not be approved if her name remained on it; she was the only woman participating in this training. Maria agreed to the removal of her name for the "good of the others." She continued to function in the parish as she had but without the certified status of the men. Later, Maria noted the irony of this stating that there had been "priestesses and training for them in the Aztec and Mayan civilizations!"

Maria did not learn about the Aztec and Mayan civilizations studying in her parish. This was to come much later:

It was mere chance really; it was just the opportunity there and I took it. I went to a wedding with a friend who had a black woman with her and she [the black woman] said to me, "Hey, have you ever thought about going to school?" I said, "Oh, yes. Many times." I had been going to adult education classes. I took sewing and then I took typing—I started when I first met Juan. I was taking typing then and he made fun of me, so I quit. I should have realized then. He made fun of me, saying, "What are you going to that school for, wasting your time?" Then I started again and took driver's education at night. . .

They told me about this woman's educational program[4] that was an experiment and so I went and here I am! We were about twenty-nine, I think, and about sixteen Chicana, about eight or nine Blacks, and only three or four Anglos. I was the *only* one of the Chicanas that finished. Of the Blacks, two transferred and the others went into the two-year Nursery Program. A lot of women went through divorces. It is funny: this one got divorced and then that one and I think I was one of the last ones. There were so many that got divorces that I lost contact.

Maria was the only Chicana to get her A.A. degree. As the time neared for her to receive her degree, she was awarded a scholarship based on academic achievement—her 3.00 grade-point average—by a Bay Area Jesuit University. Juan felt Maria was not "a good wife" and demanded that she quit. Maria explained that she had accepted the scholarship and would have to attend the university for the fall semester. As spring wore on and graduation neared the conflict increased and Juan began to drink heavily. Maria refused to quit, and Juan left her and moved in with one of his sisters the week following Maria's graduation. Maria worked in the cannery that summer, certain that she would have to quit after the fall semester. Pressure from family and relatives was intense and negative: all (except her children) thought she should quit. These interviews took place as Maria was completing her first semester at the university. This is a contemporaneous not a retrospective account:

My teachers would encourage me. Sometimes I would look at it and ask if it was all worth it. If it hadn't been so close to graduation I would have quit; I don't want to now, but I will have to, I think, if I go back to Juan—I will have to quit school. I do and I don't want to go back. I see it . . . I want to be a good wife, a good mother—mainly at this point a good mother because I don't think I'll ever be the kind of wife that Juan wants. I don't think I'll ever be that. I have lived with him for twenty-four years and I could do it—why make the kids more miserable than they have to be? I think I have a certain obligation to them and it is not fair to them and yet I say, if I have that attitude I know that eventually I will leave him anyway—as soon as the kids are old enough. Then, I say, well, that would be better than now.

I don't know. I get very hung-up trying to decide. I have started at the university and I'll finish the semester. That is for sure. The situation with Juan—I just take that as it comes. I don't want to encourage him. If he wants to come back and feels that we can make a marriage—then—because it takes the wanting. That is what I think, but it is difficult because he is really set on having his way. He is really not what I want for a husband either.

You know, the more I think about it the more it scares me. . . . if I am not really happy with him, what is going to happen? He is not what I want as a husband. I have known that all along, mainly, because I couldn't please him as a wife. I couldn't play the role that he wanted me to. But now I see that there could be some other man that would be more understanding. I don't know? Then I say, but I really don't want to put up with another man, so. . . .

It's hard to study with all this because I find my mind wandering back to the problems. School was very important to me because I felt I was going somewhere. Now I feel like the foundation has been knocked out from underneath of me and then I say, well, I need it [education] now. The more education I have the better job I can get to give the kids a better life if I have to stay with them alone. Then I kind of lose interest in school because I say, if I reconcile with Juan I am going to have to quit anyway. So I am in that boat.

But I enjoy school so much when I am there; I love it. When I get my homework done I feel like I've accomplished so much and I am ready to tackle the next thing. I think I am the only one struggling in the class. I have never had a litera-ture class before. There are big gaps—I have big gaps—so somethimes I was staying up all night because I had been lax. Now I work like crazy. The university is hard. I con-stantly have to keep reading because there is a paper due each week. At first I thought I couldn't do it. I had never read any philosophy and here I was in philosophy. There were two texts and the lectures and each week there were four questions he would put on the board and we had to write an essay. I didn't know what an essay form was. My papers looked like a third-grader's—all erased and messed. I was embarrassed; I didn't want to hand them in . . . the first one I didn't hand in.

After about the third week I went in to talk to him. I said, "I'm embarrassed, ashamed. You must think I'm an idiot, with these papers that look like a third-grader's. . . ." I didn't know what to expect. That's something I can never forget—his attitude. He said, "I understand that you are nervous. I know you are a good student." He said that over to me. I talked about big gaps and my feelings that the others were way ahead of me. He said, "Don't worry. You are a good student. You will learn." Just his attitude; that meant everything. He wasn't being judgmental and after that I could learn. The hardest thing was not having some-one to discuss it with. At the Community College we [women] were together. There isn't any of that at the uni-

versity and there is no advisor to help me fill in the gaps—
you are shifted from person to person.

Maria became increasingly involved in Chicano
problems on the campus and questioned the system of
the Jesuit university as oppressive and discriminatory
toward the Chicano student. Her own belief system—
the rules, as she calls them—became a question:

It wasn't hard and fast. I don't know, but I find when I am
trying to make decisions—I find that I'm sitting there, thinking. I read about sex and I thought, where did sin ever enter
into sex, especially between married couples? You know,
that is one thing I see that I have a different outlook on. And
what is bothering me is that more and more I am saying,
well, why should I follow the rules of the Catholic establishment? That worries me: that I think about these things!
Those rules about going to Mass on Sunday and the rest. I
think I have lost respect for the rules; I have lost respect for
the clergy. I don't think they practice it. They are saying
"love one another and do unto others and give money for
the missions."

There is so much to be done right here! Right here
under their—all you have to do is look. I was doing a report
on the high school [a high school in a Mexican-American–
low-income neighborhood] and I find that two-thirds of the
girls don't finish. It's right here and they don't look. It has
become a business; it is not preaching love the way Jesus
was doing it at all.

I feel that if I could find something that would attract me
I might leave, but I found myself and God in the Catholic
Church and I say, "So why leave?" Besides I look at others
and there is establishment there and rules there, too. So out
of frying pan into fire. But I see priests—now—as just selfish
men that look down, making no attempt. If they were Chris-

tians but then they aren't and it worries me when I see that—how I feel about how they are. I ask, "Have I gotten so involved with Chicano problems that all my bitterness and resentment is coming out that was way down deep inside?"

They give us so little; they give us these little token things—that's what makes me so mad right now: That *we* are *satisfied* with so little. We have no say as Church members! No control.

The issue of control had become central to Maria as she experienced discrimination at the university. More important to her was the issue of control in her family. Maria's children supported her in her attempt to educate herself. Her sisters and sisters-in-law as well as other relatives placed near-daily pressure upon her to quit and return home. In facing this pressure Maria also faced her own attempts to control others:

I think a number of things enter in. You can control to an extent, yes, but there is a danger in saying that we can control people and control their emotions or situations. I think we should be able, as a rule, to control ourselves—but not others, because I found that very, very dangerous when you feel that you have had control and now you don't have any. That is the most horrible feeling that there is.

Like with my daughter—you get desperate because all this time you were the one that controlled and now all of a sudden you didn't have any say because she isn't even here! Just thinking, what is she doing? I felt too much in control. You have to let go of them before so that doesn't happen. I don't think I am domineering; I could be but I fight it so that I don't have that horrible feeling that comes over a person when you feel that you have had control and now you have lost it.

Shortly after Juan left Maria, her daughter, Inez, decided to move out and "be on her own." Inez's leaving was far more stressful to Maria:

Much more so than Juan. A man I can find anywhere. What I can't find is a daughter or my children. With my daughter, I couldn't replace her even though I had the others—they weren't her. How horrible it must be when parents lose a child. How terrible. In death there is an emptiness and no matter how many you have around. I don't want—I never want to love anyone that way, you know, that you keep control—not even my own kids. I say things like that—not wanting to love that way—make you hard, but I don't think so. I think it makes you alert too, you know, that you don't control people. They don't belong to you so enjoy them and do what you can for them and have the attitude: Well, God bless you. Go your way.

That is a hard fight to do that. It is desperate when you can't control and you are not allowed to and you are forced to letting go. With our son who just got married—too young at nineteen. We let him make the decision because we couldn't make it for him. It was gradual. I see that Juan was very, very stressed. He didn't want to lose his son and didn't want him to get married and couldn't stop him.

When my daughter left—well, you don't know what to do because the Mexican tradition is that daughters don't leave home because then they are not good girls. After I thought about it, I thought that is very stupid because it is a natural thing for everybody to want to go out. So, okay, if they do wrong, they do wrong. But it has to happen—they have to go and I fight it: that old feeling that she shouldn't go. I fight it and I say, "Is it the culture or is it a frame of mind or what's right and what's wrong? Should I let her go?" I end up saying, "Well, she is intelligent; she is a good girl; she has to experience life." And then I worry. I think maybe I am too loose—that's what my family says.

I find that I am becoming aware as I am faced with problems, that my approach to them is different than what it used to be. It used to be, I more or less used to go by what I was feeling. You know, I feel I should do this. Now I try to reason it out. I think about it. I read—for my daughter—*The Art of Loving* [Fromm]. It is not being a mother just by raising them. If I should die tomorrow are these kids prepared to face life and take on responsibility? I say, "Gee, you have to prepare them." I'd rather see them be more aggressive and I like them to go after what they want. If we shelter them so much they can't do anything. If they are sheltered they can't function. I don't want that for my kids.

I guess that is why I am in such a turmoil all the time. And my family: They say I have a different way of thinking and they think I am wrong, that I am bad. I am more confused because the more that I am aware the more I have to probe and ask myself, "Is it the right thing? Are you going in the right direction? Or are you just being unrealistic?" I have always criticized people for being unrealistic and I keep saying to myself, "I wonder if I am getting to the point that I am unrealistic?" I worry about that.

I want to understand, for example, my daughter and so I ask questions of others: "What would you do?" Then I decide and I read and I find that *this* is why I am reacting the way I am—you know, following a tradition. I want to do what is right and I say to myself: "All right, now do you get it out of a book or do you get it by instinct—like I used to—or do you what?"

It worries me, figuring what's right and conscious of the fact that a lot of things that we do are just a matter of habit or culture or tradition and no questions. I want to do away with that. I don't want it. You know, like the Mexican tradition that a girl isn't good if she leaves home. Leaving home isn't right or wrong.

Maria's period of "turmoil" lasted nearly a year. Juan decided to return and they remarried, after Maria began her second semester at the university. During this period of separation and divorce Juan continued to support his family. Maria continued in school and as she became more involved in Chicano community concerns Juan's opposition lessened. When Maria had completed her A.A. degree and received some publicity Juan was taunted by his co-workers because he "couldn't keep his wife at home." Juan was suspicious and unable to understand Maria's enthusiasm. Maria experienced a similar lack of understanding and suspicion when she was interviewed for a position as a job and instruction counselor with a poverty program. The interviewer, a Mexican-American male, asked her if her husband would be jealous if she went to business meetings. The question made Maria angry and she decided that the interviewer had no right to ask her such a question. She obtained the position and again was working as well as attending school.

Maria obtained her B.A. and entered graduate school and received her M.A. degree at the same time her oldest daughter received her B.A. and the next daughter graduated from high school. Maria's oldest daughter dreams of medical school and awaits the results of her applications. Maria hopes to obtain a Marriage, Family, and Youth Counseling credential and began her internship at a community college in the fall of 1975. Maria would also like to "teach ethnic studies as well as help the young people stay in high school and to make the Mexican-Americans aware of their identity and their contributions to the whole culture of the West." Maria is committed to helping her people —*La Raza*—as well as achieving her own personal goals.

Enriqueta Longauex y Vasquez writes that the "response of the Mexican-American woman to the call of *La Raza* is directly related and dependent upon how the *macho* Chicano is treated when he goes out into the 'mainstream of society.' If the husband is so-called successful, the woman seems to become very domineering and demands more and more in material goods. I ask myself, Why are the women so demanding? Can they not see what they make of their men? But then I realize: this is the price of owning a slave." Thus, "a woman who has no way of expressing herself . . . of realizing herself as a full human has nothing else to turn to but the owning of material things. She builds her entire life around these, and finds security in this way. All she has to live for is her house and family; she becomes very possessive of both. This makes her a totally dependent human. Dependent on her husband and family. Most of the Chicana women in this comfortable situation are not particularly involved in the movement . . . [from] fear of censorship in general. Censorship from the husband, the family, friends, and society in general. For these reasons she is completely inactive."

A second response to *La Raza* comes from "the Chicana woman whose husband was not able to fare so well in society, and perhaps has had to face defeat. This is the Chicana who really suffers. Quite often the man will not fight the real source of his problems, be it discrimination or whatever, but will instead come home and take it out on his family . . . his Chicana becomes the victim of his *machismo*. . . . Much of this is seen . . . in the city. The man, being head of the household but unable to fight the system he lives in, will very likely lose face and for this reason there will often be a separation or divorce in the family. It is at

this time that the Chicana faces the real task of having
to confront society as one of its total victims." She
must find employment, feed and clothe her family, find
a place to live, arrange child-care while she works and
above all she must conform to, at the same time she
recognizes—possibly for the first time—the inherent
racism of the society in which she lives. She must conform "because her existence and the livelihood of the
children depend on her conforming, she tries very hard
to conform. Thus she may find herself even rejecting
herself as a Mexican-American. Existence depends on
this."[5]

She suffers, as Longauex y Vasquez states, the
double oppression of being "a woman in the market of
humanity" as well as that of being a "minority person
with a different set of values." If she survives, as
Maria's mother did not, she is a very strong individual.
A source of strength and of oppression is her large family. To suggest to her—as one might to Maria—that she
leave others behind and go ahead is to be ignorant of
her culture. To Maria, all must rise together, not the
few who have gained privilege.

Maria's husband was successful but she did not
build her life around "the owning of material things"
nor did she live for her children alone. She did not remain inactive even though she was, relatively speaking, economically secure. Juan did not face defeat in
his work; he did lose face as Maria became known in
the Chicano community. He was and remains a victim
of his *machismo* and Maria knows this, remarking: "I
feel sorry for him in his desperation to prove what a
man he is; I cannot help him unless he helps himself."
Maria also recognizes that Juan has suffered because
of her choices and she stays with him; "otherwise he'd
have nothing."

Elizabeth Martinez takes the white-middle-class militant woman to task for her lack of any "gut understanding of the positions of women from a colonized—not merely oppressed—group. . . ." This woman is sensitive "to the damage done to the men [from economic discrimination] . . . and feels reluctant to risk threatening their self-respect even further. This may be a short-range viewpoint involving false definitions of manhood, but it is created by immediate realities whose force cannot merely be wished away."[6]

These considerations make Maria's decisions more readily understood. Maria eventually involved most of her and Juan's family in Chicano activities and at the same time lessened their suspicion of her activities. On one occasion where she was asked to run a Spanish-speaking workshop at an out-of-town location she invited Juan's sister to come along, telling her: "We are going to talk about employment for women and you work in the cannery so why not come along for the day?" Later the Mexican-American community had news of the workshop in a pamphlet and Juan's co-workers brought it to work to show to him, telling him, "You ought to feel proud of your wife." Juan has adjusted to Maria's schooling and she simply tells him she has another course or two to finish before she can start working. She is not preoccupied with her unique status, nor is she interested in publicity.

At the same time she is unafraid to take an unpopular position if she thinks justice is involved. During hearings before county officials on the abortion issue—whether to support the state law or to recommend prohibition of abortion on demand—Maria related that she went to the meeting "on the fence" and not really certain of her position other than the knowledge that she could not imagine herself having an abortion. Pro-life advocates, including clergy, were adamant in their opposition to abortion for any reason. Maria said their opposition changed her thinking: "I couldn't have an abortion myself and I don't know if I would recommend that someone have one, but now I feel it is wrong not to let other women make that decision themselves. . . . If she decides to have one, that is her right."

Faced with clerical opposition, Maria wondered if she would have to leave the Church. "People have a right to decide and the Church can't take that away." The issue encompassed the meaning of Church to Maria as she asked: "Do I have to let that go (the Church)? If I let that go, everything goes."

I am thinking differently. The more I learn the more aware I am. . . . I am more in tune with people's reactions. I can perceive where they are coming from. I used to sense whether people liked me or didn't like me and now I have lost that, but maybe I don't pay attention to it. I am aware of people's attitudes—where they are at and I react to it but I don't pay as much attention to how they react to me. I'm more perceptive about their feelings about things.

For Maria this long process—thinking about things—began when she was thirty and subsequently became involved in the Legion of Mary and the Cursillo.

Thirty is a good age. . . . You have enough experience to have learned from your experience and you take a more serious interest in things. It seems that when I got to be about thirty my mind opened up!

Maria retrospectively equates her growing sense

of acceptance by her peers with the period when she experienced herself as beginning to think reflectively. Gradually she felt herself to be an equal—her poverty and early annulled marriage were not held against her and she was treated with respect by her peers. Her abilities as a leader gradually emerged as she was given positions of leadership and then assumed them for herself. Nearly a decade passed before Maria embarked on an undertaking that was completely of her own choosing—reentering school. All her previous positions entailed some form of clerical sanction. The move to enter school in itself was seemingly casual; the decision to take it seriously and herself seriously as a student—to think of going on and becoming a professional—was radical and brought her world and relationships into critical consciousness. Areas opened where she could now exercise choice.

Once Maria stated, "I like to get involved; I like change; I try to make change. . . ." She knows a self-fulfilling and self-affirming direction is possible and the passivity and hopelessness of the culture of poverty does not bind her as it did. First Maria finds herself "worthy of being taken seriously" as a moral and social equal; a sense of being "potent and efficacious" come almost a decade later, *after* she had acquired cognitive as well as interpersonal skills.

The reentry program sensitized Maria to her oppression as a member of a Spanish-speaking minority in an Anglo-dominated society and gave her a sense of solidarity with other similarly oppressed women. Her transfer to the university placed her in a new situation with different demands. It is difficult to overestimate the role of her instructor who recognized her abilities, was direct and explicit in his acknowledgement of those abilities, and non-judgmental as she expressed her embarrassment at the smudged paper. He stated the obvious—"I understand that you are nervous"—in non-evaluative language. Given Maria's earlier experience as a child where school consisted of one humiliation after another: being forbidden to speak her own language on the playground and being punished when she did; never quite knowing the context of the subject matter because of continuous transfers and absences to help in the fields; being older than her Anglo classmates when she was in an integrated school; and always the experience of being considered "stupid;" her experience with this instructor was probably crucial. Interestingly, it is the *only* such experience she relates. Empathy is not only an affective disposition, but a conceptual tool as well. Maria knew there were gaps in her knowledge and her own assessment of her work was accepted in an atmosphere of mutual concern that made it possible for her to continue, knowing her work would improve.

Other factors are important in Maria's development. First, Maria was not overwhelmed by childbearing and parenthood was an impetus to growth. Maria's children, with one exception, are spaced at two to three year intervals, were desired, and did not consume her energies even though one has a moderately severe neurological handicap. Rhythm worked for Maria and she was also employed between births of her children. Next, her first marriage was annulled and this enabled her to remain in the Church in "good standing" rather than as an excommunicated person who was "living in sin." Granted, education *now* enables her to dismiss any such categorization as un-Christian; but that would not have helped her twenty-five years ago. It is doubtful whether she could have participated as a *peer* given the stigma attached to the divorced woman or man in the Roman Catholic Church prior to the 1970s; it is even more doubtful that she would have been selected for leadership roles.

In addition, Maria has always been a fighter. It is impossible to capture Maria's proud bearing. However, it was probably this pride that displayed itself in her adolescent street fighting and that later enabled her to risk joining groups where she was uncertain of acceptance. Most recently she refused to quit school in spite of severe conflict and uncertainty. Maria is a fighter—not just for herself but for her cultural identity and her people—a greater good than her own advancement alone.

The line between delinquency and rebellion is a fine one. It is drawn at differing points along a continuum of socially expected and socially desirable behavior. Frequently the expected is equated with the desirable, and the nonconformist—particularly if she or he is a member of an ethnic or racial minority—is labelled "delinquent." Delinquency is not considered socially desirable and its outcome is perceived to be a career of vandalism, crime and eventual incarceration.

Having a probation officer now is not quite as much a matter to be hidden as it was fifteen, twenty, or thirty years ago. Thirty years ago Maria Garcia was picked up by the police for street fighting in a small town in the San Joaquin Valley and placed on probation after a few days in juvenile hall. Shamed to the core, fearing others would know of her disgrace, and harassed by social workers from welfare, it would have been impossible for Maria to understand her own resistance to a demeaning existence as an act of self-affirmation. She is still unable to do so: in her culture—as in most—fourteen-year-old girls do not fight in the streets and grow up to challenge society as well as to be productive and caring members of it. Maria did so in the face of very nearly insurmountable odds—perhaps partly because of a pride and courage that she expressed in the streets.

Maria would not attribute her present self-determination to the factors I have outlined. She considers much of it to be the result of "economics." When Maria returned to school she had been employed for thirteen months and had just gone on unemployment insurance. Thus she had an income while attending school and she had this employment insurance extended while she was in the re-entry program. Maria states this was not true for the other Chicana women who were either on welfare or totally dependent on their husband's income. In addition, even though Juan did divorce her, he continued to support his family until they remarried, so that Maria was never without limited financial security. As Maria states it,

In the poor family education goes first. If you are hungry and have to work you are too tired and you cannot study and so you quit. In Mexico, education—beyond the sixth grade—is not free and must be paid for by the parents. It is a luxury only the rich can afford although the poor value education for their children. I have never met parents—Mexican-American parents—who did not value education. It is the economic and racial discrimination in the United States that prevent it. Education goes first here too, in the poor family. It is an economic issue and there is confusion and insecurity so they [students] don't know how to go on; they don't see any value in it.

Maria's critical thinking is evident in her analysis of her social context. It is obvious she does not think the lot of the poor is ordained by fate but is the result of "changeable human arrangements." She understands that power, status, and wealth are merely human phenomena. They "can be scrutinized without sacrilege . . . can be criticized, perhaps even opposed. [This] awakening . . . is a crucial point in the genesis of 'psychic empathy.' Before this point is reached, 'underdeveloped' [persons] are indeed aware of their poverty, of the misery it brings to their lives, and of its hopelessness. . . . But only after the poor acquire a new consciousness do they clearly see that: (a) their own state is one of *underdevelopment,* situated *below* what ought to be and what can be; (b) their condition relative to that of others can be changed and (c) they themselves can become agents of that change."[7]

The "shock of underdevelopment" sensitizes one to one's own and other's diversity; at the same time, it raises ethical questions of common good. Maria asks, "Where do you get it [knowledge of right and wrong]? Is it the culture or a frame of mind? Do you get it from a book or do you get it by instinct—like I used to? So, [now] I ask others and then I decide and I read and I find that this is why I decide and I question. . . . And I dream."

The vicious circle is broken.

12
Implications

To be human is to be a particular kind of person because people differ:

> We must, in short, descend into detail, past the misleading tags, past the metaphysical types, past the empty similarities to grasp firmly the essential character of . . . the various sorts of individuals within each culture, if we wish to encounter humanity face to face . . . The road lies, like any genuine Quest, through a terrifying complexity.[1]

Development *is* complex; adult development peculiarly so. Nevertheless, it is possible to take persons, their interactions, and their historical context as existing givens; to recognize and organize dimensions[2] particular to the person, the interpersonal, and the cultural matrix; and to ask some questions about the interplay between these dimensions. Thus, it is possible to come to some very tentative findings about the processes that mediate development in adult life and to say something about what development consists of by reference to its diversity.

Personal Dimensions

The diversity of personal growth manifests itself intellectually, as a succession of more differentiated and comprehensive grasps of self and world and their

236

interrelation; emotionally, as empathy and vulnerability increase the person's capacity and ability to experience and express feeling; and holistically in the development and clarification of a centering meaning or theme that pervades the life and is the person's distinctive way of being in the world. The person comes to a knowledge of how he or she is thinking, apprehends that knowledge, empathizes with and appreciates the self, accepts the particular self that one is choosing to be. Self-appropriation[3] seems to me to be as useful a term as self-actualization in thinking about these dimensions of personal development.

Language forces a false and arbitrary distinction between thought and feeling—as though they are separate realms and one could think without affect or have a contentless feeling. Thought and feeling blend together but this blending may be lost on the printed page. With this qualification I will discuss some of the dimensions of the development of intelligence in adult life.

These life histories show people grasping the concept of culture as significant for the self-interpretation of their own lives. Each person expresses this apprehension differently—"the outline for the ideal person" (Anne Sienna), or a correct way of being "assimilated without question" (Ruth McCarthy)—but grasps the idea that he or she has been socialized and now must confront both the content and context of that socialization. Grasping this concept occurs over time as, at first, its voice "is a soft one"[4] and the insight is perceived to relate to what is immediately before one. For example, Maria's questioning of the Mexican tradition that good girls do not leave home occurred in the context of her daughter's leaving. Acting on this apprehension of enculturation begins with "simple things," as Anne Sienna noted, and then carries over into other situations, becomes a succession of added comprehensions.

Piaget's concept of de-centering is helpful here as it directs attention to the person's ever-increasing ability to recognize and take the view of the other—to recognize one's own socialization and the possible differing socialization of others. It is as though constraint is grasped and out of the knowledge of constraint grows the possibility of choice. Diffuse relativism—everyone has a right to do his or her own thing and should do it—does not appear in these life histories. In these lives the criteria for judgment change as morality is redefined as more complex and encompassing, demanding knowledge, risk, and commitment.

As the person discovers that he or she has been socialized, he or she retains an aspect of that socialization—a commitment to the good or worthwhile—that must now be rethought and relived, in uncertainty. Anne Sienna speaks of moving away from a previous way that one has learned was good and not knowing if one is letting go of the good. The problem of good and evil is present in these lives on many levels. The richness of David Henry Smith's discussion of the purpose of society—to liberate the individual rather than to oppress by its structure—and his role in that process simply cannot be conveyed by referring to a stage of moral judgment.

I have lingered on a single dimension of the development of intelligence in adult life—the apprehension of the concept of culture—and have pointed to people's application of this concept while maintaining their "fragile commitment to the good." In adult life

the decidings that confront these persons take on a
deeply moral connotation and cognitive development
is manifested in their description of wherein the good
consists and how they have come to know that. (The
salience of moral considerations may be higher among
these persons who were selected because of their participation in the Cursillo movement than it would be,
say, in a group identified through their participation in
the arts.) As I noted earlier, a high level of moral development may appear to be fuzzy or irritatingly
imprecise—"Things are grey, aren't they?" The judgments underlying behavior may seem so self-evident
to the individual that they are not set forth in detail and
cannot be categorized. So—Ronald Seaforth's decision not to fund a war he considered to be immoral
and his subsequent refusal to pay his taxes. While
many of these persons are actively involved in social
concerns, they are aware of the complex interplay of
factors in social problems; they take part in civil dissent,
as did Ronald Seaforth and Ruth McCarthy, without
expecting any instant solution. Increasing cognitive
complexity takes very different forms in the life histories of David Henry Smith and Melanie Roberts.
Both are very articulate: David criticizes society at a
very high level of abstraction; Melanie's social critique
appears almost glib and is almost entirely focused
upon interactions—her own and those of groups, pre-
senting an entirely different cognitive complexity, at
times hard to follow.

Emotional development, as I have delineated, in-
creases empathy and vulnerability, and augments persons' capacities and abilities to experience and express
feeling—to own their feelings and grow with them.
Barron has described the creative person as "both

more primitive and more cultured, more destructive and more constructive, occasionally crazier and yet adamantly saner. . . ." I do not agree that the persons whose lives are interpreted here are more destructive; they do, however, question themselves about their possible destructiveness as did Ruth McCarthy, Robert Duncan, and Anne Sienna. Some—Melanie Roberts, Richard Wring, and Robert Duncan—have undergone periods lasting from a few weeks (in Melanie's endogenous hyperthyroid episode) to eighteen months or two years (Richard Wring and Robert Duncan) when they have questioned their own sanity. They have had moments when they felt they were "going crazy," and had been suicidal. Each appeared to have experienced a re-integration and stronger self after the episode or period.

The ability to experience and express a complex and rich inner life is perceived as increasing in each life history as each person comes to differing terms with his or her own feelings and feelings about the self. One of the given values of our culture is the idea that the person is unique, an individual with a distinct and separate identity unlike that of any other person. This concept of a distinct and unique realizable self is grasped as a positive value. The importance of uniqueness is conveyed by culture and felt and grasped by the person. Discovering or sensing one's own uniqueness may be a developmental landmark. Several of these life histories—in particular, those of Ronald Seaforth, Anne Sienna, and Melanie Roberts—suggest that this landmark or milestone may require a developmental process before feeling unique creates positive feelings within the individual. Ronald Seaforth noted that being different carried with it an imperative; Anne Sienna felt uniqueness first as differentness, then as feeling special, and finally converted that feeling into being "especially different," a process that she thought occurred in her late twenties. Feeling oneself to be different or unique would appear—in these lives—to encompass childhood and adulthood. It is not perceived as equivalent to identity. It is probably discovered and rediscovered as both an alienating and a vital self-creative force at different times. Here the interplay of thought and feeling is suggested as the person experiences himself or herself as different, marginal, special, and is unable to identify with others in one's environment. The sense of apartness may provide the detachment necessary to create a new understanding of the self and new tasks for that self. This occurs in the life histories of Maria Garcia, Melanie Roberts, and Tom Van Dyke.

Earlier I suggested that empathy and vulnerability may increase persons' capacities and abilities to experience and express feeling. Vulnerability suggests the capacity to be affected, almost injuriously. This capacity is portrayed by Tom Van Dyke as he describes the feeling of being "stunned." It may involve retention of some of the child's ability to be "surprised" and wholly affected by experience: the growing person is fully present to his or her experience and is able to be informed by feeling—as is Melanie Roberts—and to move with feelings but not to be controlled by them. Ruth McCarthy's life history depicts this child-like aspect of affective surprise and its accompanying counterpart, the knowledge of what she had to let be destroyed within herself in order to grow: the cumulative fantasy of ontological security. Affective surprise is abrupt, spontaneously perceived and diversely expressed. The breakdown of personal meaning is more gradually perceived and is attended by a variety of feelings rather than a single affect. For David Henry Smith the collapse was quite exciting, although confusing at times; for Robert Duncan and Richard Wring, doubt, despair, depression, and anxiety were present; for Ruth, Anne, and Melanie, feelings of dying accompanied loss of previously held meaning.

In these accounts there are feelings that do not appear. In each of these life histories there is certainly cause for rage and anger and these feelings are evident; bitterness or hatred is not. Powerlessness is experienced in some form by all—most obviously by Melanie Roberts (who describes her extreme dependence upon her husband and inability to cope with a "difficult" child); hopelessness is only momentarily present, if at all. An ability to face mistakes and own them is present; guilt does not appear very salient.

Their modes of coping are as diverse as the persons and reflect individuality of personality. Ronald Seaforth plays handball and occasionally plunges in the ocean; Melanie walks in the early morning and does paper sculpture while envisioning a more powerful metal piece; David Henry Smith plays Mozart and occasionally curses, loud and articulately; and Anne reaches for her center and that of others in the quiet of nature and in the midst of a crowd.

The final dimension of the personal is the centering meaning or theme that pervades the life and is the person's self-interpreted way of being in the world. Here, too, we find diversity. Each person's life appears to have a direction that is less a trajectory and more a matter of self-appropriation, directed by meaning and pursued in a particular style. The content of meaning may change but the fact that the life is directed by meaning does not. Style or quality of being in the world is more difficult to capture. Some lives appear to unfold slowly, almost logically; others have a more eruptive quality. Ruth McCarthy perceives "a developmental lacuna" in her life that lasted for ten years before she "began to grow." Similar gaps are perceived by Melanie, Tom, and Ronald Seaforth. It would appear that development is perceived by some as having ebb and flow. Maria's life appears to be an encompassing movement, as it steadily progresses toward autonomy. Robert Duncan's conversion experience occurs over a fourteen-year span, but in that span are three or four cycles of intense pursuit and quest. Thus, the time span of "turnings"[5] varies with the individual as does perception of time as quick or protracted within a turning or a cycle. David Henry Smith's four years at North Beach were "quick," exciting, and tumultuous as everything collapsed for him. Melanie's few weeks of hyperthyroidism were interminable— "you don't know you won't be crazy forever." Ruth McCarthy's six years as Mother General were the most difficult and growing. So each person can point to a span of *years* during which he or she perceives growth, a period when growth occurred at a speed that set time apart from the rest of his or her life, a time that the theme pervading the whole of the life was clarified.

Two aspects of centering meaning or self-interpretation are apparent in the whole and in the times of turning: first, a visual imagery[6] of one's own process occurs in three of the life histories; secondly, each life is characterized—differently—but with an open-ended future that is explicitly stated. The visual imagery is of being on the edge of an expanding circle with increasing room to walk (Ruth McCarthy); of a spiraling up and out and up (Melanie Roberts); and as a force that pulls her in and pushes her out and is real everywhere she goes (Anne Sienna). The second aspect that is diverse in its expression but common to these lives is an open-ended future. These persons do not know what they will be doing five years hence; their hopes are evident as is their comfortableness with a lack of any certitude—none are in civil service, tenured positions, or otherwise somewhat "secure" work situations. The essence of their centered meaning is a trust in their own process, evident in the dynamic quiet of Anne Sienna who is concerned with peacefully making decisions and allowing life to have its part in showing directions and ways. A similar, but not so quiet, trust is evident in Melanie's "Hey" as she notes what is going on that she hadn't formulated before and perceives herself continuing that in the future. Here it appears that "trust" is hardly settled in childhood; it more nearly resembles a process whose developmental outcome is the recognition, acceptance, and trust in one's own process: in its "turnings" and in its direction. Learning to trust oneself in adulthood is explicitly stated as a process over time by Ruth McCarthy.

A further aspect of self-interpretation I present most tentatively. My purpose in this book is not to generalize but to point to diversity of being and to present a method of bringing to light patterned diversity. Nevertheless, each woman in this study explicitly stated a sense of growing up late. Ruth McCarthy notes that she did not begin to grow until she was twenty-eight or so; Melanie Roberts stated her adolescence lasted until she was twenty-six or twenty-seven and apologized for her lack of ability to pin down when it ended; Anne Sienna picked her own values and made decisions that were hers at about twenty-seven; and Maria Garcia said her mind came alive at about thirty. Obviously, one cannot generalize from four life histories. Nevertheless, such an anomaly can be noted, reflected upon.

In concluding this discussion of the personal dimensions of growth I am drawn to question stage conceptualizations—whether psychoanalytic or cognitive-developmental. Can we pick any stage to explain the person? Both Piaget and Erikson are oriented to conflict resolution (as was Freud). I would not deny that conflict is a factor in development—as when values collide with acknowledged behavior—but the conflict cannot be specified as hot (Freudian) or cold (Piagetian) because it is of a whole.

Interpersonal Dimensions

It is quite arbitrary to think of the person first as alone and then as an interacting person. Relationships never end; even though one of the persons may die, the relationship is re-interpreted throughout one's life as the person changes. People do not exist *in vacuo;* they exist in interaction with other persons, ideas, and events.

Out of the diversity of these person's lives, aspects of interpersonal meaning present themselves. People perceive themselves to have anchors, supports, challenges, communities, peer groups, significant others; they perceive themselves to be loved as good by some and judged to be wrong, even bad, by others, both by peers and those in positions of authority. Their relationships are exceedingly important to them; at the same time they are able to leave friends and familiar surroundings to do work they feel called to do. Institutional decisions moved Tom Van Dyke, Richard Wring, Robert Duncan, Ruth McCarthy, and Anne Sienna; they then left those institutions, and made subsequent geographic moves of their own choosing.

Growth out of—after recognition of—dependency is perceived as a developmental task in these lives; the depended-upon varies. Loevinger notes that the person in higher stages of development recognizes emotional dependence as separate from physical or financial dependency, and as a problem. "To proceed beyond [emotional dependency] a person must become more tolerant of himself and of others. This toleration grows out of the recognition of individual differences and of complexities of circumstances at the Conscientious Stage. The next step, not only to accept but to cherish individuality, marks the Autonomous Stage."

These life histories suggest that proceeding "beyond emotional dependency" involves much more than the recognition and tolerance of individual differences. Entrenched dependency—the need to possess, control, or model oneself on others—involves a nest of interrelated feelings and ideas about the self and others and one's being in the world. Its essence, in my opinion, consists in the *belief* that one could not exist without a particular person, system of beliefs, or institutional identity. One fears loss of self in loss of one's depended-upon person, status, or belief system and clings to it, even modeling oneself upon the other. This defines dependency in its extreme manifestations. Nevertheless, dependency is not interdependence nor independence. I would agree that there are times when all of us are deeply dependent and needful of others, particularly when illness or tragedy enter our lives. The issue is one of *continual* dependency; it is recognized with great difficulty, painful awareness in the lives of Ruth McCarthy, Richard Wring, Robert Duncan, and Melanie Roberts.

The depended-upon varies with the individual and the process of moving beyond it is diverse. Robert Duncan moves through a series of intense career commitments, each encompassing a wider identity and calling into question the previous one. Melanie Roberts carries on an internal and external dialogue whose explicit intent is to empower herself. Maria Garcia struggles over control of her children and her dependency upon their being present.

Loevinger notes that manipulative and exploitive relationships are common interpersonal styles at the Self-Protective Stage, a stage particular to early childhood. Manipulation, control and exploitation are *ongoing* questions in these lives with the recognition, as on the part of Maria Garcia, Tom Van Dyke, and Ronald Seaforth, that one is *less* manipulative now. However, the matter is not settled just as moving beyond dependency is not settled. As one woman commented, "It's like, oh, here too, here too, and here too, I have to work out that insight."

In this regard some people can be useful anchors while one grows; others can "hold one" in place and the difference is not readily determined, as Ruth McCarthy retrospectively notes. The same dual aspect of anchors or belongingness applies to peer groups. The growing person is frequently forced out of relationships or groups by the deviant nature of his or her growth. The alternative to isolation is multiple peer

groups, hardly an easy undertaking but one that
Ronald Seaforth accomplished when his close friends
found his opposition to the war "too far out." His relationships were strained, as were Ruth McCarthy's and
Tom Van Dyke's, but were maintained along with new
groupings. The type of interpersonal support evident in
these lives, as in those of David Henry Smith and Anne
Sienna, is characterized by the feeling of being deeply
loved and, at the same time, challenged to grow.

Another aspect of growth arising out of interaction
is that of direct tuition: Melanie Roberts began—
obediently—to decide for herself at the behest of her
philosophy instructor; Maria affirmed herself as able to
learn through a direct relationship with a perceptive instructor. Indirect tuition is evident in the discussion
groups that Tom Van Dyke, Ronald Seaforth, Richard
Wring, Ruth McCarthy, Melanie Roberts, and Maria
Garcia participated in. Each grouping was focused differently (the issues varied) but the context of all these
groups appears to be a questioning of the given social
order in particular and the nature of authority in general. A common theme in these lives is getting oneself
unhooked from arbitrary authority as a condition of
growth. The people I selected highlighted this aspect of
growth, given the nature of traditional Roman Catholicism and of the Cursillo. It is a major theme that might
not appear so central with another group of growing
people.

Interactions with younger persons—those young
enough to be one's own children—can have a powerful effect and be a re-socializing context, as Ronald
Seaforth and Ruth McCarthy make explicit. Parenting
is perceived by Melanie Roberts and Maria Garcia as
an impetus to growth. Equally of interest is the near

total absence from the interviews of Richard Wring, Ronald Seaforth, and Robert Duncan of mention of their children. Tom Van Dyke discusses two of his daughters, but not by name. These four men have a total of twenty children who seemingly are present in shadowed form.

Cultural Dimensions

What are the triggers, key events, that brought about or initiated development? The lives we have seen were all lived in a time that included the late sixties and early seventies, periods of extremely rapid social change in the society and of course in the Roman Catholic Church. It is as though the culture reversed or aborted normative expectations for many of these persons in the middle of life. Revered roles were no longer revered. Role expectations changed and people like Richard Wring and Ruth McCarthy acquired new roles, relationships, and a new self-understanding from that "turning about" in mid-life.

The Cursillo was a trigger event for Ronald Seaforth, David Henry Smith, and Maria Gracia, and they remain intensely involved in that movement. It was perceived as more peripheral by the others (with the exception of Robert Duncan) and they remain interested but no longer work on Cursillos. For Robert Duncan the Cursillo came at a "right moment"—the aspect of Kairos referred to earlier (chapter 8). He was intensely involved for a number of years and then moved out of that involvement. Whether these lives would have taken these directions at a different time—placed ten years earlier or later—we cannot know. Ruth McCarthy noted it would have been easy to be mother general ten or twenty years ago.

If we think about this period of rapid change and ask what really changed, it does not appear that daily life has been dramatically affected. Most of us come and go—perhaps to different places and with different persons—rise, eat, and go about our work much as we did. What has changed is the meaning of things and the meaning of our lives in a world no longer secure against destruction. We still have authority but the meaning of authority has been questioned and—for many—changed. Our society thinks it necessary to arm itself but the meaning of being a soldier has changed. Parents have children but a large family of eight or nine children does not evoke the same feeling and attitude it did twenty years ago.

If changes in meaning do, in fact, mark off great epochs, then such change is of great importance. It may be hinted at by an insightfully conceived statistical survey. It may also be partially interpreted in its diversity as it occurs in the person, a task I have attempted in this book.

At the outset of this book I noted Camus's remarks that "the aim of art, the aim of life can only be to increase the sum of freedom and responsibility to be found in every [person] and in the world." Camus goes on to emphasize that this aim "cannot, under any circumstances, be to reduce or suppress that freedom, even temporarily. There are works . . . that tend to make man conform and to convert him to some external rule. Others tend to subject him to whatever is worse in him, to terror or hatred. Such works are valueless to me. No great work has ever been based on hatred or contempt." A humanly valuable work adds to the inner freedom of those who know it. It is this freedom that Camus commends to us. He says, "It is what helps me through life." In this respect we cannot speak of success or the failure of our work; we can ask if it "has eased or decreased the various forms of bondage" that weigh upon persons. The aim of art and of life is "not to divide reality into good and evil and thus indulge in melodrama. The aim of art, on the contrary, is not to legislate or to reign supreme, but rather to understand first of all."[7]

13
Understanding and Interpreting Lives

With the main substance of this book behind us, comment is now appropriate about how these accounts of lives were written and how they might be read and interpreted. My intent, in the interviews, was to follow and to be led by the person's interpretation of his or her own life, then to help articulate and clarify that interpretation. This perspective with its focus upon personal and social meaning is one that I think is necessary if we are to understand persons on their own terms; it is also a perspective that would be denied by many psychologists and social scientists in their pursuit of the natural science ideal outside of its appropriate domain. Nevertheless, the thing to be asked is what is getting said about this life and what is its importance to the person saying it and to us as we try to interpret and make sense of it. In the life history, we meet a person saying something to us; what people say grows out of their own social reality and reaches out to ours. Thus, for example, to talk about Ronald Seaforth's picketing on the streets of San Diego (to protest the sailing of the *Connie*) in terms of "repressed rebellion" or some other abstract and impersonal construct would be to distort the meaning of the event for him, and to neglect its connection with the social reality of the Vietnam War, a reality for him and for us.

We want to grasp both the event/part/detail and the social reality/life/whole and render both comprehensible. It is clarification of meaning we are after and any "operational" approach that circumvents personal meaning or does not involve collaboration with the person in establishing it—tests to infer psychological traits and motives unformulated by the person, for example—seems quite out of place in this endeavor. Nevertheless, we need a framework within which to construct the life history, to understand it, interpret it, and question its meaning without reducing or trivializing the life of this particular person. In order to focus upon both the social reality and the person's self-understanding in that context, I have turned to a tradition in modern philosophy—dialectical hermeneutics[1]—as a discipline or method for thinking about meaning, bringing it to light in individual lives and questioning its presence for us.

Hermeneutics is a discipline based on the premise that the fundamental task of the human or social sciences is the interpretation of meaning; the dialectic—or speaking between—is the method of this hermeneutical discipline. The speaking-between suggests a dialogue, yet the life history is fixed, inscribed, as it is taped and then transcribed. The task is to find a way to a real dialogue that does not attempt to argue about, but rather to unfold the experiences of the other and thus to find their importance and meaning in the person's life. This dialectic is not conducted in an antiseptic vacuum. In fact, hermeneutics suggests that we can not actually begin with the life we are about to construct or to make sense of, but have to start rather with our own "pre-understanding"—the presuppositions that we, as interviewer, interpreter, and reader, bring to the task of understanding and reading a life history. Understanding, like interpretation, is continually directed by the manner of questioning and by what the question is about. Consequently, it is never without presuppositions. Understanding is always directed by and grounded in our prior ways of understanding. We have a standpoint—a frame of reference—from which we question and interpret. Certainly, this book has been grounded, from its inception, in the presupposition that significant growth and development occur in adult life and that the meaning of that growth is accessible to the person.

Just as a hermeneutical inquiry is acknowledged to be guided by our presuppositions, so too, the hermeneutical perspective holds that both inquiry and understanding operate within a context, a *hermeneutical circle*, in which the part informs the whole and is, in turn, informed by the whole. We enter an ever-broadening circle with the recognition that understanding an event in a life cannot be achieved separated from the whole life of which it forms a part related to other parts. The whole includes not only the details of the life but also the sociocultural context of that life and of our own as well. Upon entering the hermeneutical circle we become aware that we understand, read, or interpret from a perspective or point of view. We take a risk as we enter the circle, and that makes it possible to get beyond the circle. Once we recognize the contextual nature of our understanding and presuppositions it is possible that they will no longer remain as "given."

In actuality, this beginning dialogue between our presuppositions and their context initiates our entry into the hermeneutical circle where the task of under-

standing the life of an other is before us. Simultaneously we are faced with the fact that there is no such
thing as "raw" data, either of a person's life or culture.
Consequently, there is no escape from the fact that the
life history is a construction—first on the part of the
other person, then by the interviewer, next by the person who transcribes the taped conversation, then by
the writer and reader. A responsible construction of the
life history is not impossible; certainly it is difficult. The
task is made possible because the life history is inscribed so that momentary recollections are turned into
an account that can be reconsulted. Events and expressions of life undergo an objectification as they are
fixed or written down. As the life history becomes a
text it is thus parted from the person whose life it is and
it can speak beyond its own immediacy. That is, the life
history as originally given to the interviewer is now
open to be heard by the audience it creates because it
is a text and can be consulted over again.

I have data recorded and transcribed from my
conversation with another person. From a hermeneutical perspective the data—the transcribed interviews—are enigmatic, fragmentary, unclear, although
in my interviews I tried to push beyond unclarity and
sometimes even to challenge the person before me.
The work of constructing and interpreting a life history
involves a continuing dialogue which unfolds and
comprehends meaning within the totality of the life. Initially, we read the life from within, immersed, saturated
in its interplay of meaning and relations. We attempt to
suspend judgment as to meaning and endeavor to
stand within the life history, enclosed, to perceive it
"thickly"[2]—to follow movement within the text, because it is the meaning of what is said that we want to
unfold, not the event of talking itself. The text speaks to

us in its contextual meaning—there is no such thing as a single element that is unrelated to anything else. We are forced to deal with both the event and its context if we are to make sense of either.

We discover, in our immersion in this particular life, the questions and meanings that concerned the person, the issues he or she confronted, the pattern and style of response, and the process and direction of the life. Indeed, we also reconstruct and share the context of the person's world in order to construct the life history. The person simply cannot be separated from cultural context.

For example, to grasp the meaning of the direction of turnings taken by Ruth McCarthy we have to denote how she perceived authority, ontological security, truth, and God as One, a belief derived from a tradition stretching back through the centuries. Only if we share this context can we comprehend the importance to her of letting "the cumulative fantasy of God's Master Plan" be destroyed within her that she might grow. At the same time if *we* judge belief systems to be cumulative fantasies then we will not be able to understand their meaning in the lives of Anne Sienna and David Henry Smith. This is what I mean, in hermeneutics, when I say we suspend judgment in order to let the meaning of the life unfold. Placing the meaning of the experience of the other in the open and letting it unfold does not mean that we step outside ourselves or separate ourselves from the life; we become more fully present to the other life as we grasp and take into ourselves the world of the other person.

Of course, in so doing and in some measure, our own self-understanding is risked, our world called into question. Thus, the "hermeneutical problem" or necessity for reconciling the existence of several worlds, including our own, may result in a self-examining and self-correcting process. The context of the life history is integral to comprehending it; as the life history is brought into being it brings to awareness the differences in horizon—the boundaries of vision—of the author and interpreter-reader and the necessity to make the conflict of horizons evident in our interpretation— that is, to preserve the differences that make a dialogue possible.

Immersion in the transcribed data enables us to grasp themes or threads which then point to a whole to be appropriated; the editing process continues and gradually a life-history-text is constructed. As we begin this construction we are bound and free at the same time; there is an immediacy to the life before it becomes a life-history text, an intensity that binds us to the tapes and pages before us; we are also free to communicate that life of another person as a life history. The discipline of hermeneutics suggests that we cannot communicate that life without getting near the immediate life and immersing ourselves in it. This is what the data of the transcribed interviews permit us to do. In the nearness to the life we begin questioning— asking what our own position is and how we might make explicit the meaning of the other life. Obviously much more is left out than is included; what is included is what seems to direct the life and point to its meaning.

I am reminded here of Ruth McCarthy's description of her annual meetings with each new first grade class over a ten-year period, which concluded with the observation that while she liked the kids, she didn't like teaching them! Her own interpretation of her experience points to the meaning of this insight in her life and

the direction she then took; it is not necessary to account for each September of that period. Similarly,
Ron Seaforth's account of the logistics involved in getting several tons of food to the farm workers at Delano
is interesting, but it is not essential to the task of reveal-
ing the meaning of his organizing and participating in
this effort. The meaning of his participation is the
thread that reveals the importance to him of this act.

Thus, in beginning to construct the life history it is
necessary to become very familiar with all that we
have—the anecdotes, stories, remembrances. We
need a thorough knowledge of all the fragments and
pieces in order to construct the life history from the
given meanings of the person—meanings that are at
first only perceived as themes, later their interrelatedness within the life becomes clear. In Melanie's life we
are seemingly referred from relationship to relationship
with descriptions of specific interactions; it is only later,
after repeated study of the several hundred pages of
interview data, that a theme emerges. Melanie is questioning not only the meaning of the relationship to her,
but also its context of implied values, normative expectations, and past behaviors. What is meaningful for
Melanie is the questioning process itself in which she
places herself in relief against a formerly given ground
of structured interactions.

Finding the theme does not necessarily interpret
that theme. Both Anne Sienna and Ronald Seaforth
perceived uniqueness; they tell us about their feeling
unique. Unless we are thoroughly familiar with the
whole of their accounts we will not know how their
perception of uniqueness is related to other meanings
and structures them; that is, how it operates within the
life to relate other meanings to itself. In the life of

Ronald Seaforth uniqueness is expressed as apartness and an unwillingness to follow the crowd or to fall for "the dangling carrot of the large corporation." As we follow uniqueness in Ronald's life it is expressed with increasing clarity as a directing influence that encompasses more and more aspects of his life.

In interpretation we are involved in an arcing dialectic; we move back and forth between many parts and many wholes. Thus, to apprehend is to construe the whole, to grasp the what, to comprehend the person; to unfold is to detect the themes, to discover the why that structures and relates meaning in this life history. Each unfolding opens up a new whole, suggesting that a more adequately informed dialogue is possible—one that will plunge us ever more deeply into the heart of the life, and it is the heart of the life— its meaning—that interpretation is about. Of course, any such interpretation is intrinsically incomplete; it is always open to challenge as it is a judgment, not a prediction nor the last word. In hermeneutics, a "final word" is called "doing violence to the text." The life history is open to many readings, many constructions, yet one interpretation of it—as a whole—seems more probable than others to the responsible interpreter.

We ask, "What are the events in this life?" and "What came to expression in these events?" This context of interweaving questions relates the meaning of part and whole to each other; it also has a referential ability: the power to disclose a world. Depth interpretation of a life necessitates that we enter the world of the person, appropriate it, make it our own. This does not mean we must identify with the person. Interpretation is not an occasion for labeling; it is a manner of relating through dialogue which remains—in the end—unfin-

ished. Meaning arises in relationship: hermeneutics
demands a particular relationship with what is to be interpreted, an openness that is willing to hear and is capable of being modified. Our presuppositions, our
data, the lives we construct cannot be taken as absolute; all are subject to change. If they are not, then we
operate within a circle of illusion that does not truly
question because we have decided that the answer is
present. In this instance it is not interpretation of meaning and pattern within a human life that we are about;
it is something else, vacuous and vacant. Interpretation, furthermore, is concerned with intrinsic meanings—meanings that arise from within the life account,
within the document—not with extrinsic ones.

A good interpretation of anything—a poem, a person, a history, a ritual, an institution, a society—takes us into the heart
of that of which it is the interpretation. When it does not do
that, but leads us instead somewhere else—into an admira-
tion of its own elegance, of its author's cleverness, or of the
beauties of Euclidean order—it may have its intrinsic
charms; but it is something else than what the task at hand
. . . calls for.[3]

Good interpretation has the power to disclose a
world just as a work of art has the power to transform
our understanding of our world. A high level of personal development embodied in a life history is a fresh
way of seeing life and is capable of expanding our
understanding. A realm of actual freedom uncovered
in a life history not only reflects its time; it bears within
itself a new world to be unfolded. The life history also
awaits new, or other, interpretations.

The interpretations given in the preceeding chapters are not the only ones possible, but those that seemed important to me. Construction of a life-history text is also an editing process which itself both depends on ongoing interpretation and facilitates the reader's further interpretations. As a pragmatic necessity, one has to stop at some point. But the hermeneutic method inevitably allows hidden and therefore biasing interpretations to alter meaning. My editing process began with my trying to grasp as clearly as I could the person's own retrospective account from his or her present life perspective, and attempted to discern, from that account, the process of broadening horizons and unfolding development. Such an approach is certainly not invulnerable; it cannot attempt "complete" interpretations. Yet the reader's participation in the hermeneutical circle can result in continuing, and humanly valuable, reverberations of meaning.

Interview Themes

These are the themes which formed the basis of my interviews. For anyone, I think they can provide the means for increased self-understanding.

Life history—the *feeling* and *taste* of childhood, relationships with parents (divorce, deaths, moves), and the atmosphere of family life. What stands out as you think about that time?

The origin of self-concept. When did you first sense your own uniqueness, differentness? What was that like?

The earliest moment of commitment—to what? At what age did this happen?

What was adolescence like, what kind of friends did you have? Was adolescence a hard time? When did you feel yourself to be an adult? Can you remember an event or situation or person present when that occurred?

The choice of life work—what given alternatives did you have to the occupation you chose? Did you actively choose an occupation or calling?

Did personal growth parallel community growth? Do you have a sense of being ahead of any others? Or parallel to others? Or were you alone?

Who has freed you? Whom have you freed? Describe and elaborate how you were freed, by whom, and when.

What was or is falling in love like? What did that mean to you? Are there any experiences that are beyond words or hard to put into words? Do you have any awareness of dread or evil?

How do you know what is good or bad? What makes something good or bad? What do you think about rules?

In what situations or with which persons do you find yourself facing the truth of self? With whom have you experienced crises? When has this happened? What was it about?

Do you sense any pattern to your growing? How do you tell yourself to grow? How do you manage when things are awful? What do you do? Where do you go? Why?

What does creativity mean to you? When have you experienced that? How are you creative?

What do you do with your feelings? Anger? Guilt? Depression? Sadness? Anxiety? Fear? Do you ever have suicidal thoughts? Are you ever ecstatic? Blissful? Gloriously happy? Disillusioned? Peaceful?

How do you handle your boredom? Or are you bored?

What surprises you or when are you surprised? When was the last time you were surprised?

Have you felt power at times? What do you do with that feeling?

What sustains you—keeps you going? Is approval important to you? Whose approval matters?

Is sexuality—related to overall growth— important?

Is money—related to growth—important?

What do you see in the future—one, five, ten years from now? What would you like to try out? Why haven't you tried those things yet?

What is beautiful to you? What form of art do you prefer?

What moves you to tears? When did you last cry?

Notes

PREFACE

1. Sheed (1974), p. 20.

CHAPTER 1

1. Camus (1961), p. 240.

2. Geertz (1973), p. 53. *Ab initio*, sexist language excludes
and dehumanizes. With few exceptions, that are obvious because
they are bracketed, I have decided not to cleanse other quoted
texts of their sexist language.

3. The quotation was part of a display at the Library of the
University of California, Santa Cruz, "Special Collections: Albert
Camus," Spring Quarter 1971.

4. Loevinger (1976), p. 26.

CHAPTER 2

1. Cursillo is a Spanish word, literally "a little course," pro-
nounced cur–si–yo.

2. The Cursillo as experienced by most of the people I studied
had already changed substantially from its European origins. Disturbed by the apathy of his male parishioners on the Island of
Majorca Bishop Juan Hervas met with a psychologist, Eduardo
Bonnin, and a group of priests and laymen. Over a period of

months this group devised *The Cursillo*, literally, "A Little Course," whose subject matter was Christianity and whose purpose was the projection of Christianity into society using the techniques of catechetics, sociology, psychology, and education—as those disciplines were conceived in 1949. The first Cursillo was held in Majorca; the movement then spread rapidly throughout Spain, Austria, Germany, France, and Italy, and was introduced into the United States by two Spanish Air Force Cadets stationed in Texas. The first California Cursillo was held in Stockton in 1962, followed in the same year by the establishment of a Cursillo Center in San Francisco.

McLaughlin (1964) describes the origins, specific content, and growth of the Cursillo movement. *Time*, (March 13, 1964, p. 61), gave a fair description of the content of the early Cursillo but ignored the difference between the Cursillo in Baltimore and San Francisco—notably the ecumenism in San Francisco.

3. Turner (1969), pp. 127–128, states: "Communitas breaks in through the interstices of structure, in liminality; at the edges of structure, in marginality; and from beneath structure, in inferiority. It is almost everywhere held to be sacred or 'holy,' possibly because it transgresses or dissolves the norms that govern structured and institutionalized relationships and is accompanied by experiences of unprecedented potency. The processes of 'leveling' and 'stripping,' . . . often appear to flood their subjects with affect . . ."

4. Sarbin and Adler (1970).

5. Of the approximately eight thousand Bay Area participants, about three thousand were on the Cursillo Center mailing list. Finances prohibited sending out a newsletter to everyone who had made the Cursillo; only those who continued to participate in the Cursillo or specifically requested to remain on the list (people who left the area) were on the "active" mailing list. A short questionnaire was mailed to every other entry on this "active" mailing list on July 1, 1974. In all, 1,500 questionnaires were mailed out and 344 were returned.

6. Responses to the brief questionnaire were scanned by myself, the former Director of the Cursillo Center and a religious sister who had been a major leader in the Cursillo movement. A longer questionnaire was mailed to 250 persons selected from those who had indicated change in their lives (whether or not they attributed it

to the Cursillo) or were publicly known to have made major changes in their lives. Of these, 146 were returned completed. For extensive discussion of questionnaire results see McDowell (1976).

7. On the bases of the questionnaires, personal knowledge, and consultation with other Cursillo leaders, I interviewed twenty persons at length for periods ranging from five to thirty hours. The nine people whose interviews are the basis for the following chapters were selected somewhat arbitrarily for the richness of the interviews, for the clarity with which psychological growth was apparent in the interviews, and for the variety of that growth.

CHAPTER 3

1. Puhl (1962), p. 169.

CHAPTER 4

1. Perry (1970).

2. Daly (1975), pp. 95–98 delineates the unusual powers exercised by abbesses in the Middle Ages.

3. McCann (1960).

4. Sr. Mary William of the Immaculate Heart. Quoted by Daly (1975), p. 137.

5. Paul Tillich quoted by Daly (1975), p. 165.

CHAPTER 5

1. Marty (1974), p. 147.

2. See Alexis de Tocqueville, *Democracy in America* (Vol. I).

3. Johnson's appeal to Congress was made on March 15, 1965. Johnson's words are quoted by Bellah (1974), p. 35.

4. Richardson (1974), p. 162, states that such an analysis legitimates means and end as related to a transcendent ideal and thus affirmed as "true."

CHAPTER 6

1. Gray (1971), p. 92. "A Gallup Poll taken at the beginning of 1966 showed that Catholic support of Johnson's Vietnam policy had a substantial lead over Protestant and Jewish support: fifty-four percent of Catholics approved of it, as against forty-one percent of Jews, and thirty-nine percent of Protestants."

2. Gray (1971), p. 85.

CHAPTER 7

1. Perry (1970), pp. 131–132, has noted that faith differs from mere belief. Only the person who has experienced doubt in the *context* of a relative world can make the commitment that constitutes faith.

2. The quotation was attributed to H. Richard Niebuhr in a lecture given by a sociologist of religion in 1970. I have been unable to locate it in print.

3. James (1902), p. 505.

4. Küng (1968), p. 2.

5. As stated earlier, the Cursillo movement in the Bay Area was unique in that it was ecumenical almost from inception. Ecumenism in other locations, national and international, within the Cursillo movement was uncommon—rare—and remained so.

6. Gregory Bateson, personal communication, May 15, 1974.

7. James (1902), p. 41.

8. Geertz (1973), p. 100.

9. Berger (1961), p. 96.

10. Camus (1961), pp. 69–74 *passim.*

CHAPTER 8

1. Camus (1961), p. 272.

2. James (1907), pp. 284–301.

3. Prior to the Second Vatican Council, the Roman Catholic Church placed books its censors did not approve on an *Index of Forbidden Books*. The custom has since been abolished.

4. The relationship of a confessor to a seminarian is similar to that of an advisor to a student in college.

5. Mandelbaum (1973), pp. 181–182.

6. Tillich quoted in Kelman (1969), p. 61.

7. Gourdon quoted in footnote by James (1902), pp. 171–172.

8. These moments are comparable to the young child's apprehension of the achievement of conservation. There is a moment when the young child first comes to understand that the amount of "substance" in a wad of dough or in a container of water stays the same no matter what shape it is molded or poured into.

9. James (1902), p. 335.

CHAPTER 9

1. James (1902), p. 74.

2. Loevinger (1976), p. 147.

CHAPTER 10

1. Palmer (1969), pp. 145–146.

2. Geertz (1973), p. 5.

3. Quoted by Geertz (1973), p. 13.

4. The language is clear; it is also sexist. Although appropriate *here*, woman, she, herself would particularize and thus exclude as does man, he, himself. Heidegger quoted by Palmer (1969), p. 150.

5. Melanie attended a noted Jesuit university on a scholarship based on academic achievement, entering shortly after the all-male institution accepted a small number of intellectually gifted women.

6. Quoted by Bernard (1972), p. 50.

7. Bernard (1972), pp. 40, 41. Bernard (*ibid.*), p. 328, has also noted that sociologists have "documented ad nauseam the dependencies of wives rather than how to overcome them. . . ."

CHAPTER 11

1. M. Brewster Smith (1974), p. 155.

2. de Jesus, *Child of the Dark* (1962), pp. 52–53.

3. *La Raza* literally means *The Race* and refers to the descendents of American Indians and Spanish colonialists.

4. During the last seven or eight years several Re-Entry programs for women have been instituted in Community Colleges in the Bay Area and San Joaquin Valley. Many are federally funded under the Consumer Education Act and provide daycare for preschool children of educationally disadvantaged women, most of whom have been on welfare and are members of an ethnic or racial minority.

5. Longauex y Vasquez (1970), pp. 380–381, 382.

6. Martinez (1970), pp. 376–377.

7. Goulet (1971), pp. 43–44.

CHAPTER 12

1. Geertz (1973), pp. 53–54.

2. By "dimension" I mean scope and breadth in development, not its measurement.

3. Lonergan (1972), p. 7, uses "self-appropriation" to refer to the self as knower.

4. Freud, *The Future of an Illusion* (1928), p. 93.

5. Mandelbaum (1973), p. 181, uses "turnings" to denote periods perceived to be landmarks or watersheds in a life history.

6. As I did not ask this question in the interviews I do not know if others would have had an image of their own process. These were expressed spontaneously.

7. Camus (1961), p. 266.

CHAPTER 13

1. See Palmer (1969) for a thorough description of the historical development of hermeneutics from Dilthey through Heidegger to Ricoeur and Gadamer.

2. See Geertz's (1973) interpretation of "thick" and "thin" description.

3. Geertz (1973), p. 18.

Bibliography

Abbott, Walter M., S.J. (Editor), *The Documents of Vatican II* (New York: Guild Press, 1966).

Allport, Gordon W., *Becoming* (New Haven, Connecticut: New Haven & London Press, 1955).

Allport, Gordon W., *The Person in Psychology* (Boston: Beacon Press, 1968).

Asch, Solomon E., "Effects of Group Pressure upon the Modification and Distortion of Judgment," in H. Guetzkow (Editor), *Groups, Leadership, and Men* (Pittsburgh: The Carnegie Press, 1951).

Back, Kurt W., *Beyond Words* (New York: Russell Sage Foundation, 1972).

Barfield, Owen, "Imagination and Inspiration," in S.R. Hopper & D.L. Miller (Editors), *Interpretation: The Poetry of Meaning* (New York: Harcourt, Brace & World, Inc., 1967).

Barron, Frank, *Creativity and Psychological Health* (New York: D. Van Nostrand Company, 1963).

Barron, Frank, "Diffusion, Integration, and Enduring Attention in the Creative Process," in R.W. White (Editor), *The Study of Lives* (Essays on Personality in Honor of Henry A. Murray) (New York: Atherton Press, 1963), pp. 235–248.

Barron, Frank, *Creativity and Personal Freedom,* (Princeton, New Jersey: D. Van Nostrand Company, 1968).

Bateson, Gregory, *Steps to an Ecology of Mind* (San Francisco: Chandler Publishing Company, 1972).

Baum, Gregory, *Faith and Doctrine* (New York: Newman Press, 1969).

Bellah, Robert N., and William G. McCoughlin (Editors), *Religion in America* (Boston: Beacon Press, 1968).

Bellah, Robert N. "Civil religion in America," in R. Richey & D. Jones (Editors), *American Civil Religion* (New York: Harper & Row, 1974), pp. 21–44.

Bellah, Robert N., *The Broken Covenant* (New York: Seabury Press, 1975).

Berger, Peter L., *The Precarious Vision* (Garden City, New York: Doubleday & Company, Inc., 1961).

Berger, Peter L., & Thomas Luckmann, *The Social Construction of Reality* (New York: Doubleday & Company, Inc., 1946).

Bernard, Jessie, *The Future of Marriage* (New York: World Publishing Company, 1972).

Block, Jack, *Lives Through Time* (Berkeley: Bancroft Books, Inc., 1971).

Brim, Orville G., Jr., "Life Span Development of the Theory of Oneself," invited address to the International Society for the Study of Behavioural Development Biennial Conference, University of Surrey, Guildford, Surrey, England, July 1975.

Buber, Martin, *I and Thou* (R. Smith, Translator) (Edinburg: Clark, 1961; originally published, 1958).

Campbell, Joseph, *Myths to Live By* (New York: The Viking Press, 1972).

Camus, Albert, "The Unbeliever and Christians," in J. O'Brien (Translator), *Resistance, Rebellion, and Death* (New York: Alfred A. Knopf, 1961), pp. 69–74, passim.

Camus, Albert, "The Artist and His Time: The Wager of Our Generation," in J. O'Brien (Translator), *Resistance, Rebellion, and Death* (New York: Alfred A. Knopf, 1961), pp. 235–248.

Camus, Albert, "The Artist and His Time: Create Dangerously," in J. O'Brien (Translator), *Resistance, Rebellion, and Death* (New York: Alfred A. Knopf, 1961), pp. 249–272.

Collingwood, R.G., *Essays in the Philosophy of History* (Austin, Texas: University of Texas Press, 1965).

Cottle, Thomas J., & Stephen L. Klineberg, *The Present of Things Future* (New York: The Free Press, 1974).

Cross, Patricia A., "College Women: A Research Description," paper presented at 1968 annual meeting of National Association of Women Deans and Counselors (mimeographed), quoted by S.D. Feldman, "Graduate Study and Marital Status," *American Journal of Sociology*, January 1973, *78*(4).

Daly, Mary, *Beyond God the Father* (Boston: Beacon Press, 1973).

Daly, Mary, *The Church and the Second Sex* (New York: Harper Colophon Books, 1975).

de Charms, Richard, *Personal Causation* (New York: Academic Press, 1968).

de Jesus, Carolina M., *Child of the Dark* (New York: E.P. Dutton & Co., Inc., 1962).

du Plessix Gray, Francine, *Divine Disobedience: Profiles in Catholic Radicalism* (New York: Alfred A. Knopf, 1970).

Durkheim, Emile, *The Elementary Forms of Religious Life* (Glencoe, Illinois: Free Press, 1947) originally published, Paris: Felix Alcan, 1912.

Erikson, Erik H., *Childhood and Society* (New York: W.W. Norton & Co., Inc., 1st ed., 1950; 2nd ed., 1963).

Erikson, Erik H., "The Nature of Clinical Evidence," in D. Lerner (Editor), *Evidence and Inference* (Glencoe, Illinois: Free Press, 1959), revised and enlarged in *Insight and Responsibility* (New York: Norton, 1964).

Erikson, Erik H., *Identity, Youth, and Crisis* (New York: Norton, 1968).

Evely, Louis, *If the Church Is to Survive,* J. F. Bernard (Translator), (Garden City, New York: Doubleday, 1972).

Farberow, Norman (Editor), *Taboo Topics* (New York: Atherton, 1963).

Feldman, Saul D., "Impediment or Stimulant? Marital Status and Graduate Education," *American Journal of Sociology,* January 1973, *78*(4), pp. 982–994.

Flavell, John H., *The Developmental Psychology of Jean Piaget* (Princeton: Van Nostrand, 1963).

Frank, Jerome D., *Persuasion and Healing* (Baltimore: Johns Hopkins University Press, 1961).

Freire, Paulo, *Pedagogy of the Oppressed* (New York: Herder & Herder, 1972).

Freud, Sigmund, *The Future of an Illusion* (London: Hogarth Press, 1928).

Friedman, Martin, "Touchstones of Reality," in M. Friedman, T. Bourke, P. Laeuchli, & S. Laeuchli (Editors), *Searching in the Syntax of Things: Experiments in the Study of Religion* (Philadelphia: Fortress Press, 1972).

Frye, Northrup, "The Critical Path," *Daedalus,* Spring 1970, pp. 268–342.

Gadamer, Hans-Georg, *Truth and Method* (translated), (New York: Seabury Press, 1975).

Geertz, Clifford, *The Interpretation of Cultures* (New York: Basic Books, Inc., 1973).

Gordon, Chad, & Kenneth J. Gergen, *The Self in Social Interaction* (New York: John Wiley & Sons Company, 1968).

Gordon, Rosemary, "Symbols: Content and Process," in J.B. Wheelwright (Editor), *The Reality of the Psyche* (New York: Putnam, 1968).

Goulet, Denis, *The Cruel Choice* (New York: Atheneum, 1971).

Greeley, Andrew M., *Unsecular Man: The Persistence of Religion* (New York: Schocken, 1972).

Greeley, Andrew M., *The New Agenda* (Garden City, New York: Doubleday & Company, 1973).

Greeley, Andrew M., and Peter H. Rossi, *The Education of American Catholics* (Chicago: Aldine, 1966).

Häring, Bernard, *The Law of Christ* (Westminster, Maryland: The Newman Press, 1963).

Hartsock, D.E. (Editor), *Contemporary Religious Issues* (Belmont, California: Wadsworth Publishing Co., 1968).

Harvey, O.J., E.D. Hunt, and H.M. Schroder, *Conceptual Systems and Personality Organization* (New York: Wiley, 1961).

Heidegger, Martin, *Introduction to Metaphysics,* R. Manheim (Translator), (New Haven, Connecticut: Yale University Press, 1959).

Heilbroner, Robert L., *The Great Ascent* (New York: Harper & Row, Publishers, 1963).

Herberg, Will, *Protestant-Catholic-Jew, An Essay in American Religious Sociology* (Garden City, New York: Doubleday & Co., Inc., 1960); originally published by Anchor Books, Garden City, New York, 1955.

Hogan, Robert, "Moral Conduct and Moral Character: A Psychological Perspective," *Psychological Bulletin*, April 1973, *79*(4), pp. 216–232.

Horney, Karen, *The Neurotic Personality of Our Time* (New York: W.W. Norton & Co., 1937).

Horney, Karen, *Neurosis and Human Growth* (New York: W.W. Norton & Company, 1950).

Illich, Ivan, in F. Eychaner (Editor), *The Church, Change and Development* (New York: Herder and Herder, 1970).

James, William, *Varieties of Religious Experience* (New York: Longmans, Green and Company, 1902).

James, William, *Pragmatism: A New Name for Some Old Ways of Thinking* (New York: Longmans, Green & Co., 1943); originally published 1907.

Janis, Irving, *Victims of Groupthink: A Psychological Study of Foreign-Policy Decisions and Fiascoes* (Boston: Houghton Mifflin, 1972).

Kaplan, Abraham, *The Conduct of Inquiry* (San Francisco: Chandler Publishing Company, 1964).

Kelley, Harold H., "Moral Education," *American Psychologist,* March 1971.

Kelman, Herbert C., "Kairos: The Auspicious Moment," *American Journal of Psychoanalysis,* 1969, *29,* pp. 59–83.

Kohlberg, Lawrence, "Development of Moral Character and Moral Ideology," in M. L. Hoffman and L. W. Hoffman (Editors), *Review of Child Development Research*, Vols. 1 and 2 (New York: Russell Sage Foundation, 1964).

Kohlberg, Lawrence, "Stage and Sequence: The Cognitive-Developmental Approach to Socialization" in D. Goslin (Editor), *Handbook of Socialization Theory and Research* (Chicago: Rand McNally, 1969).

Kotre, John N., *The View from the Border* (Chicago: Aldine-Atherson, 1971).

Küng, Hans, *The Church* (New York: Sheed & Ward, 1967).

Küng, Hans, *Truthfulness: The Future of the Church* (New York: Sheed & Ward, 1968).

Kuhn, Thomas S., *The Structure of Scientific Revolutions* (Chicago: University of Chicago Press, 1962).

Lessa, William A., and Evon Z. Vogt (Editors), *Reader in Comparative Religion* (New York: Harper & Row, 1965).

Lifton, Robert Jay, *Thought Reform and the Psychology of Totalism: A Study of "Brainwashing" in China* (New York: Norton, 1961).

Loevinger, Jane, *Ego Development* (San Francisco: Jossey-Bass, 1976).

Loevinger, Jane, and R. Wessler, *Measuring Ego Development,* Vols. 1 and 2 (San Francisco: Jossey-Bass, 1970).

Lonergan, Bernard F., *Insight—A Study of Understanding* (New York: Philosophical Library, Inc., 1957).

Lonergan, Bernard F., "Papers by Bernard Lonergan," in F.E. Crowe (Editor), *Collection* (New York: Herder & Herder, 1967).

Lonergan, Bernard F., *Method in Theology* (New York: Herder & Herder, 1972).

Longauex y Vasquez, Enriqueta, "The Mexican-American Woman," in Robin Morgan (Editor), *Sisterhood Is Powerful* (New York: Random House, Inc., 1970), pp. 379–384.

Lynd, Helen M., *On Shame and the Search for Identity* (New York: Harcourt Brace, 1958).

McCann, Justin (Editor and Translator), *The Rule of Saint Benedict* (London: Burn Oates, 1960).

McDowell, Virginia H., "Explorations in Adult Development: A Study in the Interpretation of Lives," unpublished doctoral dissertation, University of California, Santa Cruz, 1976 (Ann Arbor, Michigan: University Microfilms).

McLaughlin, John, S.J., "Opinion Worth Noting: I Made a Cursillo," in *America,* January 18, 1964, pp. 94–101.

Mandelbaum, David C., "The Study of Life History: Gandhi," *Current Anthropology*, June 1973, *14*(3) pp. 177–209.

Martinez, Elizabeth S., "Colonized Women: The Chicana," in Robin Morgan (Editor), *Sisterhood Is Powerful* (New York: Random House, Inc., 1970), pp. 376–379.

Marty, Martin E., "Two Kinds of Civil Religion," in R. Richey and D. Jones (Editors), *American Civil Religion* (New York: Harper, 1974), pp. 139–157.

Maslow, Abraham H., "Peak-Experiences as Acute Identity-Experiences," *American Journal of Psychoanalysis*, 1941, *21*, pp. 254–290.

Maslow, Abraham H., *Toward a Psychology of Being* (New York: Van Nostrand Company, 1962).

May, Rollo, *Power and Innocence* (New York: Norton, 1973).

Milgrim Stanley, *Obedience to Authority* (New York: Harper & Row, 1974).

Morgan, Robin (Editor), *Sisterhood Is Powerful* (New York: Random House, Inc., 1970).

Naroll, Raoul, and Ronald Cohen, *A Handbook of Method in Cultural Anthropology* (Garden City, New York: The Natural History Press, 1970).

Neugarten, Bernice, *Personality in Middle and Late Life* (New York: Atherton Press, 1964).

Neugarten, Bernice, *Middle Age and Aging* (Chicago: University of Chicago Press, 1968).

Novak, Michael, "Social Concreteness in American Theology," in T. O'Meara and D. Weisser (Editors), *Projections: Shaping an American Theology for the Future* (Garden City, New York: Doubleday, 1971), pp. 78–92.

O'Meara, Thomas F., and Donald M. Weisser (Editors), *Projections: Shaping an American Theology for the Future* (Garden City, New York: Doubleday, 1971).

Palmer, Richard E., *Hermeneutics* (Evanston, Illinois: Northwestern University Press, 1969).

Perry, William G., *Forms of Intellectual and Ethical Development in the College Years: A Scheme* (New York: Holt, Rinehart & Winston, 1970).

Piaget, Jean, *The Child's Conception of the World* (New York: Harcourt, Brace, 1929).

Piaget, Jean, *The Child's Conception of Number* (New York: Humanities, 1952).

Piaget, Jean, *Six Psychological Studies* (New York: Random House, 1967).

Piaget, Jean, "Piaget's Theory," in P. H. Mussen (Editor), *Carmichael's Manual of Child Psychology*, Vol. 1 (3rd ed.) (New York: John Wiley and Sons, Inc., 1970), pp. 703–732.

Piaget, Jean, *Structuralism* (Chicago: Chicago University Press, 1970).

Polanyi, Michael, *Personal Knowledge* (New York: Harper & Row Publishers, 1958).

Puhl, Louis J., S.J. (Translator), *The Spiritual Exercises of St. Ignatius* (Westminster, Maryland: The Newman Press, 1962).

Redfield, Robert, *The Little Community: Viewpoints for the Study of a Human Whole* (Chicago: University of Chicago Press, 1955).

Richardson, Herbert, "Civil Religion in Theological Perspective," in R. Richey and D. Jones (Editors), *American Civil Religion* (New York: Harper, 1974), pp. 161–184.

Ricoeur, Paul, "The Conflict of Interpretations: Essays on Hermeneutics," in *Studies in Phenomenology and Existential Philosophy* (Evanston, Illinois: Northwestern University Press, 1974).

Ricoeur, Paul, *Freud and Philosophy: An Essay on Interpretation*, D. Savage (Translator) Terry Lecture Series (New Haven, Connecticut: Yale University Press, 1970).

Ricoeur, Paul, "The Model of the Text: Meaningful Action Considered as a Text," *Social Research*, 1971, *38*, pp. 529–562.

Ricoeur, Paul, *The Symbolism of Evil*, Emerson Buchanan (Translator), (Boston: Beacon Press, 1969).

Rooney, Patrick, "Educational Processes and Theology," in T. O'Meara and D. Weisser (Editors), *Projections: Shaping an American Theology for the Future* (Garden City, New York: Doubleday, 1971), pp. 208–220.

Sanford, Nevitt, "Whatever Happened to Action Research?" *Journal of Social Issues*, 1970, *26*(4), p. 3.

Sanford, Nevitt, and Craig Comstock, *Sanctions for Evil* (San Francisco: Jossey-Bass, Inc., 1971).

Sarbin, Theodore R., and Nathan Adler, "Self-Reconstitution Process: A Preliminary Report," *The Psychoanalytic Review*, 1970–71, *57*(4).

Sheed, Wilfred, "America's Catholics," *New York Review of Books*, March 7, 1974.

Sheehy, Gail, "Catch-30 and Other Predictable Crises of Growing Up Adult," *New York*, February 18, 1974, pp. 30–51.

Slater, Philip, "What Hath Spock Wrought?" *Washington Post*, March 1, 1970.

Smith, Charlotte, *Carl Becker: On History and the Climate of Opinion* (Ithaca, New York: Cornell, 1956), p. 117.

Smith, M. Brewster, *Social Psychology and Human Values* (Chicago: Aldine, 1969).

Smith, M. Brewster, *Humanizing Social Psychology* (San Francisco: Jossey-Bass, 1974).

Smith, M. Brewster, *Edited Transcript AHP Theory Conference*, remarks from conference at Tucson, Arizona, April 4–6, 1975 (San Francisco: Association for Humanistic Psychology, 1975), p. 53.

Spiegelberg, Frederick, *Living Religions of the World* (Englewood Cliffs, New Jersey: Prentice-Hall, 1956).

Sullerot, Evelyne, *Woman, Society and Change*, translated from the French by Margaret S. Archer (New York: McGraw Hill Book Company, 1971).

Taylor, Charles, "Interpretation and the Sciences of Man," *Review of Metaphysics*, 1971, pp. 3–51.

Tillich, Paul, *The Protestant Era* (Chicago: University of Chicago Press, 1948).

Tillich, Paul, *The New Being* (New York: Scribners, 1955).

Tillich, Paul, *Dynamics of Faith* (New York: Harper & Row Publishers, 1957).

Tillich, Paul, "Kairos," in *A Handbook of Christian Theology* (New York: Meridian Books, Inc., 1958), pp. 193–196.

Tillich, Paul, *Theology of Culture* (New York: Oxford University Press, 1970; originally published in 1959).

Tocqueville, Alexis de, *Democracy in America*, Vol. I, The Henry Reeve text as revised by Francis Bowen and edited by Phillips Bradley (New York: Vintage Books, 1960).

Turiel, Elliott, "Developmental Processes in the Child's Moral Thinking," in P. Mussen, J. Langer, & M. Covington (Editors), *Trends and Issues in Developmental Psychology* (New York: Holt, Rinehart & Winston, 1969).

Turiel, Elliott, "Adolescent Conflict in the Development of Moral Principles," expanded version of paper presented at the Loyola Symposium on Cognitive Psychology, Loyola University of Chicago, Chicago, Illinois, May 12, 1972.

Turiel, Elliott, "Conflict and Transition in Adolescent Moral Development," *Child Development*, 1974, *45*, pp. 14–29.

Turiel, Elliott, "The Development of Social Concepts: Mores, Customs and Conventions," in D. J. DePalma and J. M. Foley (Editors), *Contemporary Issues in Moral Development* (Potomac, Maryland: Lawrence Erlbaum Associates, 1975).

Turner, Victor W., *The Forest of Symbols* (Ithaca, New York: Cornell University Press, 1967).

Turner, Victor W., *The Ritual Process* (Chicago: Aldine, 1969).

Wach, Joachim, *Sociology of Religion* (Chicago: University of Chicago Press, 1944).

Watzlawick, P., J. Weakland, and R. Fisch, *Change: Principles of Problem Formulation and Problem Resolution* (New York: Norton & Co., Inc., 1974).

Wheelis, Allen, "The Place of Action in Personality Change," *Psychiatry*, May 1950, *13*.

Wheelis, Allen, "How People Change," *Commentary*, May 1969, *47*.

Wheelis, Allen, *The End of the Modern Age* (New York: Basic Books, Inc., 1971).

White, Robert W., *Lives in Progress*, Third Edition (New York: Holt, Rinehart and Winston, 1975).

White, Robert W. (Editor), *The Study of Lives* (New York: Atherton, 1963).

Yankelovich, Daniel, *Ego and Instinct* (New York: Random House, 1970).

Index